The Kyoto School

The Kyoto School

An Introduction

Robert E. Carter

with a Foreword by
Thomas P. Kasulis

Cover image courtesy of the author.

Published by State University of New York Press, Albany

For information, contact State University of New York Press, Albany, NY
www.sunypress.edu

Production by Kelli Williams-LeRoux
Marketing by Michael Campochiaro

Library of Congress Cataloging-in-Publication Data

Carter, Robert Edgar.
  The Kyoto school : an introduction / by Robert E. Carter; foreword by
Thomas P. Kasulis.
      pages cm
  Includes bibliographical references and index.
  ISBN 978-1-4384-4542-7 (pbk. : alk. paper)
  ISBN 978-1-4384-4541-0 (hardcover : alk. paper)
  1. Philosophy, Japanese—20th century.   2. Nishida, Kitaro, 1870–1945.
3. Tanabe, Hajime, 1885–1962.   4. Nishitani, Keiji, 1900–   5. Nothing
(Philosophy)   I. Title.

  B5241.C37 2013
  181'.12—dc23   2012011074

10 9 8 7 6 5 4 3 2 1

For Deanie, Pal, and Rita

Contents

Foreword   ix

   Thomas P. Kasulis

A Note to the Reader   xix

Acknowledgments   xxi

Introduction   1
   A Different Kind of Philosophy • The Buddhist
   Background • The Kyoto School

Chapter One
Nishida Kitarō (1870–1945)   13
   Background • The Early Years: Education • Pure
   Experience • A Unifying Power • The Place of Doubt •
   Becoming the Thing Itself • Absolute Nothingness •
   On Becoming Enlightened • Self and World •
   Ethics and Evil • Ethics • Nishida and Mysticism

Chapter Two
Tanabe Hajime (1885–1962)   61
   Life and Work • Metanoetics • Mediation • Mediation
   and Absolute Mediation • The Logic of the Specific •
   The Centrality of Ethics • Critique of Reason •
   • The Ethics of Metanoetics • Society Transformed

Chapter Three
Nishitani Keiji (1900–1990)   91
    Life and Career • Nietzsche and Nihilism • The Ten
    Ox-herding Pictures • The Meaning of "Nothingness" •
    A Way Out • Enlightenment • Relative and Absolute
    Nothingness • The Self • Selfless Ethics

Chapter Four
Watsuji Tetsurō (1889–1960)   125
    Life and Career • *Climate and Culture* • *Ethics as the
    Study of Man* • Double Negation • The Importance of
    Relationships • The Confucian Background • In the
    Betweenness • *Kokoro* and *Aidagara* • Watsuji and
    Nothingness • Back to the Everyday World • The
    Importance of the Body • Conclusion

Chapter Five
Conclusion   153
    Nishida and Tanabe • Tanabe's Critique of Nishida •
    On Original Goodness • Nishitani • Watsuji

Glossary   173

Notes   183

Selected Bibliography   201

Index   209

Foreword

Thomas P. Kasulis

In this book Robert E. Carter performs a great service to the study of modern Japanese philosophy in the West. To appreciate the significance of his contribution, it is useful to begin by reviewing briefly the introduction of modern Japanese philosophy to the English-reading audience. In the years following World War II, a few translations of modern Japanese philosophical works—a couple of books and several papers in scholarly journals—began to appear in English. In the next decade or two, several more volumes of translations appeared, the writings of Nishida Kitarō (1870–1945), Japan's most famous modern thinker and the founder of the so-called Kyoto School of philosophy centered in Kyoto University. The effects of those early translations were subtle, not attracting much attention from Western philosophers. Yet, the translations did provide resources, however limited, for the occasional interested Western reader. Moreover, once the interest in Japanese philosophy began to grow in the West, there was a foundation on which to build.

With Japan's rise in the 1970s and '80s as a global economic power, a curiosity about "Japanese thinking" took hold in the West, and a broader audience began to wonder what Japan might offer on the philosophical front. While many Anglo-American philosophers still resisted the invitation to engage any thought originating in languages other than English, others were not so provincial. Furthermore, there were Christian philosophical theologians interested in interreligious dialogue. The roots of such dialogue go back at least to the discussions begun by D. T. Suzuki and Alan Watts, but after Suzuki's death in 1966, philosophical theologians sought an East-West encounter more sustained and probing. The publication of the English translation of Nishitani Keiji's *Religion and Nothingness* in 1982 quickly became a focal point for Buddhist-Christian dialogue, and it led to a broader interest in the Kyoto School by Western Christian theologians. By the end of that decade, there were enough materials available in English that Robert Carter was able to write his first book addressing the Kyoto School: *The Nothingness Beyond God: An Introduction to the Philosophy of Nishida Kitarō* (Paragon House, 1989). I was pleased when Bob asked me to write the Foreword for that volume since it was a benchmark study for modern Japanese philosophy in the West: a Western philosophical ethicist was able to engage Nishida's philosophy in an insightful and provocative way on its own terms based entirely on works available in Western languages. Since then, Carter has spent the bulk of his time working with Japanese materials, both in commentaries and as a co-translator, providing many fresh perspectives on an array of ideas from Japanese thought, both modern and traditional. Meanwhile, translations of Kyoto School thinkers have continued, and there are also at least a dozen more scholarly books in English on some aspect of the Kyoto School, most nota-bly James W. Heisig's groundbreaking *Philosophers of Nothingness* (University of Hawai'i Press, 1991).

As the scholarly works in English now accumulate, there is a call for a good, concise, accurate introduction that will map the intellectual terrain. We need an appropriate starting point so readers new to the field will get a sense of what is available and be able to decide for themselves what interests them and where to turn next for deeper study. This is where the present volume finds its niche. It is what is called in Japanese a *nyūmon*, a term for "introduction" that literally means "entry gate." Every great Japanese institution has a *nyūmon*. For example, one readily thinks of the "mountain gates" giving access to Zen temples, the *torii* at the entrance to Shintō shrines, and the entries to every major Japanese academy such as the "Red Gate" leading to the heart of the University of Tokyo. A *nyūmon* has three main functions: to give access to outsiders, to define the boundaries of a place or field, and to be an invitation to enter more deeply into its heart. The term *nyūmon* is, therefore, appropriate to an introductory work in philosophy. Many of Japan's great modern philosophers, including Nishida Kitarō and Tanabe Hajime (each the focus of a chapter in the present work), wrote a *tetsugaku nyūmon,* "an introduction to philosophy." The Japanese assumption is that writing such a work is not a task for a young scholar, but, rather, is to be reserved for one who has developed an expert knowledge gleaned from many years in the field. Robert Carter has reached that point in his career, experienced enough to have seasoned insights of his own, but not so far from his own first entry that he has forgotten the importance of the *nyūmon.* Thus, his book serves as an excellent introduction to the Kyoto School.

In that same spirit of *nyūmon,* as a historian of Japanese philosophy, I will offer a few comments how each of the four philosophers in this book related to premodern Japanese thinkers. As Carter explains, the modern period in Japanese philosophy was not only a departure from the past triggered by the influx of Western thought, but also a return to ideas and values traditional to Japanese culture for many centuries. So, how exactly did each of the four philosophers relate to specific premodern Japanese or East Asian thinkers? A few details may help contextualize the situation for the reader new to Japanese philosophy.

Nishida Kitarō. In many ways, Nishida's links to the premodern Japanese philosophical tradition are the least obvious of the group. Of the four philosophers discussed in this book, he is the only one not to have written at least one volume explicitly about a premodern Japanese thinker. His direct references to Asian thought are few and far between and, more often than not, not much more than an epigram or phrase such as his repeated references to the "form of the formless" from the Buddhist (and Daoist) tradition. For example, Nishida almost never mentioned

Dōgen (1200–1253), whereas the other three modern philosophers in this book all wrote about Dōgen, indeed, often extensively. Since Dōgen is generally considered today to be one of the two or three most philosophical thinkers of premodern Japan, Nishida's omission may seem puzzling. Did he simply, like his lifelong friend, D. T. Suzuki, not like Dōgen's thought? Nishida once wrote that if he were banished into exile and could take only two books with him, they would be the *Record of Linji* and the collection of Shinran's sayings known as *Tannishō*. Linji was the Chinese founder of the Rinzai Zen tradition and Shinran the Japanese founder of the Pure Land sect of Shin Buddhism. We might expect, therefore, that Nishida's philosophical writings drew extensive connections with those two thinkers, but they did not. It seems, then, we cannot take the number of citations to be an indicator of what in premodern Asian thought might or might not have influenced Nishida's philosophical perspective. I suspect his omission of premodern Japanese philosophers in his analyses reveals more about his rhetorical, than his philosophical, position.

If this is right, what was Nishida trying to accomplish rhetorically? His primary goal, I think, was to write philosophy in the modern Japanese language for the first time. Given his wish to contribute to global, rather than merely Japanese, philosophy, he probably thought Japanese philosophical texts should read more like a Western (usually German) philosophical text translated into Japanese than a native Japanese text. The difference, of course, would be that the *content* of his text would be in many respects critical of the very Western philosophy it rhetorically resembled. He would, as it were, engage Western philosophy on its own playing field with its own terms and rules, but to that field he would bring his own Japanese style of play. In that context, any detailed discussion of premodern Asian thinkers would only distract the reader from Nishida's main project.

Nishitani Keiji. As the student of Nishida and a second-generation member of the Kyoto School, Nishitani was no longer constrained by the rhetorical limits his master had imposed on his own writing. Thanks to Nishida's efforts, no one any longer questioned whether "philosophy" could be written in Japanese. In matters of style as well as content, therefore, Nishitani could find his own voice, taking some cues, perhaps, from his German mentor, Martin Heidegger. In fact, the transition from Nishida to Nishitani resembles in some ways the transition from Husserl's phenomenology to Heidegger's existential "fundamental ontology" (without, of course, the animosity that fractured the personal relationship between the two German philosophers). Let us see how this is so.

Nishida's first book, *An Inquiry into the Good,* followed the spirit (and, to some extent, the writing styles) of William James and Henri Bergson by taking "experience" for his point of departure. As he rethought that work, however, he came to feel that it ultimately seemed too "psychologistic" and "mystical." So, he turned his attention from the American and French thinkers to the German Neo-Kantians. Like those German philosophers, Nishida wanted to develop the overall structure of rationality—the "logic"—through which he could then explain the experiential process of judging and analyzing. Although he found the Neo-Kantian philosophies inadequate, throughout most of his later writings (except perhaps the very last essays known as his "last writings"), he continued to seek the Holy Grail of logical systemization, hoping to find the formal structures for understanding the kinds of experiences that had interested him in *An Inquiry into the Good.* To that extent, Nishida's quest was in some ways analogous with Husserl's phenomenological efforts to develop a "pure science" (*reine Wissenschaft*) of consciousness. Husserl was a cartographer of consciousness, trying to map with scientific objectivity the nooks and crannies of every form of consciousness.

Heidegger, however, was not interested in continuing Husserl's cartography. He realized that Husserl's maps could be a treasure map, showing the route through the thicket of beings (*Seindes*) to the clearing of Being itself (*Sein*). Heidegger's project was not to develop more Husserlian categories, but rather, to use those categories to reach "authentic existence." This quest undoubtedly had a profound impact on Nishitani. He saw that Nishida's "logic" did not so much need further development, but rather, application to the most profound problems of human existence. Like Heidegger's reaction to Husserl, Nishitani turned Nishida's philosophy into a more explicitly spiritual quest for existential authenticity. The aforementioned book translated as *Religion and Nothingness* was entitled originally *Shūkyō to wa nanika* (What is Religion?) and its title fits this model well. Nishitani also published a series of lectures on Dōgen, wrote about Meister Eckhart, compared Shinran and Western spiritual views of temporality and faith, and so on. Further, as Heidegger's later writings broke the pattern of the dry scientistic writing style of Husserl, Nishitani also tried to write in a more "existential" manner, actually more like the French and American style of Nishida's maiden work than his later more Germanic rhetoric. As the topic of experience again came to the fore in Kyoto School philosophy, Nishitani never hesitated to draw explicitly on the traditional philosophies of East Asia in his writing, somewhat as Heidegger drew on and celebrated the ancient philosophers of the Western tradition, especially the pre-Socratics.

Tanabe Hajime. With Nishida, his senior, Tanabe was the other major first-generation member of the Kyoto School. As this book explains, we find two phases in Tanabe's thinking. After his early work in Kant and the philosophy of science, Tanabe turned to the structure of the "logic" that Nishida had been developing. According to Tanabe, Nishida had fallen into a problem that he had inherited from Hegel's logic, namely, construing the dialectic in terms of two moments, the universal and the individual (or the genus and individual). Missing was the level of the "specific" (or the species). Our human existence, Tanabe claimed, is most manifest not in the dynamic between our universal humanity and our individuality, but in our specificity, the medial plane that is the home of culture, ethnicity, and society. It is only there that language, thought, meaning, and value emerge. Indeed, the universal and the individual are abstracted and articulated from this plane. That is, we become individuals in a society or culture and we discover our universal humanity in the language and meanings learned within our social and cultural milieu. Tanabe's critique of Nishida's logic had much philosophical merit, but it turned out to be the right idea at the wrong time. The ethnocentrists and jingoistic ideologues quickly appropriated his theory and used it to buttress their idea of the "primacy" of being "Japanese" as superseding "individual" needs or any universalistic morality based in our "common humanity." Witnessing the application (misapplication?) of his ideas transformed into the tragedy of Japanese militarism and its inevitable defeat, Tanabe's underwent a "repentance" or "change of heart" (*metanoia* in Greek; *zange* in Japanese). The work of one of his graduate students at Kyoto University, Takeuchi Yoshinori, turned Tanabe to a deeper appreciation of the philosophy of Shinran (1173–1262), the aforementioned founder of the Pure Land tradition of Shin Buddhism. Inspired by that premodern Japanese philosopher, Tanabe wrote his *Philosophy as Metanoetics*. Because Shinran's philosophy is probably not as well known in the West as Zen philosophy, it might help the reader unfamiliar with that tradition if I very briefly sketch Shinran's theory of human existence as it pertains to the problematic of Tanabe's later philosophy.

Shinran maintained that human existence is so embedded in the karmic results of evil that even our attempts to be egoless, rationally objective, or altruistic end up being self-deceptions that only feed the ego further. How can "I," Shinran asked, eliminate "my" ego? If "I" succeed, has the ego really been eliminated? The only truly good deed is one I do with no self-interest. Yet, when I try to act altruistically, do I not inevitably see myself as a "do-gooder," a virtuous person deserving of enlightenment? Is this not just ego again, albeit in a disguised form? In response to this predicament, Shinran claimed, we must completely relinquish all presumptions that we can reach the wisdom and compassion of enlightenment through our own efforts. To do so, we turn over all agency to a power outside us, no longer trusting ourselves to "figure things out" (*hakarai*) or to transform ourselves through our own efforts (*jiriki*) and talents. This *shinjin* ("faith" or "true entrusting") turns over agency to the working of another, the cosmic Buddha Amida. Amida is in itself immeasurable light that illuminates our egos, highlighting our karmic habits of self-deception and ego-serving delusions. As compassion, that light takes the form of a Buddha who establishes a dimension, a Pure Land, where enlightenment is possible. Once our trust in Amida is complete, therefore, the ego dissolves and rebirth into that Pure Land is assured. No longer seeing oneself as an "I," there is no longer the need to relinquish the self and there is no need for an Amida to be a personal source of a power to which one surrenders. So, Amida as well disappears into suchness, a "spontaneous" or "natural" (*jinen*) working in which there is no individual agency, neither mine nor Amida's.

In light of this medieval Japanese model of *metanoia* (in Greek) or *zange* (in Japanese), Tanabe argued that philosophy should always recognize its own inherent corruptibility. To the extent a philosophical system is successful, the danger is that its success will feed the ego of those who accept the system, supporting delusions of power and grandeur. In its quest for "figuring things out" and achieving truth, philosophy loses sight of its limits and assumes the mantle of absolute truth. This absolutizing tendency distorts whatever conventional, limited, relative truth the philosophy had discovered, making it into a totalizing ideology that denies its all-too-human, finite origins. Therefore, Tanabe argued that a philosophy should integrate an awareness of its own limitations, expressly showing how it *cannot* be absolutized. Philosophy can never transcend its provisional and relative status. That is what Tanabe learned from his reading of Shinran.

Watsuji Tetsurō. As Carter points outs, depending on the context, Watsuji can be considered as either an insider or just beyond the periphery to the Kyoto School proper. He was both personally and philosophically indebted to Nishida and the Kyoto University Department of Philosophy, where he held his first major academic position. We see his Kyoto School ties most obviously in his use of the idea of nothingness, for example. Yet, in many respects after he returned from Germany and then took the chair in Ethics at the University of Tokyo, his trajectory of interests were tangential, rather than central, to those of the Kyoto School. We are interested here, however, mainly in his treatment of premodern Japanese thinkers.

Watsuji had started his career in Japan as the country's foremost specialist in Schopenhauer, Kierkegaard, and Nietzsche. In fact, precisely because of those interests, Nishida recommended he spend some time doing research and studying in Germany. At about the same time, however, Watsuji's father, a physician in the Chinese tradition steeped in Confucian values, urged him not to abandon his own cultural roots, especially as Japan was undergoing such a radical social and cultural upheaval. Therefore, from the late 1920s until his death, at least half of Watsuji's writings were analyses of, and reflections on, traditional Japanese ideas and values. He wrote many volumes on such topics as the history of Japanese ethical ideas, the pragmatic character of early Indian Buddhism, and the aesthetics of various traditional Japanese art forms such as Noh drama, temple architecture, and Buddhist sculpture. His 1926 book, *Shamon Dōgen* (Dōgen, the Monk), might be considered the single most influential work in modern Japanese philosophy's engagement with traditional Japanese Buddhist philosophy. For the first time, a modern Japanese philosopher had treated a great Japanese religious thinker not as saintly figure shrouded in the aura of sectarian veneration, but as a fellow human being driven by philosophical questions. This started a trend in modern Japanese philosophy that continues today.

With these few comments in mind about what Japanese philosophers brought with them as they developed modern Japanese philosophy, we can now turn the task over to Bob Carter, who will take us through his entry gate into the Kyoto School. Readers will feel fortunate to be led by such a talented and experienced guide.

Thomas P. Kasulis
The Ohio State University

A Note to the Reader

The many endnotes in this book can be bypassed without significant loss of meaning. They are there for those who wish to check a source in more detail, or who require references for research purposes. Those who simply read the text straight through might wish to consult the Glossary from time to time to be reminded of the meaning of a word or phrase, or to check on the details of a school of thought.

Readers who simply wish to read straight through will, hopefully, find a narrative that is accessible from beginning to end. I have attempted to simplify difficult concepts and ideas, and to leave out technical scholarly details. It is my hope that this Introduction to the Kyoto School will make available to the general reader four rich and exciting cross-cultural explorations which continue to challenge and inform readers both in Japan and abroad. I regret that an important fifth figure is not included. Ueda Shizuteru clearly ranks among the most important Kyoto School figures, and he is still very active. Unfortunately, most of his writings are in Japanese or German. Some of his essays available in English are listed in the "general background" section of the bibliography.

A major reason for including the four philosophers included here is that each of them has at least one major book-length text available in English: Nishida's *An Inquiry into the Good,* Tanabe's *Philosophy as Metanoetics,* Nishitani's *Religion and Nothingness,* and Watsuji's *Rinrigaku (Japanese Ethics).*

I have adopted the Japanese custom of placing the surname first: Nishida Kitarō, not Kitarō Nishida. To adopt the traditional

Western habit of first name before last, might appear as though you were on a first-name basis with the authors.

Finally, as mentioned in the text, the Nanzan Institute for [the Study of] Religion and Culture, in Nagoya, Japan, has recently published seven volumes of essays on the Kyoto School and Japanese Philosophy. They are listed together at the very end of the bibliography. Noted as well is the recently published *Sourcebook in Japanese Philosophy*.

Acknowledgments

A manuscript becomes a published book only because of the many helpful interventions along the way. Nancy Ellegate, of the State University of New York Press, first suggested that I undertake this *Introduction to the Kyoto School*. My friend and colleague, Pal Dosaj, was to write portions of the manuscript, but Pal unexpectedly became seriously ill just as the writing began. As healing gradually took place, he offered suggestions and advice on numerous issues.

Prof. Thomas P. Kasulis, of the Ohio State University, wrote the Foreword that serves as an excellent introduction to my Introduction to the Japanese Kyoto School. Given that he is currently in the midst of writing the complete history of Japanese philosophy, it comes as no surprise that his Foreword displays the best of scholarship coupled with an admirable ability to communicate in an easily accessible form. My first book on Japanese Philosophy, *The Nothingness Beyond God: An Introduction to the Philosophy of Nishida Kitarō* (Paragon House, 1989 and 1997) contained a brilliant Foreword by a much younger Tom Kasulis, then at Ashland College, in Wisconsin. Friends from even before then, it gives me great satisfaction that Tom has introduced both my first and my latest book on Japanese philosophy. In spite of the spatial distance between us, we have continued to be linked in a variety of ways, personally and professionally, in the betweenness (*aidagara*) between us.

Prof. James W. Heisig, Director of the Nanzan Institute for [the Study of] Japanese Religion and Culture, at Nanzan University

(Nagoya, Japan), proved a great help, both through his writings and his e-mails in response to my queries.

My wife, Deanie LaChance, and my friend and former student, Jerry Larock, read the manuscript more than once, offering many helpful suggestions and correcting errors of one kind or another. Deanie has a keen editorial eye for maintaining continuity of thought, and for spotting grammatical issues. Jerry was indispensable in editing, preparing the Index, and attending to details too numerous to estimate.

Tomio Nitto, Toronto artist and friend, created a distinctive and modern rendering of the "Ten Ox-herding Pictures" which appear in the chapter on Nishitani Keiji. In Zen fashion, they have the quality of direct communication. Tomio, recently retired, spends his time painting in watercolors and oils.

Toby Tyler offered word processing assistance at a time that I was unable to move due to a back injury. In addition to typing, as a professional chef he brought with him each time a gourmet meal which he prepared in our kitchen. Thank you for those gifts, Toby.

To all of you I express my deepest thanks. The book is a far better book because of you.

Introduction

For nearly two and a half centuries (1633–1853), Japan was shut off from the rest of the world. *Sakoku* ("locked or chained country") was the foreign relations policy of Japan that allowed no foreigner to enter Japan, nor any Japanese to leave the country, except on penalty of death. It remained unlawful for a Japanese to leave Japan until the Meiji Restoration in 1868. While limited trading was allowed with a very few countries at five main ports, during more than two centuries the vast majority of Japanese never even caught a glimpse of a non-Japanese. "Dutch learning" was a term to describe the few books and limited information gained from Dutch traders who were allowed to use Dejima, an artificial island port (measuring 600 x 240 feet) just outside Nagasaki, but such information was anything but widely disseminated. In fact, a small stone footbridge was all that connected Dejima to Nagasaki, an entrance that was always heavily guarded. For all intents and purposes, Japan was closed to the entire world and, for the most part, unaware of any of the industrial and technological advances made elsewhere.

The Japan that existed before 1853 was a feudal society, with warlords controlling specific regions, where "vassals" were required to show submission in the form of payments and loyalty. The pre-contact Japanese worldview was an eclectic mix of Confucian, indigenous Shintō, and Buddhist values. Japan had shunned European technological advances from the 1600s onward, if they were even aware of them, and remained unindustrialized to any significant extent. From the perspective of European and American officials, Japan was a "primitive" country, believing in nature spirits, religious magic, and the adequacy of the sword as protection.

In 1853, the United States forced the opening of Japan to "free trade" at gunpoint, when the four "black ships," armed with cannons, made it clear that the Japanese sword was all but useless against foreign armaments. The warships *Mississippi, Plymouth, Saratoga,* and *Susquehanna* steamed into Tokyo Bay, known then as the Bay of Edo, under Commander Matthew Perry of the U.S. Navy. Brandishing weapons, Perry made clear the United States would not take "no" for an answer. Wintering in the Ryukyu Islands, Perry returned a few months later with seven ships, essentially forcing the signing of the "Treaty of Peace and Amity," thereby establishing diplomatic relations between the United States and Japan. Treaties were soon signed with other countries as well (England, Russia, Holland), but in each case the Japanese felt that these treaties were unfair and unequal, granting "favored nation status" at gunpoint while giving Japan considerably less in return. Western nations assumed control of tariffs on imports, and all visiting nationals were granted the right of extraterritoriality. Given that it was a time of rampant Western imperialism, Japan soon knew enough to fear that Western nations sought more than trading and visitation rights.

Militarily, Japan could do nothing to defend itself against the superior power of its new treaty "partners." Nevertheless, among the rank and file the cry was "expel the barbarians," and not long after, "honor the emperor—expel the barbarians." However, the Tokugawa Shōgunate, which had been in power for 250 years, realized that they must submit to the unreasonable demands of the United States and other Western nations. Over the past hundreds of years, the emperor had been all but forgotten by the Japanese in favor of the Shōgun, but now that the power of the Tokugawa Shōgunate was crumbling, the emperor summoned the Shōgun to Kyoto and the Shōgun immediately complied. This "imperial" show of muscle was important given that the new government of 1868 would place the emperor at the forefront of Japanese minds, even though political power would actually lie elsewhere.

It was in 1867 that the Tokugawa Lord of Mito voluntarily gave over the actual political rule of Japan to the emperor. After centuries of feudal rule, the Shōgun collectively gave over all power, and all of this occurred virtually bloodlessly. It had become clear to all that reform was necessary. The "Restoration" of imperial rule was now a fact, even though the emperor himself was but a boy of fifteen. Among those who advised the young emperor was a group of young and very poor samurai who actually wielded political power. By 1868, the reform was in place and the "Meiji Restoration" was a fact: emperor "Meiji" was now the titular head of the country and a new government was in place. To this energetic group it was clear that Japan had to reform, but lasting reform would require adequate knowledge and perspective, and the most desirable knowledge had to be gained by learning from the recognized leaders in any given field. With this in mind, in 1868, the "young Turks" who guided the Meiji "restoration," sent sixty-eight of Japan's brightest young minds to study Western ways at the various centers of excellence: law in France and England, commerce in the United States, the army and medicine (and philosophy) in Germany, the navy and merchant marine in England, and so on. From the earliest times, the Japanese manner of progressing in knowledge and skill was to go to the "state of the art," and then to adapt and improve on it. Prince Shōtoku did just this in the seventh century AD,[1] attempting to bring Chinese excellence to Japan in the form of city building, art, literature, philosophy, poetry music, history—and the Meiji officials were simply repeating this tradition. The slogan, "catch up, overtake" was presented to the Japanese people as an urgent demand for hard work, open minds, and self-sacrifice. The Japanese accepted the challenge with determination. There was no time to waste if Japan was to resist being swallowed by those stronger and more advanced countries that were already taking control of nations in the Far East. Even today, the Japanese post–World War II "economic miracle" is still spoken of, since Japan climbed from nearly complete isolation and industrial, technological, and military inferiority, to become one of the industrial, technological, and military giants in but a handful of decades. The dash from feudalism to modernism was made without going through any of the intervening stages that were typical of the development of Western nations. This rapid development was both unprecedented and astonishing.

Nishida Kitarō, Japan's first world-class modern philosopher, the founder and focus of the "Kyoto School," was born in 1870, just two years after the Meiji Restoration. How remarkable it is that, in a generation or two, Japan produced a philosopher who not only read several Western languages but engaged the giants in the Western philosophic pantheon with an ease that suggested that such musings had been occurring for centuries. Moreover, Nishida attempted to use Western philosophical ideas and techniques in order to describe the spirit of Eastern culture and thought and, in particular, the genius and uniqueness of Japanese thought.

While many still think of the Japanese mind as inscrutable, how much more so did it seem in the 1860s when Japan was first opened to the rest of the world. The Japanese language was not well studied, nor were Japan's cultural values and practices familiar. "Inscrutability" was an understatement. Yet, in 1911, Nishida published his *Inquiry into the Good*, a book that captured the imagination of the Japanese because it introduced them to full-blown Western ideas while stating with remarkable clarity and force what was distinctive about Japanese ways of thinking. Nishida's aim was to state in precise Western-style philosophical language what the Japanese standpoint was: what it was like to see things from a Japanese perspective. So in forty years, from isolation to encounter, Japan had produced its first modern philosopher of world-class significance; an incredible achievement. And because of the excitement surrounding his rather difficult contributions, a school or stream of agreement and reaction to his philosophy began to form. The Kyoto School arose both from Nishida's immense contributions and out of a national spirit that encouraged citizens in every possible field to catch up and overtake the more advanced nations of the world.

Nishida took as his challenge the presenting of the Japanese perspective in a way that would be understandable to Western readers. He tried to present the Japanese way of being in and thinking about the world in Western terms. Not all Japanese, then or now, agreed with his characterizations, and some might think that what Nishida presented was in fact Nishida's way of looking at things. Such a perspective on his work is not without merit, but it fails when compared to his own intentions. He simplified his approach when he wrote that the Western cultures are cultures of being, while Eastern cultures are cultures of nothingness.[2] The primacy of *being* in Western culture was not present in many Eastern cultures, and certainly not in Japan, where *nothingness* was the focal concept. But how to convey to Western readers just how nothingness plays itself out systematically in many Eastern perspectives: Daoism, Buddhism, Zen Buddhism, Hinduism, and even to a degree in Shintōism? Hence, there is not one perspective but rather many that together make up the Japanese experience. Yet all of these do give preference to nothingness. And given Nishida's own training as a Zen Buddhist, one might expect that his outlook would be heavily influenced by that training. Nonetheless, he does not write as a Zen Buddhist but, rather, as an interpreter of what he takes to be the Japanese mind-set generally and, even more generally, the mind-set of Eastern peoples. The complexity of the East means that we must take into account the many strands that make up the Chinese mind, the Korean mind, the Thai mind, and the many minds that constitute India. However, Nishida did capture a way of understanding that was widespread in all of these traditions. It is still insightful enough to stimulate interest and excitement, not only in Japan but the world over. The Kyoto School continues to attract scholars and religious leaders who wish to dialogue on the insights of Nishida, and with the successive Kyoto School members.

A Different Kind of Philosophy

James Heisig, in his *The Philosophers of Nothingness,* reminds us that "the first time the designation 'Kyoto school' seems to have appeared in print was in a 1932 newspaper article by Tosaka Jun entitled 'The Philosophy of the Kyoto School.' "[3] The designation did not so much refer to a school, but rather to a sequence of appointments in philosophy at Kyoto University during and after Nishida's tenure there, who shared a common focus on at least several of the key ideas of Nishida's philosophizing. Beginning with Tanabe Hajime, those who followed Nishida at the university were, at least in part, either interpreters or critics of his work. In any case, as Heisig himself affirms, "the best that the Kyoto philosophers have to offer sets them squarely on a par with the best western philosophical minds of the time."[4]

A salient characteristic of Japanese philosophizing is the lack of any sharp separation between philosophy and religion. Indeed, those individuals from the West who became interested in the work of the Kyoto School consisted of both philosophers and theologians. The separation (more or less) of philosophy from religion, which is so important to Western academics, was out of sync with the Japanese understanding of philosophy and its content. Viewing the range of philosophies in the Far East, in what sense can we say that Confucianism, Daoism, Buddhism, or Shintō were religious philosophies, in the broadest sense of a common understanding of "religion" in the West? Confucianism has been termed a system of ethics, Buddhism an atheistic philosophy, Daoism nothing more than abstract philosophy and/or mere magic, and Shintō (wrongly understood) mere animistic superstition, making it difficult to know precisely what qualifies as philosophy or religion. Generally, religion in Japan is not about belief, whereas belief is often central and sufficient in defining religion in the West. Instead, religion in Japan is about consciousness transformation.

The situation is not much clearer with respect to philosophy: are Confucianism and Buddhism, for example, instances of true philosophy? Both philosophy and religion in Japan are providers of transformational experience, so again any line between them is anything but sharp. It is my contention that philosophy is, at the very least, thinking that is both rigorous and consistent, leading to clarity. If such thinking leads to self-transformation, then it is in line with what the Japanese believe philosophy ought to be.

Philosophy can take many forms, but it is not necessarily a specific canon of writings (the established texts of philosophy), or style of deliberation that makes philosophy philosophy, for it is a systematic rigor and consistency that best describes it./It might be argued that religion is faith-based, while philosophy is truth-based./Yet, Augustine, Anselm, Aquinas, and Descartes are clearly, at times, faith-based in their deliberations. Be that as it may, for the Japanese, religion is not a matter of faith or reason, belief or dogma, but of experience, the sort of experience that is truly transformative, the kind that can truly be said to cause one to see oneself and the world differently. Such philosophy cannot simply rest content within a web of analysis and conceptual distinctions if it does not transform the individual. The problem is that "religion" means something different in Japan, as does "philosophy." With the Kyoto School, the issues at stake here melt away considerably, since the consistent and rigorous thinking undertaken and presented are, for the most part, in Western philosophic style, while the content is decidedly Japanese. It is a fresh face on the philosophic scene, presenting systems of thought heretofore outside the canon, in language and form in harmony with the canon itself, and in deep dialogue with many of the key authors of the Western philosophic canon, from the pre-Socratics to Heidegger and beyond. The Japanese perspective had to be analyzed and justified as a legitimate philosophical and logical one. Yet the starting points were so different!

/Furthermore, not only did the Japanese not separate religion and philosophy, but they deemphasized the central importance of reason and placed the emphasis on experience./The Western emphasis on reason alone tended to make philosophy a "purely cerebral affair," while the starting point for the Japanese was that knowledge is also an experiential affair which can be achieved and honed through *practice* rather than reason alone.[5] Moreover, what comes to be experienced through the practices of self-cultivation (using techniques gained from such practices as meditation, the way of tea, the way of flowers, the martial arts, calligraphy) is an awareness that can only be achieved by annihilating the ordinary ego-self's perception of reality. Reason chatters away at the surface of understanding, but there is a level beneath ordinary awareness, a deeper self that emerges through meditational practice. It is in this sense that philosophy ends in an awareness of the interconnectedness of all things, and it is philosophy that must stand back from this awareness and the practice that led to it, in order to analyze the entire trajectory of awareness and its basic structure. Religion takes us to a fundamental insight that philosophy itself cannot achieve, and yet it is this insight that is the fundamental basis on which philosophy rests and from which it begins the arduous task of the analysis of the structure of knowledge and reality. Religion and philosophy, on this understanding, are inseparable yet distinct, complementary yet opposed, or in Nishida's words, self-contradictory and yet identical. Just as religion and philosophy are one and yet distinct, so, too, are intellectual knowledge and the knowledge gained through practice (such as through sustained meditational practice) one and yet distinct. Taken together, intellectual knowledge (gained through the mind) and the knowledge gained through practice (which is achieved through the use of the body), yields the "oneness of body and mind" that is so emphasized in Japanese culture. Nishida refers to it as an "eastern" phenomenon, that is, the "unity of knowledge and practice."[6] From such a perspective, religion is the background or foundational experience to philosophy's foreground or rational superstructure. Reason cannot reach this foundation for it is *experiential* and dependent on losing the self and its ordinary sense of things. Philosophy is the rational edifice that arises from and through an analysis of what can follow from (can be built upon) this foundation. Japanese religion, in its several forms, is about such experience.

While academics may continue to argue about the quality of the work offered to the world by the Kyoto School, Heisig, who is not uncritical of the Kyoto School philosophers, concludes that "the philosophers of the Kyoto School have given us a world philosophy, one that belongs as rightfully to the inheritance as much as the western philosophies with which they wrestled and from which they drew their inspiration."[7]

The Buddhist Background

The Kyoto philosophers do not present a Buddhist or a Zen Buddhist philosophy, although it will be evident soon enough that the Buddhist and Zen Buddhist perspectives supply the context out of which their thinking arises. Tanabe Hajime rejects the Zen approach and utilizes Shin (Pure Land) Buddhism as his background inspiration. Nishitani Keiji, Nishida's student, is perhaps the most Buddhist-centered, yet even there the attempt is not to create a neo-Buddhist philosophy, but rather to use Buddhist insights in order to accurately depict the Japanese cultural perspective. He, like Nishida, was a student of Zen. During his early years, Nishida attended intensive Zen workshops (*sesshin*), and continued this practice for a decade; Nishitani continued his Zen practice throughout his life. Watsuji Tetsurō does not explicitly adopt a religious perspective, although some scholars argue that his philosophy arose out of a Buddhist perspective, however implicit it might be.

The Kyoto School

While it is still open to debate as to who qualifies for "membership" in the Kyoto School, the four philosophers selected for this *Introduction* were chosen partly because of the availability of translations of their work in English (to allow for textual research), and partly to give a more comprehensive view of topics and issues covered. Takeuchi Yoshinori has commented that a definition of the Kyoto School should be made by "triangulating" it around the three central figures—Nishida, Tanabe, and Nishitani.[8] No one would question whether these three were "members." Most would cite Watsuji as a "marginal" figure, both because his work was original and independent of "Nishida philosophy" and because he taught at Kyoto University for a relatively short time. Nevertheless, original and independent as his philosophy was, there is no doubt that many of the ideas he worked with he shared with the undisputed members of the School, most notably the idea of *nothingness*. Davis writes that "the most fundamental of their shared and disputed concepts is that of 'Absolute Nothingness,' a notion that has, in fact, most often been used as a point of reference for defining the School."[9] But Davis goes on to say that Watsuji (and another philosopher named Kuki Shōzō [1888–1941]) "were brought to Kyoto University by Nishida, and both developed philosophies that were more or less influenced by Nishida's thought . . . and yet, both their thought and their activities remained too independent to count them among the inner circle of the School. It should be kept in mind, however, that these two "associate members" in particular are first-rate philosophers in their own right, whose original work outshines that of many of the less original though "full-fledged" members of the School."[10] Watsuji offers an original perspective on Japanese ethics and culture that, while on the periphery of the Kyoto School, enriches an understanding of a time in Japanese history when philosophical ideas were generated in so very many directions. Watsuji was an important contributor to Japan's philosophical renaissance.

Disagreement about who is to be included in the Kyoto School is mild compared to the continuing debate as to whether there is such a thing as Japanese philosophy at all. Indeed, many are suspicious about the so-called philosophies of the Far East in general and, often including the entire East, India as well. But India's was the first Eastern tradition to gain an approving, if qualified, nod from Western philosophers, particularly because of the logical rigor of Buddhist thinkers such as Nāgārjuna, and in the twentieth century, J. R. Malkani and K. C. Bhattacharya. Still, the "nod" was a qualified nod because Indian philosophy was "religious" philosophy. It has taken time for Western scholars to discern that the dichotomy between religion and philosophy was, for the most part, simply nonexistent in the East. Not only that, but religion in the East has qualities that are quite different from the institutional religions of the West. For example, it is not at all unusual to find a Buddhist and a Shintō shrine in a single home, and not unheard of for a Christian altar to be added to the mix. One takes what one needs from each and every way of thinking, religious or otherwise, in building one's philosophy of living well. One simply has no need to choose between religion and philosophy, or between one religion and another. As Heisig points out, "For the Kyoto philosophers, thinking either transforms the way we look at the things of life or it is not thinking in the fullest sense of the word."[11] The approach to philosophy taken by the Kyoto philosophers was to inquire into culture in its many forms, religious and nonreligious, and to abstract from them a coherent, philosophically rigorous account that would stand the test of criticism. Philosophy, understood in this way, is a transformative activity and not just a cerebral exercise in logic or the analysis of words or propositions. Philosophy, like religion, seeks to transform the way we view ourselves, others, and the world. It is always more than an intellectual activity, and yet, unlike religion, there is no limit as to what is to be investigated and no prescribed texts or rules to be followed in one's inquiries except to be true to the evidence. Even reason, while important, is not the final arbiter of truth, for truth is to be found in experience as well. The goal of such philosophizing is some personal transformation, akin to enlightenment, which alters our way-of-being-in-the-world for the better. Anything short of this is mere mind-play or intellectual gymnastics. Philosophy is an ultimately serious and vital activity: it seeks a "transformation of awareness."[12]

Almost all attempts to *define* the Kyoto School include the observation that its members were, each of them, involved in a systematic attempt to think philosophically on the basis of "nothingness."[13] Some list several other defining characteristics such as a close connection with Nishida's philosophy, association with Kyoto University, a strong emphasis on Buddhism, and so on. But if "nothingness" is the essential defining quality of Kyoto School thinking, then Watsuji has "associate membership" at the very least. Be that as it may, it is helpful to follow Ōhashi Ryōsuke's grouping of possible Kyoto School members as follows: (1) Nishida and Tanabe constitute the first generation; (2) Hisamatsu (1889–1980), Nishitani,

Kōsak Masaaki (1900–1969), Shimomura Torataro (1900–1995), Koyama Iwao (1905–1993), and Suzuki Shigetaka (1907–1988) constitute the second generation; (3) the third generation includes Ueda Shizuteru (1926–), Tsujimura Kōichi, and Abe Masao (1915–2006). A fourth (4) generation scholar, Ōhashi Ryōsuke (1944–), and several others currently researching the Kyoto School offer hope that its philosophy is still alive and well. It will be noted that Watsuji's name is not included in this list.

The creation of a Department of the History of Japanese Philosophy, in 1998, at Kyoto University, under the direction of Fujita Masakatsu, makes evident that Japanese academics will continue to research the history of the Kyoto School and beyond. However, at present there is no one among the fourth generation of the stature of Nishida, Tanabe, or Nishitani to continue the creative thrust of the previous Kyoto School thinkers. It would be all too easy for the growth of the Kyoto School to be curtailed by rendering it a historical focus of academic research rather than a living tradition setting off in new directions. Only time will tell whether the Kyoto School tradition has the lasting power to produce original and provocative ideas. It has been only twenty years since Nishitani's passing, leaving the rest of us to ponder the future of the tradition which he continued with such depth and passion. The depth of Ueda Shizuteru's work, a member of the third generation, which offers both originality and clear interpretive and critical skill in assessing the work of the Kyoto School, provides some evidence that the Kyoto School continues to produce ongoing results of quality and real interest.

Additionally, through the guidance of James Heisig of the Nanzan Institute for [the Study of] Religion and Culture, in Nagoya, Japan, a seven-volume series of essays on the Kyoto School and Japanese philosophy has recently been published. More than one hundred essays are presented in these volumes, representing a giant step forward in Kyoto School scholarship. As well, a *Sourcebook* has just been published that contains translated readings on virtually every significant figure in Japanese philosophy (see bibliography). The *Sourcebook* and the essays cannot help but catapult the scholarship in the field to a higher level, and to make available translations of works heretofore inaccessible to all but Japanese readers.

1

Nishida Kitarō
(1870–1945)

It is no exaggeration to say that in him [Nishida Kitarō] Japan has had the first philosophical genius who knew how to build a system permeated with the spirit of Buddhist meditation, by fully employing the Western method of thinking.

—Takeuchi Yoshinori, "The Philosophy of Nishida,"
in *The Buddha Eye: An Anthology of the Kyoto School*

Background

At about the same time that Japanese men were sent to the West to study the centuries of advances made since the closing of Japan, a small but steady flow of Western academics came to Japan to teach Western ideas and accomplishments. Two German philosophers who taught in Japan (Ludwig Busse and Raphael von Koeber) contributed to the trend toward German "romantic" philosophy and away from the increasingly less popular English philosophers (J. S. Mill, Spencer, Darwin, and Huxley). The affinity that the Japanese had for German authors continued well into the twentieth century: Martin Heidegger's *Zein und Zeit* (*Being and Time*), for example, was translated into Japanese before it was translated into English, and upon Heidegger's death, the national radio service, NHK, broadcast a tribute to Heidegger that was several minutes in length. It was in this intellectual climate that Nishida was educated.

Kant, Hegel, Schopenhauer, Nietzsche, and Hartmann were key figures in the rush to understand the West and its ways. Yet, as James Heisig observes, Nishida "did not simply seek to *preserve* Japan's traditional self-understanding in the face of the onslaught of foreign ideas and ideals, but to submit it to the rigorous critique of philosophy."[1]

The account of Nishida's philosophy that follows is not meant to be complete, but only introduces the reader to the thought of this foundational thinker by drawing out some of the major themes in his lifelong pursuit. The early Nishida is dominant in this account, although themes from his middle and later periods are also present. As a questing philosopher, he continued to rewrite his position time after time, trying to overcome shortcomings or simply reviewing an issue from a new perspective. His first period was dominated by the notion of "pure experience"; his second by "self-consciousness"; his third by the notion of *basho*, or *topos* (a notion that he borrowed from Plato), perhaps best rendered in English as "place," or "field" (as in "field theory"), or simply as that in which something is located; and the fourth by the complex notion of "the absolutely contradictorily self-identical dialectical world of the one and the many."[2] Not only does much of the material from the middle and later periods remain untranslated, but these writings tend to be extremely dense and notoriously difficult to read. Thus, while I think that the following account of Nishida's philosophy is accurate, it represents but a small portion of his thinking and rethinking about issues that continue to reverberate in the minds of scholars the world over. The point is that readers should not be misled into thinking that they "know" Nishida's philosophy from reading this account. What I have tried to provide is a basic look at the greatness which he created.

What Nishida took to be Japan's traditional self-understanding was a perspective heavily colored by his own interest in Zen Buddhism. Noda Mateo reported that Nishida often stated in his lectures that his aim was to establish "a rational foundation for Zen."[3] Having been a practitioner of Zen for a decade from his mid-twenties, and even though his philosophic writings hardly make mention of Zen, one must assume that his aim continued to include an acceptable rendering of the Zen perspective, although he often remarked that his philosophy was not tied to that perspective. Perhaps it would be more accurate to say that Zen continued to provide the lens through which he saw the world.

The Early Years: Education

Nishida's secondary education included an intense study of Chinese language and literature, and mathematics. While he did well, he increasingly felt stunted by militaristic and rule-oriented administrators. Nonetheless, he found some excellent teachers and studied a wide range of subjects including Japanese, Chinese, English, German, history, mathematics, geology, physics, and physical education. As he developed intellectually, he was torn between mathematics and philosophy, eventually selecting philosophy as his focus. In July 1889, he learned that he had failed his first year of the main division because of his poor class attendance and bad classroom conduct, although his academic achievement was not in question. Unwisely, he decided to drop out of school in 1890, unhappy with the constraints imposed on students and intent on self-learning. He read incessantly on his own but, in doing so, damaged his eyes to the extent that he was ordered by his doctor not to read for a year. It was becoming more and more clear that educating himself was not the realization of the ideal of freedom that he sought. He needed the guidance of strong, educated minds, and the requirements of ordered learning.

Realizing that trying to educate himself on his own was more difficult than he had thought, in 1891 Nishida took the entrance examination to apply to become a "limited status" student at Tokyo University, the reduced standing being the direct result of having dropped out of high school before completing the requirements. He found the exam for this "second best" academic entrance easy and was admitted to the Department of Philosophy. In 1894 he wrote a graduation thesis on Hume's theory of causation. After graduating, he was unable to find a teaching job either in Tokyo or his hometown of Kanazawa and spent the rest of 1894 unemployed. He used the time to compose an essay on T. H. Green's theory of ethics, which was published in three installments in 1895 in the "Education Times."

In 1897 Nishida acquired a job as head teacher at the branch campus of a Middle School in Nanao, which was about sixty kilometers northeast of Kanazawa. His duties included walking great distances in an attempt to attract students to the school. In that same year he married his cousin, Takuda Kotomi. Later that year politicians voted to close the school, and in 1896 Nishida obtained a position as instructor in German at his old school in Kanazawa, the Fourth Higher School. That same year also marks the birth of their first child, a girl whom they named Yayoi.

Nishida's new status as a father, now responsible for supporting a family, seemed to push him toward a more intense practice of Zen. But it was not an easy time for him, for his wife abruptly left with Yayoi, and as a result of this their parents ordered them to be separated for an unspecified time. Furthermore, on the teaching front, Nishida was dismissed due to a "reorganization of the teaching staff" by the Ministry of Education, the result of internal disagreements at the school. He spent much of the summer that year in intense Zen practice in Kyoto. To practice Zen one had to meditate for long hours each week at the monastery. It required diligence and endurance. News came at the end of his intensive Zen involvement that a one-year teaching position in German, in Yamaguchi, a rural community at the southwestern end of the main island of Honshu, was his if he wanted it. A year later he returned to a position in philosophy and German at the Fourth Higher School in Kanazawa. He and his wife and child were reunited, and a second child was born, a son whom they named Ken. All the while Nishida continued his Zen practice. Yusa's translation of Nishida's letter to a friend, on September 15, 1899, makes evident that he struggled with his many duties, family life, and Zen practice: "I'm ashamed that I have made very little progress in my Zen practice. Although I want to, it is really hard to practice Zen when I have a job in the outside world and a wife and children at home."[4] In another letter he makes plain his determination: "so regardless of whether I attained awakening or not, I intend to continue practicing Zen for the rest of my life."[5] To "awaken" in Zen means to break through the surface level of awareness, to a deeper level of self-awareness: to knowing who you really are, one might say. In 1903 he finally passed his *kōan* (*mu,* emptiness, nothingness—a *kōan* is a mental puzzle one is given as a challenge to solve, except that it has no mental or intellectual solution) and had his *kenshō* (seeing into one's true nature) experience.

In 1904, his brother Kyōjirō was killed in battle in the Russo-Japanese war, leaving a wife and child. While it took Nishida a long time to recover from this loss, nonetheless he saw to it that a husband was found for the widow, and he and Katomi adopted the child, raising her as their own. While Zen once again proved a comfort to him through a lengthy depression, it was at this time that he ended his formal practice of Zen. He now gave his full attention to philosophy and, in particular, to the study of ethics. His attention also turned to reading on psychology and to the writing of an essay entitled "Pure experience, cognition, will, and intellectual intuition," which became part one of his first book.[6]

In 1909 Nishida accepted a position teaching philosophy at Gakushōn University, in Tokyo. Nine months later he was appointed lecturer at Kyoto Imperial University, where he remained until his retirement in 1928. His career at Kyoto University was an illustrious one. In 1913 he was awarded the Doctor of Arts, granted tenure, and promoted to full professor. Through it all his melancholy personality was severely tested by a string of family tragedies: he himself succumbed to several lengthy bouts of illness. But in addition, "in 1918 his mother Tosa died at seventy-seven years of age. In 1919 his first wife Kotomi suffered a brain hemorrhage and was confined to bed in a paralyzed state. In 1920 their eldest son died of acute appendicitis at twenty-three years of age. In 1921 and 1922 their second, fourth, and sixth daughters were stricken with typhus. On January 23, 1925, Kotomi died. Six of his children were to die before him. These difficult years served to deepen Nishida's philosophical and personal integration acquired through his Zen training. His later writings featured the point that true religion and true philosophy issue forth from personal suffering."[7]

Pure Experience

It was in 1904 that Nishida read William James's *Varieties of Religious Experience,* finding it a "deep and delightful" work.[8] He took from James not only the term "pure experience," but also James's insistence on grounding philosophy on experience, rather than abstract theory. These insights would provide Nishida with the seminal concepts for his early work, and remained foundational insights for Nishida throughout his philosophical career. He took James's "radical empiricism" to be confirmation that all empiricism ought to be experientially based, that is, that the temptation to add nonexperiential ideas to an empirical philosophy ought to be avoided. It also meant that ideas that were grounded in experience must be included in any empirical philosophy. Hence, the Zen experiences of seeing into one's true nature and enlightenment were also empirical matters that had to be included in a truly empirical philosophy. Both James and Nishida doubted the adequacy of the intellect and its concept formation to deliver a true picture of the complexity of everyday human experience. Together with the fact that concepts are already once removed in our attempt to "represent" experience, James further argued that "experience *as experience* outstrips our capacity to conceptually or linguistically articulate it."[9] James posited a "primal stuff," a "big blooming buzzing confusion," and out of "this aboriginal sensible muchness attention carves out objects, which conception then names and identifies forever—in the sky 'constellations,' on the earth 'beach,' 'sea,' 'cliff,' 'bushes,' 'grass.' Out of time we cut 'days,' 'nights,' 'summers' and 'winters.' "[10] As Edward Moore puts it, for James "the world consists of a flux of pure experience out of which man—by observation and inspiration—carves isolable chunks to which he gives names.

These chunks have no identity in reality as chunks. They are simply artificial cuts out of what is in reality a continuum."[11]

For his part, Nishida maintained that "meanings and judgments are an abstracted part of the original experience, and compared with the actual experience they are meager in content."[12] James called concepts "static abstractions" taken from the original "given" in experience: concepts are like the "perchings" of birds in flight, just temporary resting places chosen to stop the incessant flight of experience. Concepts are fixations on a limited aspect of that flow for practical purposes. But there are more smells, colors, textures, and shapes in experience than we have names for. The color chips in a paint store, for example, while outstripping previously limited color choices, can never reach a full display of the infinite color variations possible. Each color chosen is a static fixation on one point in the color spectrum, while the additional experiences of color variations are inexhaustible. If texture and shape are added to the mix, the possibilities expand exponentially. Furthermore, as Zen training makes apparent, to divest oneself of concepts, meanings, judgments, and other mental additions renders one capable of "just experiencing." Taken to its goal, learning to just experience is to encounter reality as it is, and to experience one's "deep" or "real" self, just as it is. As Krueger explains, "Pure experience for Nishida is both the primordial foundation of consciousness *and* the ultimate ground of all reality," as absolute nothingness.[13] The aim of Zen training is to become one with ultimate reality in the sense that one comes to "grasp" the oneness of all things, a unity that is ineffable, unspeakable, because it is what it is prior to all distinctions, all carvings and conceptual fixations. It has no qualities, characteristics, or form. If followed far enough, pure experience ends in enlightenment, the awareness of the primal flow of reality as it is prior to all intellectual impositions upon it. To grasp this ineffable oneness is to understand that all things that exist are but manifestations or expressions of this original oneness, in which case it is to view the entire universe, in all its parts, as sacred, because all things are manifestations of this one source. All things are "kin," because they all have the same ancestry. Thus, the view from pure experience is that of a transformed world: one can never simply see the surface of reality alone, for all things have a deeper richness and worth that far surpasses the superficial surface view. As with Japanese philosophy generally, enlightenment is always transformative.

James did not take pure experience this far, resting content to propose it as a heuristic "limiting" concept in that it brought philosophy back to experience and posited a state of being prior to such distinctions as monism and dualism. But as a limiting concept, it did not need to be a fact of ordinary experience itself. James goes so far as to state that "only new-born babes, or men in semi-coma from sleep, drugs, illnesses, or blows, may be assumed to have an experience pure in the literal sense of a *that* which is not yet any definite what"[14] For Nishida on the other hand, pure experience was both given in experience, served as the basis of all possible experience, and was a real and definitive experience available to any and all who followed one or more of the meditative arts. Pure experience was directly available to those wise men and women, in a meditative culture, who sought it out.

But it was his reading of the French philosopher Henri Bergson on "immediate experience" that he found to be central to the development of his notion of pure experience: "It was only after I familiarized myself with Bergson's thought that I was able to formulate my idea of 'pure experience' and publish my *Zen no Kenkyō* [*Inquiry Into the Good*]."[15] Bergson believed that thinking distorts already given experience because it selects from, emphasizes, and deemphasizes portions of the whole of experience. Reason selects what is most useful to us, then discards the rest and, in doing so, falsifies reality as given to us as a continuous flow or flux. "Duration" is the term Bergson chose to capture this unceasing flow of experience. Only "intuition" is capable of apprehending the whole of our experience from within, rather than as objectified as though existing outside of us. In order to return to a true sense of reality-as-experienced, it is necessary to undo the work of the intellect, leave behind its categories, comparisons, abstractions, and part-by-part analysis, and return to the richness and vibrancy of the flowing and changing experience in its immediacy. "Duration" is the feeling of flow, in contrast to the constructed second-by-second time of the clock. Intuited duration is a return to the richness of the world as experienced, not to the world of scientific constructs or useful abstractions with much of the rich detail removed. Zen, too, teaches that the world as experienced is infinitely rich in properties, and its formal meditation practices have as one of its aims the stilling of the intellect's reformations of given experience.

To take an example, Zen monasteries often open to children during the summer months. The story is told of a Zen monk ushering young children into the temple grounds, gathering them around a goldfish pond, providing them with paper and pencils, and asking them to draw what they saw. Upon completion of a drawing, he would ask them not to move, but to compose a different drawing of the same scene. This would be repeated several times. Hopefully, the penny would drop, and the students would come to see that there are an indefinite number of perspectives of a single subject matter if one continues to drink in aspects not seen at first. For Bergson, this is to intuit the larger whole of experience from within, rather than prejudging it through assumptions of reason or a simplified constructed map of interpretation. Intuition offers a glimpse into reality that is always changing, thrusting, moving, expanding. Reality displays this force, this energy—this *élan vital* ("vital force")—which incessantly creates by forming matter as a resistance to which it responds in various ways. Nishida would have found nearly all of this remarkably similar to his own developing standpoint arising out of his Buddhist heritage: the Buddha taught that all is impermanent and that impermanence or change is the only reality.

Bergson's call to return to experience, stripped of all additions, is echoed by Nishida's opening words in his *Inquiry*: "To experience means to know facts just as they are, to know in accordance with facts by completely relinquishing one's own fabrications. What we usually refer to as experience is adulterated with some sort of thought, so by *pure* I am referring to the state of experience just as it is without the least addition of deliberative discrimination."[16] The years of Zen training that he underwent were years of forgetting—of stilling, and then emptying the intellect—remembering what it is to experience the flux of reality directly. Yet it is not an abandoning of the intellect, for we must make plans and create maps of convenience and discernment, but rather a recovery of that originary awareness out of which reason, science, religion, and so on, carve out their domains of understanding. A map of intellectual understanding is always an impoverished selection taken from an original richness.

Pure experience is the starting point, for it is through pure experience that knowledge of what is comes to be known, and all other knowledge derives from or arises out of pure experience as it is given to us. Experience is an event of consciousness and, therefore, the I (the experiencer) is always a part of what is experienced. Nishida's former student, Nishitani Keiji, writes "that I see with my own eyes and feel with my own heart, or at any rate that I am myself present in what is going on, is an essential part of the experience of 'knowing facts as they are.'"[17] Nishida offers examples of pure experience, such as seeing a color or hearing a sound. Before one interprets the color as belonging to a "thing," or as akin to similar colors seen in the past, there is just the awareness of color. Later, one can assign the term *red* to this seeing, and *cherry* to the object that is before us, or that it is a darker red than usual, or any number of intellectual modifications. To take another example, when you first awaken, before you have established where you are or who you are, pure experience is present. Then, you carve up that experience, thankful that you have another day before you, now aware of the day's obligations as you focus on the blankets, the sunshine or its lack, and the aches and pains in your body or a vibrant sense of good health. It could be that all or most of this was available in the first instance of awakening, but was just not yet abstracted from the immediacy of the whole.

What follows from this is that our best chance to grasp reality in its richness is through pure experience. Furthermore, all other knowledge necessarily begins with this wholeness. It is our first and most basic apprehension of what is. Nishida suggests that "all experience, including such simple things as seeing a flower, hearing the sound of a frog diving into the water, or eating a meal, consist in 'knowing facts as they are.' "[18] His mention of a frog diving into the water is a reference to the poet Bashō's famous haiku poem:

> The old pond
> A frog jumps in—
> The sound of the water.[19]

The final line could equally well be translated as "splash" or "plop," but in the translation chosen here, one is left to imagine, in one's own way, what the sound of water is. Closer to the original Japanese, it leaves undecided what the sound is. Either way, this haiku poem is a superb example of a pure experience. The poem itself is reflective and constructed, but it captures well what Nishida means by pure experience. Before reflection and discrimination, one supposes that there was merely a sound. The heart of the poem is the sound of water: the rest of the poem simply sets up the experience. Perhaps, initially, Bashō was meditating or resting by the pond, or writing another poem, when suddenly he heard a noise. It is not yet a splash, and there is not yet a frog or water in mind. Just a noise. Surprised, Bashō comes awake and provides the context to explain the noise. The mere seventeen syllables that constitute a haiku forces the conveying of the experience in a minimum of words. Ideally, the words will not get in the way of the conveying of the experience. Did you hear the sound when you read the poem? Did you actually experience it as though you were there?

Nishida concludes the first paragraph of the *Inquiry* by noting that "when one directly experiences one's own state of consciousness, there is not yet a subject or an object, and knowing and its object are completely unified."[20] Prior to judgments, or any other mental manipulation of the original seamless awareness, prior even to the subject/object distinction, awareness simply is, and it is completely unified. Such experience is a simple, single experience. However complex a pure experience is as viewed upon later reflection, at the moment when it occurs it is a "simple fact," a unified whole. And it is always in the present. Even memory of the past is a remembrance in the present. Nevertheless, within pure experience it is possible to shift focus of the experience over a period of time; creating a "perceptual train," and each act of focus "gives rise to the next without the slightest crack between them for thinking to enter."[21] It remains a strict unity, as in a well-practiced performance of a musical piece, or the skilled demonstration of a martial artist attacked by a half-dozen fellow martial artists. A strict unity, amid shifts of focus, allows a remarkable spontaneity to arise. Whether a unified musical phrase, or a seemingly effortless over-coming of the attackers, the fluidity achieved is of a single, unified awareness. Nishida cites Goethe's "intuitive composition of a poem while dreaming"[22] as a further instance of a unified complexity.

Nishida maintains that pure experience "is the intuition of facts just as they are and that it is devoid of meaning."[23] The addition of meaning or judgments about pure experience add nothing to the experience itself, but are mere abstractions from it, or additions to it, as in comparing one experience with another, or taking an abstracted aspect of the experience and comparing it to other such experiences. The result might be, "This is the brightest blue I have ever seen," which is comparing one experience to another, but adds nothing to the original blueness as experienced. Furthermore, the extracting of meaning and the making of judgments about a pure experience cause the pure experience to "break apart" and, as a result, it "crumbles away."[24] Knowing things as they are is, for Nishida, a genuine "grasp of life" to be gained only through intuition.[25]

A Unifying Power

Pure experience is, therefore, the bedrock of Nishida's metaphysics, his more systematic account of reality. We have already seen that pure experience is always a unity, that it may be complex, and that while always occurring in the present, it may extend as a unity over a stretch of time. It is prior to the subject/object distinction, and prior to the division of consciousness into the aspects of knowing, feeling, and willing. While this unity is a unity of conscious experience, it is, therefore, our conscious self at its basic starting point, but it also forms the basic structure of all reality. Nishida maintains that "since both material and spiritual phenomena are identical from the point of view of pure experience, these two kinds of unifying functions must ultimately be of the same sort. The unifying power at the foundation of our thinking and willing and the unifying power at the foundation of the phenomena of the cosmos are directly the same. For example, our laws of logic and mathematics are at once the basic principles by which the phenomena of the universe come into being."[26] Furthermore, the unifying power at the "basis of our thinking and willing (the world of the subject) is 'directly identical' with the unifying power in the phenomena of the cosmos (the world of objects)."[27] In other words, while we can never know a flower as it is in itself apart from human consciousness, the fact that we, along with the flower, are self-expressions of God, or the originating energy, should indicate to us that the same unifying power is at work throughout the universe. Hence, I can know the unifying power that is the flower by means of the same unifying power that is my mind, and my perception. This is not a stringent proof, of course, but a reasonable deduction from the metaphysics of becoming which Nishida adopts. It is not, as with Descartes and Berkeley, that God would not deceive us, but more pragmatically, that as self-manifestations of a creating energy, we are of the same stuff, and exist by means of a unifying activity that extends throughout the universe. Thus, the macrocosm is reflected in the microcosm; and the reverse also holds. This principle of unity is found in all things, mental or material and, indeed, is that which spawns them both.

The importance of pure experience in Nishida's lifelong intellectual output is disputed. Some consider it to be an early approach, later superseded by more potent concepts such as "self-consciousness," "topos" (field, basho) and "identity of self-contradiction," representing chronological advances in his philosophic development.

However, I side with those authors who view pure experience as the root notion, significantly present throughout his development, although continually refined and amplified throughout the unfolding of his increasingly mature and complex thought. Pure experience is our access to what is real, and that insight necessarily pervades his entire collection of writings. It also reveals our own deep (or true) self. By looking within, our depth is revealed, as is the depth of trees, rocks, waterfalls, birds, and cicada when apprehended as pure experience. All of these are now grasped in a more robust fullness than when ordinarily perceived abstractly through one or more stripped-down categories of expectation. When the self is free of ego, one is able to comprehend the ultimate reality, which manifests as every thing that is, has been, or will be. Ordinary perception rarely breaks out of habits of expectation, making the richness of seeing things as though for the first time, each time, quite impossible.

Gathering together some key ingredients in understanding the force and nature of pure experience, we might focus on the following excerpts:

> For many years I wanted to explain all things on the basis of pure experience as the sole reality. . . . Over time I came to realize that it is not that experience exists because there is an individual, but that an individual exists because there is experience [pure experience is prior to the distinctions of things and self, so the experience had by a self is carved out of the unity which is pure experience].[28]

Again:

> It is not that there is experience because there is an individual, but that there is an individual because there is experience. The individual's experience is simply a small, distinctive sphere of limited experience within true experience.[29]

/ He adds that he is neither a materialist (the view that matter is fundamental), nor an idealist (the view that mind or consciousness is fundamental):/

> Materialists consider the existence of matter an indubitable, self-evident fact, and from this starting point they attempt to explain mental phenomena as well. . . . From the perspective of pure experience, there are no independent, self-sufficient facts apart from our phenomena of consciousness.[30]

At the same time, it would be a misunderstanding to suppose that phenomena of consciousness are "true reality." The better position is that "true reality is neither a phenomenon of consciousness nor a material phenomenon."[31] And because reality is always reality for consciousness, and since consciousness always includes feeling and willing, "it is the artist, not the scholar, who arrives at the true nature of reality."[32] It is the artist who does not concern him or herself with subjectivity or objectivity, who, in order to create must be fully engaged in a creative event through knowing, feeling, and willing, and who is ever aware that artistic reality "is a succession of events that flow without stopping."[33] Thus, your pure experience and mine are the doorways to reality.

Pure or direct experience is prior to all distinctions, including the distinction between seer and seen. It arises before there is an individual self as distinguished from the experience and presupposed as having the experience. It is prior to distinctions of self, other, thing, internal or external. "A direct experience goes beyond the individual—it is fundamentally trans-individual."[34]

Perhaps it is now clear that Nishida's philosophical strategy was to grasp reality through pure experience rather than through experience as already structured by a subject looking outward to objects already identifiable and dualistically separate from subjects, or by means of rational deduction or empirical induction. The way forward is to go back, to the beginning, to experience in its purest form. It is a strictly unified awareness grasped through what Nishida calls "intellectual intuition," or direct seeing.

Nishida uses the term *intuition* in two different ways (with a third use insofar as he adopts Kant's use of the term to mean sense perception. To taste an apple is, for Kant, to sensuously "intuit" the apple's taste—in this way Kant uses intuition in the way we normally speak of "sensation." Kant also uses "intuition" to refer to the a priori *forms* of intuition: space and time, while given in experience, are not gained from experience. Rather, they are our contributions to the *matter* of experience). The first of the two terms that Nishida introduces is "intellectual intuition." It is not a form of sense perception, but a grasping of "ideal" objects, such as the "unity" that underlies all awareness. Nishida tells us that it is an enlargement or deepening of pure experience. But because such awareness is not logical or inferential, some scholars have suggested that Nishida ought to have referred to it as "*creative* intuition," a direct seeing of artistic, religious, or moral insight. It is related to inspiration, an immediate seeing of a correct conclusion without calculation in any form. It is a state of awareness that has transcended the subject/object distinction, resulting in a unified experience out of which subject and object are carved. The unity that intellectual intuition grasps underlies all other experience.

"Action intuition," a feature of Nishida's later work, emphasizes that we do not just contemplate the world, but that we act in and on the world. Whereas "intellectual intuition" is more a *psychological* analysis, "action intuition" involves the body in the seeing and acting mode of our awareness: such intuition does not simply refer to the state of our consciousness, but to our engagement with the historical, physical world. Here, theory and practice are joined together. One is informed in order to act, but there is no space between the knowing and the doing. Models of "action intuition" include the master painter, or master swordsman, who act without having to deliberate. Their integration is such that there is no intervening moment discernable between seeing and acting— all calculation is absent, all concerns about goals or the future are absent—and there remains only the seamless seeing-as-acting in the moment, in the here-and-now instant.

The Place of Doubt

Since pure experience is prior to meaning and judgment, there is as yet no self and no world. How, then, do these distinctions arise, and can they be trusted? Like Descartes, Nishida begins with doubt, questioning assumptions of whatever stripe: "The independent existence of mind and matter is generally considered an intuitive fact, but on reflection we realize that this clearly is not the case."[35] We cannot know things apart from our consciousness. All that we can know with a certainty that is beyond doubt are the phenomena of consciousness, as pure experience, "intuited" without inference or assumption. Even our bodies are phenomena of consciousness, "for it is not that consciousness is within the body, but that the body is within consciousness."[36] Nishida further clarifies this by stating that there are only phenomena of consciousness, and not both phenomena of matter and mind: "Material phenomena are abstractions from phenomena of consciousness that are common to us all and possess an unchanging relation to each other."[37]

Recall that Nishida argued that since neither the mind nor material objects can be said to exist as independent entities apart from pure experience, hence, reality as given is neither a phenomenon of consciousness nor is it a material phenomenon. Reality is an activity and this activity is a unifying activity. As an activity within consciousness, it includes feeling and willing. When we retrospectively unpack the "meaning" of the content of pure experience and make abstract judgments about it, notions of objectivity and subjectivity together with the distinctions of knowing, willing, and feeling are all present.

There is a unifying factor or principle behind all of reality. Nishida's continuing attempts to put his understanding of the unifying principle into rigorous and precise language are to be discerned throughout the *Inquiry*. He repeatedly writes of "intellectual intuition" or of a "grasp of life" to indicate how we come to know of the existence of this unifying principle. Such "knowing" is not the knowing of ordinary thinking or of ordinary perceiving. The unifying principle can only be known by becoming it, or appropriating it. It appears that what he has in mind is a pure experience that is prior to the distinctions of mind and matter, and so on, but that reveals the ultimate source of all that is. It cannot be objectified, for while it makes objectivity possible, it cannot itself be objectified. We can only know it intuitively, that is to say, directly. To fix this point, Nishitani quotes Zen master Dōgen (who in turn cites an ancient Chinese sage) who asks, "How do we think what lies beyond the reach of thinking?" The answer given is that "we do not think it."[38] Leave the thinking self behind and *become* the unifying principle. Meditate on it, but do not think it, nor should you struggle to not-think it. Let pure experience come to the fore *without* thinking.[39]

Put in more religious terminology, remembering all the while that Nishida rejects what he refers to as an "infantile" notion of God as a being outside the universe, affirming instead that "God is the unifier of the universe," for the universe is God's manifestation.[40] Given that each of us is a part of the universe as God's manifestation, then the unifying power is within us as well, as an expression of the unifying power of reality.[41]

In emphasizing that our deepest understanding of reality is gained not through reasoning or sensation, Nishida offers a new kind of metaphysics. Neither rational, nor empirical as given through the senses, his solution is radically experiential. Knowledge of reality is gained intuitively in and through pure experience. It is not posited, nor can it be grasped through the five senses, but it can be grasped intuitively as pure experience. To know it is to be it. To be it is to live it. To live it is to feel the oneness or unity of all things, one's own kinship with ultimate unity and to acquire closure and joy by having satisfied one's desire to comprehend this ultimate unity. God is the "greatest and final unifier of our consciousness; our consciousness is one part of God's consciousness and its unity comes from God's unity."[42] It is love that seeks unity, and "love is the deepest knowledge of things." Analytical knowledge and inferential knowledge are "superficial," and "cannot grasp reality." Therefore, "we can reach reality only through love. Love is the culmination of knowledge."[43]

Becoming the Thing Itself

The theoretical aspects of Nishida's philosophy take on a more concrete result when applied to ordinary living. He concludes that what Japanese people "strongly yearn for" is to become one with things and events: "it is to become one at that primal point in which there is neither self nor others."[44] What is required to achieve this oneness is to negate the self and become the thing itself: "to empty the self and see things, for the self to be immersed in things, 'no-mindedness.' "[45] The haiku poet who becomes one with the frog or the water, the Zen monk who experiences an ecstasy of oneness when immersed in the glory of a dewdrop on a rose petal, "see" by becoming the thing seen. Pure experience necessitates that one let go of all subjective conjectures in order to unite with the basic nature of something else, hence, "those who have extinguished the self—are the greatest."[46] One experiences the flower (of course, experience is always in consciousness), but it is within this experience that one achieves union. Union is a kind of love, and this union with an object is, like all unions, an instance of such loving. For, as has been said already, "love is the culmination of knowledge," and not a detour from it.[47] Here, Nishida is not describing a process that is foreign to those from the East or the West: to focus solely on a mathematical problem, a complex dance step, learning a musical piece, or on making love is an occasion to totally forget the self and everything else except the experience at hand. It is a merging with the "other" such that, at best, subject and object are totally united in a single awareness. While such experiences are not uncommon, it is the Japanese who have refined the methodology in pursuit of such experiences. The Japanese arts, from the martial

arts to poetry, flower arranging, the way of tea, landscape gardening, and so on all have as their goal "enlightenment." This means
that one forgets the self and becomes one with either something
or everything. Such a mystical vision, the world over, is a "seeing" of the oneness of all things. But the artist need not be a true
mystic to enter into a relation of intimacy with another (animate
or inanimate). To take an example, the world-renowned landscape
architect and Sōtō Zen priest, Masuno Shunmyo, whom I had the
opportunity to dialogue with at length at his temple in Yokohama,
meditates before he begins to create in order to become focused
and tranquil: "When I encounter a stone or a tree, I communicate
with it; I ask it where it wants to be planted or placed."[48] He
believes that everything that exists has *kokoro,* spirit or, at the very
least, some sort of awareness that is to be respected. The Japanese
have long held rocks in high esteem, and expensive rock stores can
be found across Japan. Not that the average Japanese homeowner
communicates with his or her garden rocks, but the status of rocks
is far higher there then in the West. Nishitani argues that rocks,
trees, grass, and animals may all be engaged in a kind of "communication" and should be treated as "thous" rather than "its," as
an "awareness" of some sort, and not just an inanimate lump of
dead matter. He writes that "to speak to a stone might sound like
a metaphor. But truthfully . . . the question of whether speaking
to a stone or to a plant is to be regarded as a mere metaphor is
something worthy of deep consideration."[49] Borrowing the "I-thou"
way of speaking of Martin Buber, he analyzes that language in
considerable detail: "Ordinarily, a second person way of thinking
is applied to the relationship between human beings. We relate
ourselves to inorganic and non-living things other than humans in
a third person fashion, in the form of 'it.'" But just as we might
name a pet, thereby referring to it as a "you" or "thou," Nishitani
maintains the view "that this is true not only of animals but also
of trees, grass, stones," and insofar as a "person loves a stone,
there takes place an exchange of communication between them."[50]
The key to understanding his position resides in language wherein
the root meaning of the Greek *logos,* like the Japanese *morotomo,*

is "to gather," or to be together with someone or something, as with a friend. There is a "deep connection" between one thing and another, as in a friendship, because "a human being and a stone are together, they stand face to face with each other" in the place (or *basho*) which is the "home-ground" of each and every thing.

Nishida's metaphor of the lining of a kimono is helpful here. If the kimono is well tailored, it is unseen. Yet one knows the lining is there because of the "hang" of the garment. It is to recognize the lining of each thing as being kin to our own lining or originating source. Substituting the Buddhist word "*Śūnyatā*" for *basho* (nothingness, place), Nishitani explains that on the field of *Śūnyatā*, there is "a most intimate encounter with everything that exists."[51] In other words, we are one with every other thing, and yet are, at the same time, distinct. Furthermore, our "oneness" is such that every thing holds up the being of every other thing. This refers to an enlightened awareness that everything interpenetrates every other thing. Nishitani quotes Musō Kokushi, who wrote that "hills and rivers, the earth, plants and trees, tiles and stones, all of these are the self's own original part."[52] In human relationships we often cannot put into words what we are feeling, and in a similar way we cannot express our experienced sense of connection with flowers and rocks. Such awareness arises from our depths where we are selves that are not ordinary selves, known only intuitively. At this deep level, our pre-self empathizes with the incredible richness of the universe, and everything in it.

The analysis provided by Nishida and Nishitani on becoming the thing itself is borne out in the work of the landscape architect Masuno and his own description of his relationship with the garden and its materials. For example, he describes the care which he takes in the initial selection of rocks: "Even when I am looking for suitable stones and other materials for a garden, I go up into the mountains and make numerous sketches in order to find stones and plants with the right degree of empathy." The term *empathy* is clearly a "thou" response, for he believes that each rock and plant is unique, important, and possessed of immense value: to think and feel this way is already to be in an intimate relationship with them. Even the garden site itself is important: "It is not acceptable to move in the earth-moving machines to fit some economic or leveling demand. The site and its history must be itself engaged as a part of the whole garden which is in the making. When I am on site, I don't simply arrange stones and things like waterfalls or cascades to suit the forms of the remaining concrete. Instead, what I try to do is to make the landscaping and such things as retaining concrete walls fit in with the waterfalls, cascades and other features that have been formed by the temporarily set out groups of stones, themselves arranged as a result of their dialogue with me." His elaboration is clear confirmation of his experience of the oneness of things. He writes, "I wonder just what kind of spirit a certain stone has and how it would prefer to be set out. This is also true of plants and I always consider how I think the plants would like to be displayed. I always feel at one with the plants, when I am planting them, and with the stones, when I am arranging them."[53] Masuno contends that to be in the moment when setting out a garden does not mean to be reflecting on gardening, but to be *in* the garden, to be an integral part of the whole. One is then truly in one's depth, in a place unreachable through reason or language but always available to one through direct experience.

When we become one with a flower, we have become one with the unifying principle of the entire cosmos, which orchestrates the flower becoming a flower. Rather than a dead, material universe, Nishida envisions reality as an "activity of consciousness."[54] A mathematician becomes one with the unifying principle of a proof, axiom, or theory. The entire universe and everything in it is aware, at least in some sense, and expressive of an activity of consciousness which, too, displays this unifying principle that makes it what it is. The same "spirit" or unifying force exists "throughout reality . . . in nature as well . . . [but] in so-called non-living things, the unifying self has not yet appeared in actuality as a fact of direct experience. The tree itself is not aware of the unifying activity."[55]

When we empty ourselves of ego and thinking and intuit experience directly, we discover our own deep self and the nature of realty itself unadorned by theory, assumption, meaning, or purpose.

Contact with our own deep reality and with the deep unifying activity of the universe Nishida often terms "God," keeping in mind that his notion of God is not the "extremely infantile" notion of God held by many, but rather a direct experience of a unity within and without. We can experience foundational unity within ourselves, hence, God is within us. God is *both* transcendent and immanent: "Because God is no-thing, there is no place where God is not, and no place where God does not function."[56]

At least in the *Inquiry*, Nishida, through pure experience, discovers a pathway to an encounter with reality that is, for him, ultimate and foundational. No doubt it is by now obvious to the reader that the only proof that Nishida has for this move from pure experience to a vision of ultimate reality is the experience of it. Yet, if Nishida is correct, then anyone can verify this claim, but only by gaining the experience for him/herself. The journey demanded is akin to Zen training; a stilling of the chattering mind, such as through meditation of some sort, and a letting-go of the ego and ordinary awareness. Then, as D. T. Suzuki gestured in an interview by moving his hands in an upward movement from his midriff, something arises.[57] As a lifelong friend and colleague of Nishida's, no doubt Suzuki would call this something "pure experience," or "god," or "absolute nothingness."

Absolute Nothingness

Nishida's *Complete Works* (*Nishida Kitarō Zenshu*) constitute nineteen volumes written over more than a fifty-year period. However influential and groundbreaking the publishing of the *Inquiry* had been, he went on to try many different approaches to the formulation of his initial quest for an ultimate reality to be found before, beneath, or behind the dualism of subject and object and all other intellectual distinctions. The *Inquiry* had established psychologically the primacy of experience and the self that captures it. In his attempt to develop a fuller picture of reality itself and to diminish dependence on the experience of it as captured by and in consciousness, Nishida began to think in terms of an "absolute nothingness," a reality that, while without characteristics, could serve as the foundation for everything else in his philosophical conception of things. It serves as the widest and utterly comprehensive formlessness from which all forms derive.

And we come to know it not through thinking—for it is unthinkable and unnameable except that we must use a minimalist term such as *nothingness* in our attempt to point it out. Like a finger pointing at the moon, the term tells you nothing except to point to a reality beyond words. The thinking involved in thinking the unthinkable is negation of what is ordinarily meant by "thinking": Recall, "How do we think what lies beyond the reach of thinking? We do not think it."[58] Instead, we become it, we intuit it in Nishida's sense of acquiring a "grasp of life."[59] It seems to me that we are still talking about pure experience. To be sure, Nishida is taking a new tack in developing further what was briefly laid out in his first work, seeking other ways of coming to grips with "pure experience." Nishida makes it plain that what he is pointing to—the ineffable nothingness—is a perspective deeply embedded in "Eastern" cultures generally, and in Japan in particular: "I think that we can distinguish the West to have considered being as the ground of reality, the East to have taken nothingness as its ground. I will call them reality as form and reality as the formless, respectively."[60] Nothingness (i.e., God) is found in pure experience, but, of course, not all pure experiences are of God or nothingness. In one sense, both God and (absolute) nothingness can be used interchangeably, for both refer to the highest and most encompassing reality. Yet, in a deeper and more profound sense, God may be left behind. D. T. Suzuki made this point when he wrote that "what we must grasp is that in which God and men have not yet assumed their places."[61] God is the penultimate notion, with absolute nothingness assuming the highest and most inclusive position. Pure experience, before it is carved up by the intellect, has no distinctions. But God has qualities, and is therefore more than just pure experience. Nothingness, as a mere pointer or placeholder, is precisely without qualities because it is prior to all qualities and distinctions. Nothingness is that undivided something out of which God arises. It is a nothingness beyond God. Still, for those without the philosophical or religious skill to grasp what is meant by "comprehending the incomprehensible," then "God" is a meaningful term to point to a reality beyond the "seen" and "comprehensible." For Nishida, belief in God can be a springboard to the incomprehensibly real, or, it can simply congeal into a set of beliefs and doctrines through which most people understand what is meant by a "higher reality." In a sense, God and nothingness are two sides of the same coin, and yet, it is the side of nothingness that reaches the farthest and most inclusive understanding. You might say that while nothingness contains God, God does not encompass nothingness. For the most part, when Nishida writes of "God," he is writing of absolute nothingness.

For Nishida, God is an experience, and the pathway that leads to such an experience is through the lifelong practice of self-cultivation, through whatever form or discipline is chosen. Religion, he writes, is "an event of one's soul," and rational proofs and blind belief have little or nothing to do with God.[62] As noted earlier, "If we seek God in the facts of the external world, God must inescapably be a hypothetical God. Further, a God set up outside the universe as a creator or overseer of the universe cannot be deemed a true, absolutely infinite God. The religion of India of the distant past and the mysticism that flourished in Europe in the fifteenth and sixteenth centuries sought God in intuition realized in the inner soul, and this I consider to be the deepest knowledge of God."[63] This ground or base of reality is to be grasped through intuition. The term *intuition* in Japanese means "direct experience," and may refer to a kind of "feeling." Paradoxically, this grasp of reality is achieved by means of a "reversed eye," that is to say, by looking inward rather than outward. Nishida, together with many of the mystics of all traditions, asserts that God is to be found within us. The true or deep self within each of us is identical with God, indeed is God's own self-manifestation. To see the divine within ourselves is, at the same time, to see God: "the unifying power of infinite reality is there," within us.[64] The claim that we are God in our depths and that we are one with God in our nature is rarely found in the three main Western religions (Christianity, Judaism, and Islam), but the idea is ubiquitous in the East. Nishitani summarizes Nishida's position precisely: "How does this [great] . . . self relate to God? Clearly God is conceived of as something inseparable from the true self. God does not transcend the true self and stand outside it."[65] The seeming duality of Creator and created is erased in our depths, allowing us to see the nondual unity of all things. Recall that pure experience is experience as it is prior to the subject/object split, indeed prior to all division and distinction making. Subject and object, self and other have to be carved out of something that is not yet so carved. Since the deep self as pure experience cannot be objectified, spoken of directly, or perceived, Nishida calls it a *basho,* an empty place, a field, or nothingness (in the sense of the *basho* of absolute nothingness: Nishida later describes three *basho*; of being, of relative nothingness, and of absolute nothingness. *Basho* is often used to mean *universal,* when used in its logical sense rather than its ontological sense as a description of reality, from which an objective self can be abstracted, but which presents itself as an awareness without one who is aware; a seamless awareness where knower and what is known are not yet distinguished. The deep self of pure experience is not a construction of consciousness, but a manifestation of that unity that lies at its depths, and at the bottom or foundation of everything else. It is a cosmic consciousness.

Nishida's conception of the ultimate, or God, is not that of a transcendent personality outside of our world. God is seen as immanent in everything that exists, and yet, at the same time, transcendent. Rather than a pantheism, what is proposed here is what contemporary philosophers of religion term "panentheism": God is in everything, but is more than everything. Pantheism—or all-is-God-ism—maintains that the universe and everything in it is God. Panentheism adds to this that God is more than that, for God also transcends and is the source of all that is. The result is an immanent-transcendence (or a transcendent-immanence); God is inherent in all things, and yet, at the same time, transcends all things. For Nishida, in order to distance his thought from the heavy baggage connected with Judaism's YHWH, Christianity's triune God, and Islam's Allah, substitutes instead the unifying factor displayed by everything that exists, yet is that in itself which is unknowable except through direct experience and remains beyond words. It might be more accurate to speak of the nothingness beyond God. In fact, the thirteenth-century Christian mystic, Meister Eckhart, came to much the same conclusion when he prayed to be rid of God in order to apprehend the Godhead beyond God.[66] For Nishida, "The unity of consciousness cannot become the object of knowledge. It transcends all categories . . ."[67]

Earlier it was noted that God or nothingness was to be found by looking inward, which is the direct path to the experience of the divine. But one who understands can also find nothingness in each and every thing. Nishida uses the image of a *kimono*, you will recall: looking at a beautiful kimono, one does not see the lining. Yet, in another more profound sense, the lining is invisibly visible, for one can detect it by the way the kimono "hangs." A well-tailored garment is lined, and while the lining should not be visible, a discerning eye detects its presence by the manner in which the garment drapes the body and holds its shape. Similarly, an "enlightened" individual who is aware of the oneness of all things will look into a flower or a stone or a songbird and grasp its divinity, its kinship with us and with nothingness; its double identity.

Expanding on this, it is not only flowers and birds that possess this kinship with the divine, but seemingly undesirable things as well. There is a well-known Zen *kōan* (a teaching tool—a puzzle unsolvable by reason or intellect, to stop the chattering mind, allowing one to focus on what is before one, here and now) that asks the question, "Why do birds shit on Buddha's head?" No doubt there are several acceptable answers to this *kōan*, but the issue is not the answer itself, it is the transformation in the student that the answer displays. Moreover, the insight behind the question is that any answer must go beyond the dualisms of good and bad, beautiful and ugly, and so on. Excrement is a natural aspect of living, an essential ingredient in the growing of food and a sought-after source of nourishment for countless bacteria, insects, birds, and animals. It is an indispensable part of the whole and a life-giving factor in the journey of existence. Here, too, the most fundamental experience (pre evaluation and judgment) is nondual experience. Such experience tells us that "there is nothing that is not a manifestation of God."[68]

On Becoming Enlightened

Nishida was engaged in Zen meditation over a period of ten years. Meditation involves both body and mind, as all of the Japanese "practices" do. Nishida's abstract theory and often complex prose offer a vision of reality that is difficult for the average person to easily comprehend. Relatively few become Zen monks, and even then the pathway can be arduous, long, and without any guarantee that the effort will bring about the hoped-for result, spiritual awakening in the form of enlightenment. Enlightenment is not the result of taking a course where hard work will inevitably bring with it a high mark. To know about unity and oneness intellectually is quite aside from the deep knowledge that actual, intuitive experience brings, and intellectual knowledge alone is rarely deeply transformative. To gain an enlightenment experience is to be transformed even though deeper potential transformations lie ahead. In Japan, the methods that may bring one to an enlightenment experience are numerous, traditional, and still readily accessible. All methods are *practices* and the practice continues to the end of one's life.[69] The practices or *dō* ("ways") include meditation, the various martial arts, poetry, landscape gardening, the way of tea (as in the tea ceremony), flower arranging, calligraphy, and any one of the many other forms of art if undertaken as a spiritual practice: pottery making, painting, woodcarving, weaving, papermaking, the making of fine swords, puppetry, dance, and so on. And to explore any of these practices seriously is to accept the challenge of lifelong transformation.

Returning to the example of Japanese landscape gardening of Masuno Shunmyo, it should be noted that, in addition to his gardening and lecturing, Masuno is also a Sōtō Zen priest. As a member of the Sōtō Zen tradition, emphasis is placed on the practice of meditation itself rather than on Rinzai Zen's focus on *kōans* and sitting meditation, with the achievement of enlightenment somewhere far in the distance. For Sōtō Zen followers, to commit oneself to meditational practice is already enlightenment: it is the practice itself that is *satori*. Enlightenment is not something elusive and far away, for it is right here now, within action. Gardening, among the many *dō*, is one method of practicing and revealing one's true nature, if undertaken with mindfulness, that is, as a meditational act. With gardening as his calling, Masuno always meditates before he begins to plan and design. "I do standing meditation for three or four minutes, at the garden site. This helps me to become peaceful, tranquil. Otherwise, with a racing mind, one would create a jumbled and out-of-control garden." One's *kokoro* (mind/heart) "must not be moving," but rather must be focused and as clear as a mirror-surfaced lake. Then, and only then, can a dialogue between the architect and the plants, rocks, and garden-site take place. Masuno explains that "everything that exists has *busshō* (Buddha-nature)." If everything that exists is a self-expression of the Buddha, or the absolute (God, nothingness), then we have to grant that rocks and plants have the same status as human beings; everything is equally worthy, of unique value. Thus, he concludes, "We must respect each other, sustain and preserve each other in a mutuality of help and assistance." Continuing with his cosmic account of things, Masuno explained his belief that "everything that exists has *kokoro* (mind/heart). There is rock *kokoro*, and there is tree *kokoro*. In whatever form it exists, *kokoro* is to be respected. One must arrange the rocks or plants to express their own *kokoro*, and also arrange the rocks or plants in such a way as to express one's own philosophy and understanding. There is a mutuality of influence and effect. To do this is extremely difficult, for it demands a meeting of *kokoro* with *kokoro*." Landscape gardening is a practice that leads one toward enlightenment, or, at least, toward the grasping of the interconnectedness of all things as divine manifestations of the absolute.

Each of these kinds of practice is designed to shift one's way of seeing and acting in the world. It is a spiritual shift in that one's outlook is now broad (cosmic), rather than narrow (individualistic, tribal, or nationalistic), with a resultant sense of being at one with the evolutionary flow of existence and wide open to its magnificent and ever-changing display.

Nishida maintains that feeling (emotion) is what is left when all content is removed from consciousness. This is most clearly seen when the self is completely absorbed in an activity, and all qualities disappear in one undifferentiated awareness which is, nonetheless, perfectly lucid and clear. The focus is in the moment, in the now. In this sense, your deep self is an undifferentiated place (*basho*) or clearing where all things arise. It is, itself, without characteristics and empty and so is "where" all things arise and take form. To say more is to lose it, to turn it into an external object and/or concept, thereby becoming blind to its essence as pure subjective awareness. It is formless awareness wherein all forms come to be known. The self is selfless. And just as the eye can see all things (under proper conditions) but can never see itself, the self can never be seen objectively, but can be known indirectly as awareness.

In a sense, then, one loses the world in the distinctionless "muchness" of pure awareness, just as one loses the permanency of the self as a fixed entity. The self is a place, a blank screen of awareness on which experience writes, and the person and the world reappear only afterward when one unpacks the incredible richness of experience. The person, the world, and the universe are all finite abstractions carved from a pure experience. You may recall that James describes this process as a carving out of objects from a sensible continuum. Thus, a once unified whole of experience becomes divided into parts and relations to which concepts are applied according to human needs and purposes. James's supposition was that "there is only one primal stuff or material in the world, a stuff of which everything is composed, and . . . we call that stuff 'pure experience.' "[70] James's insights are almost perfectly echoed by Nishida, except that it was Nishida who went on to construct and develop a comprehensive worldview on this foundation, a foundation that is not a supposition, but an attainable experience.

Self and World

Pure experience is the foundation of Nishida's philosophy, but out of it he develops a complete view of the human self and of the world. The "carving out" which James describes offers us a world of things, but it is Nishida, not James, who goes back to the beginnings in order to clarify the relationship of self and world to the original Oneness of everything. The religious West begins with the biblical depiction of the Garden of Eden. The various interpretations of this story all emphasize that Adam and Eve disobeyed God's command not to eat the fruit of the tree of the knowledge of good and evil. Why God would have so commanded is certainly less than clear. Nevertheless, for this "original sin" human beings were expelled from "Paradise" and, as a result, have hardship, suffering, pain, and death to look forward to. Nishida's take on the Garden of Eden story underscores just how different his position is from Western religious interpretations.

To begin, human beings, as represented by Adam and Eve, did not disobey God but, in fact, followed God's will precisely. The background to the story, as Nishida may have understood it, is that in the beginning there was absolute nothingness, a Oneness without a second of any sort. Absolute nothingness became many, while remaining One, in order to reflect itself to itself. It did so out of an urge to create, and out of an urge to know. Knowledge requires a knower and a known, and the many knew the One. But this separation of the many from the One was not an expulsion from the One, but an individuation of the One: it was an expression of the One's nature as creator and truth seeker. In this sense, Adam and Eve, representing the many, became separate individuals not in opposition to the One, but as an act of the One. The original Oneness of things—the true reference of "paradise," that is, being one with God—was surrendered in order for God to create. Creativity is the essence of the original Oneness, nothingness, or God. Imagine a singular, throbbing energy that needed to express itself, to evolve, to give birth. In order to do so the One had to become many. But this is contradictory! Indeed it is, if left without elaboration, and one of Nishida's later insights is that self and world are themselves self-contradictory identities stemming from an absolute that is self-contradictory. The One, in becoming many, was no longer one, *and yet*, remained One at the same time that the many were created. For the One to be truly creative, Oneness had to be "emptied" (or broken) in order for the many to arise, *and yet*, in so doing, remained One, but now encompassing the many. The "and yet" is a rough translation of *soku hi*, used often by Nishida to point out that something is other than itself and yet remains itself. By differentiating itself into many the One remains one, a oneness that now includes and embraces the many as itself. Moreover, the many, while "other" than the One, are at the same time part of the One. The One is many and the many are one. Nirvana is samsara; samsara is nirvana, as the oft quoted Buddhist mantra puts it. The real (nirvana) is to be found in the creation of the many in this world (samsara), and one can discern in the many, the One—one can look through the empirical form of a thing, and "see" or "intuit," or "feel" its formless heritage. This self-contradiction expresses the identity or nature of things as they are actually experienced. We live by dying, writes Nishida, and we die by living. To say less is to give an incomplete account of actual human life. Each of us is a seemingly self-contradictory identity. We live by expending our lives, minute by minute, day by day, and we die progressively by choosing to live our lives, minute by minute, as we do. How we choose to die by living makes all the difference, of course. We can fritter it away, enjoy it, fear it, resent it, or be creatively who we really are in using it up. As sons and daughters of the One, we, too, are creators.

We ourselves and the world can be viewed in two directions: as one with the One, or as one of the many. This "double aperture" is a unity, but also a self-contradiction. The contradictions are preserved in their differentiation, and yet there remains an underlying unity. This is Nishida's dialectical logic of *soku hi*: the simultaneous acceptance of both is and is not as pertaining to the same thing. In symbolic representation, A is A; A is not A; therefore A is A. I see the mountains; I see that they are not mountains; therefore, I see the mountains anew. The mountains are not just particular mountains, for they are also one with the One: the formless whole is what formed particulars rest within. This is the background to the logic of *basho,* of the nothingness as the formlessness out of which all formed things arise: the enlightened seer sees both aspects at once, a kind of stereoscopic vision. In Nishida's own formulation, "the correspondence of the world and self, namely, of whole and one in the logic of *basho* is linked up with the self-identity of contradiction because if we keep saying 'One becomes the many, and the many becomes One' they will be forever opposed to each other. . . . The Absolute is what embraces both of these opposite directions as the Self-identity of contradiction."[71] Opposition remains, but at the same time the One embraces the many as the formless *place* (*basho*) out of which they arise. The forms, therefore, are self-expressions of the formless. The many are contained in the formlessness of nothingness, the One, while they still maintain their status and nature as distinctly what they are.

Nishida rejects the supremacy of an either/or logic, where experience must be one or the other of two opposites and proposes a both/and logic. To more fully capture what we experience, we must speak the language of opposites: we both live, and at the same time we are dying; or again, everything is what it is, *and yet* is lined with nothingness; a thing is distinctly what it is, *and yet* it is (a part of) the One. The nothingness of anything is infinitely rich in properties, for it is the pure experiential muchness from which particular things are abstracted. Abstractions are stripped-down carvings from the original richness. Any assertion merely captures but one, or a few, of the infinitely rich whole from which it is abstracted. What follows from this is that one needs to be a flexible observer who realizes that all views are partial views and that the observer is rather like an artist who sees the same vista anew each time, now emphasizing these qualities and, at another time, quite different qualities. Many different paintings are possible from a single vantage point. Cézanne returned again and again to Mt. St. Victoire, near Aix en Provence, painting more than sixty versions of that wonderful rock-mountain. One must look again and again, "without prejudice," with no expectation that there is a definitive painting to be done. The haiku form of poetry captures this truth so well, for it never pretends to present the whole, but instead highlights important facets of a thing or scene.

Nishida's strength is that he did not try to resolve the contradictions of experience, but saw them as inescapable descriptions of the way the world is, as it is known by us. The result is not a synthesis, but a unity-in-contradiction, an identity of opposites. Ordinary consciousness, likewise, is predictably self-contradictory.

In part, all of this is a result of having left "Paradise," the Garden of Eden, the original Oneness, for as differentiated individuals we see the various parts but not necessarily the whole. Each of us contributes to the whole a perspective that is utterly unique. No two people see the world in exactly the same way, and even day by day our perspectives change. As the ancient pre-Socratic, Heraclitus, taught, one cannot step into the same river twice, for fresh water has already replaced the old, and you yourself are slightly different, even if only because you have already experienced the cold current of the river. Each of us contributes a unique perspective on the whole and its parts, and each of these perspectives provides a perspective of difference that together contribute to the whole itself, that is to say, to nothingness (to God). It is not too much to claim that we are the eyes of nothingness (of God) on this earth.

Ethics and Evil

Nishida approaches the subject of ethics and evil through his remarkable reading of the biblical account of Adam and Eve. As noted earlier, it was in the Garden of Eden that evil, as disobedience to God, first arose. With the arrival of evil, issues of an ethical nature flood to the fore, as symbolized by the utterly new recognition that Adam and Eve stand naked before one another. Prior to that dawning awareness, nakedness and other potential moral issues simply did not arise. Adam and Eve simply went about living in a paradise untroubled by such distinctions as evil and good, moral and immoral. Nishida bypasses the conventional reading and begins by observing that the differentiation of forms and related distinctions arises from the divine and self-contradictory act of the formless becoming form. That God is the differentiation of the One into many on one level of understanding does not entail the destruction of unity on another. Unity and differentiation are one and the same activity. Nishida consistently argues that each individual person or thing is a self-expression of the creative force, or God. No one was expelled from the Garden of Eden, for it was the will of the One to create (to become other than itself as One, or to break the oneness in order to create the many), thereby coming to know its nature in and through an indefinite number of new and unique ways through the myriad of entities that, while remaining united at their depths, are nonetheless distinct from the One. All of these unique apertures reflect back to the One, its nature now perceived through the many. Humanly speaking, it is through each of us that the One, God, continually comes to know Him/Her/Itself. The One became many because "in God there is accordingly no reflection, memory, hope, and hence no special self-consciousness. Because everything is the self [One, God], there is no consciousness of the self."[72] The self-consciousness of the One necessitates differentiation, or the creation of "others." Paraphrasing the thirteenth-century Christian mystic, Meister Eckhart, Nishida asserts that "God's altruism is God's self-love."[73] To love the other is also to love oneself, since the other is oneself as well. Nishida describes this relationship beautifully through an analogy: "In a painting or melody . . . there is not one brush stroke or one note that does not directly express the spirit of the whole. For a painter or a musician, a single inspiration instantaneously comes forth and becomes an extremely varied landscape or an exquisite complex melody. In this way, God is none other than the world and the world is none other than God."[74] In leaving the Garden we become estranged, distant, even forgetful. We need to be reminded of our origin and of our inescapable connection. And it is here that evil arises. As we increasingly forget our divine heritage—our connection—we begin to act as isolated individuals, concerned primarily with our own selves, while developing a strong sense of estrangement from the world. Other people are "strangers," and the world becomes either an obstruction to our desires to be fought against, or mere material-at-hand for us to exploit as we chose. Separation has now reached its zenith, as we deem ourselves alone in an alien and mostly inert and uncaring universe. The Garden, no longer even a dim memory, is but a facile consolation for the weak-minded.

Borrowing another analogy, Nicolas of Cusa imagined an infinite sphere on which every point is the center.[75] Nishida then modifies this image, referring to a "self-contradictory sphere" that bears at least two directional tendencies. First, the centrifugal direction is a movement away from God, from the whole, which is represented by the center of the sphere. This direction represents evil, for it is the movement of separation from God, of individuality as independent objective existence, of estrangement from the center or source of all things, including estrangement from one's own self-contradictory self. Second, the centripetal direction, the direction inward toward the center, represents the direction of goodness because it is toward God and unity. If everything is God, then evil, and even "Satan," are aspects of God. The absolute is itself self-contradictory, and were this not the case, all change, growth, evolution, and diversity would be quite impossible. As manifestations of the absolute, we, too, are similarly self-contradictory. Thus, the "good" is to be thought of as a movement toward God—toward remembering or recollecting our oneness with the whole—and evil as a movement away from the original oneness, a radical independence with little or no awareness of the profundity that lies within each of us, and within all things. Denying this depth within things, the world becomes a monochromatic flatland where mostly dead material is manipulated by life forms that just happened to have come into existence and feel threatened by the world. "We, the centers of this bottomless contradictory world, are both Satanic and divine."[76] But the direction of spirituality is centripetal, and is characterized by an abandoning of the self as separate. The centrifugal direction represents the ego at an increasing distance from the now forgotten source. On the other hand, estrangement is a partial, superficial understanding of our nature, cut off from its deeper core. So movements toward the deeper layers of self, culminating in the realization of a bottomless self-contradictory identity as the place where absolute nothingness arises and becomes uniquely conscious of itself, is contrasted with movement away from our essential nature, which is increasingly evil (estranged) as its deeper nature becomes hidden. Delusion, the traditional cause of evil in Buddhist thought, occurs when we mistake the separate objective self for the real or deeper self.[77] Just as the absolute is endless, so our deep nature is, as Nishida observes, "bottomless" or limitless. Because of this endless potential, we, like the cosmos itself, can transform and evolve without limit or end. It is little wonder that the Japanese saying, "the Buddha is only halfway there," has such meaning in Japan.

Ethics

In the *Inquiry*, Nishida examines several approaches to ethics before stating his own position.[78] An ethical action is a willed action, and not a mere reflex, and it is the will that most clearly expresses the self.[79] For Nishida, the standard of good conduct is to be found in direct experience—in our consciousness.[80] The drive toward the good must be an "internal demand": "at the base of the will are innate demands (the cause of consciousness) that appear in consciousness as goal concepts which unify consciousness, when such unification reaches completion—when ideals are realized—we feel satisfaction."[81] Along with Plato and Aristotle, Nishida labels his position "energetism."[82] The goal of life is happiness (*eudaimonia*), and happiness can only be achieved through perfect action, not through the pursuit of pleasure. It is happiness that we should pursue, not pleasure, and happiness is achieved by realizing our ideals. The highest good "is for our spirit to develop its various abilities and to achieve a perfect development."[83] This perfect development is the expressing of our innate nature. The good is the development and the improvement of the self. Over a lifetime, consciousness is organized into a system of unity as the "self," and since our demands "never arise alone," our own internal demands necessarily involve others. Following Plato, just as the external goal of the self is to achieve its own harmony or unity, so externally its goal is community. Harmony is to be defined by means of reason, as rationality is the highest capacity we have to relate ideas in accordance with the laws of reason. Once again this echoes Plato's urging that the rational part of the "soul" control the appetites and enlist the will in its aspirations. The "unifying power" is an expression of this control within the self, and it is manifested as "personality." It is with this insight that Nishida is finally able to establish the ethical standard as those internal demands for ethical action, for "the true personality comes forth when a person eradicates [highly subjective hopes that function at the center of each person's superficial consciousness] and forgets his or her self."[84] The result is a personality that is unique for each individual, *and yet* "our personalities are the particular forms in which the sole reality . . . manifests itself according to circumstances."[85] The demand to actualize personalities is, for Nishida, "the greatest good."[86] Personality is the basic value, the end to which all other values—"wealth, honor, authority, health, skill, and academic knowledge"[87]—are subordinate: not good in themselves. To seek any other value "contrary to the demands of personality" is evil. The standard of ethical choice is the actualization of personality. Moreover, good conduct results from internal necessity. We can grasp this internal necessity "only in the state of direct experience prior to deliberative discrimination":[88] we encounter our true self only in pure experience. Sincerity is the expression of this personality: it emerges spontaneously and effortlessly when consciousness of the ego-self disappears. Nishida offers the example of a natural artist whose years of struggle, patience, and practice has led him to the point where his brush spontaneously and effortlessly follows his will. He could equally well have used a martial artist, or any other kind of practiced artist as his example. Such an achievement represents a union, with one's own selfish self under control, and then one's deep personality can unite with its object, and such unification is love: "Love is the feeling of congruence between self and other, the feeling of the union of subject and object."[89] Therefore, good conduct is a merging of subject and object. One's self is now large enough to embrace the universe, for one is the universe, and the universe is who I am. Ethical action is now effortless and spontaneous, for one has become the goodness that is in one's own depths, and one now acts in accord with the force of love, of divine unity.

And yet—*soku hi* (that is, that something both is and is not)— within the unity there still is diversity, and Nishida argues that the greatest human beings are those who display the greatest individuality.[90] They are individuals because they do express their own personalities, but not out of selfishness: "Individualism and egoism must be strictly distinguished." To be an individual is not to take pleasure as one's goal, but rather to act as a self-actualizing expression of increasing unity: out of love. Although one commonly hears the opinion that the Japanese individual is sacrificed at the expense of societal uniformity, Nishida holds that "a society that ignores the individual is anything but a healthy one."[91] The healthy individual is a uniquely robust aperture who has, nonetheless, discovered that his or her personality is increasingly inclusive in its concerns, and the inner demands of the self become increasingly social. As G. B. Burch wrote, "Greatness of character is measured by the extent of one's concern."[92]

How wide should be the individual's concern? The following assertion makes evident just how inclusive Nishida's position is on this: "[T]he nation is not the final goal of humankind. A meaningful purpose runs consistently throughout the development of humankind, and the nation appears to be something that rises and falls in order to fulfill part of humankind's mission. . . . Genuine universalism, however, does not require that each nation ceases to be. Rather, it means that each nation becomes increasingly stable, displays its distinctive characteristics, and contributes to the history of the world."[93] The nation is not the final goal of realization, but merely a step along the pathway to self-realization. Nevertheless, stable nations, distinctive in so many ways, should continue to thrive, but each with a sense of "world spirit," of the unified goal of humanity.[94]

The self and the universe share the same "ground," or rather, they are the same thing.[95] To know reality is to know the true self, and to know the true self is to know reality. In the depths of our differences as individuals, "no matter how small the enterprise, a person who works out of love for his or her fellow humans realizes the great personality of all humankind."[96] Socrates maintained that the foundational good was to "know thyself." Nishida echoes this when he writes that "our true self is the ultimate reality of the universe."[97] By listening to our deep selves, we encounter a desire to unite with the good of all humankind, fuse with the essence of the entire universe, and unite with the will of God. Religion and morality are united in Nishida's thought. But this unity is not based on the authority of a scripture, or on the dictates of reason, but on personal experience itself. As the Buddha himself taught, do not accept what I say because it is I who said it; find out for yourself.

Nishida offers a mature summary of his views on God, good, and evil in his *Last Writings*, completed just months before his death. In it he maintains that his concept of God goes farther than that of Eckhart's Gottheit (Godhead) insofar as God, too, is an identity of self-contradiction. Indeed, the self-contradictory quality pervades all possible existence, including the Creator: God negates his oneness by self-manifesting the many in existence. What results is a "dynamic equilibrium" of 'is' and 'is not.'[98] What drives continuous creation forward is the increasing self-contradictoriness of goodness hidden in the depths of the most evil, and evil is always present in the good, again at the depths of our being: "The human self, God's own image, is similarly a contradictory identity of good and evil."[99] Nishida goes so far as to assert that God, as the true absolute creator of all that is, must be Satan, too.[100] A truly omniscient and omnipotent God must include within Him/ Her/It self all that there is./The conundrum of a totally good God who creates a world in which evil exists is, therefore, laid to rest./Opposites *drive* the creative world, and without "evil" in some form, evolution would come to a standstill, as would matters of personal self-transformation, including progress toward enlightenment and involving the recollection of our origins. Creativity would come to a grinding halt. The idea that God is engaged in a struggle with evil yields only a relative God, not an absolute God. Such a struggle divides reality into God and the "other" (not God). Nishida's God embraces evil, Satan and immorality as part of His/ Her/Its very nature as creator of all that is. As human beings, we, too, represent this same inclusion: hence, "our hearts are essentially this battlefield between God and Satan."[101] To move toward God, centripetally, is the good: to move away, centrifugally, is to move toward Satan, that is, toward a Godless world of inert matter and purposelessness. God is not indifferent to good and evil but, rather, a force toward increasing goodness as a quiet call to remember who we are. We are a part of absolute nothingness, and "to exist while being absolutely nothing is the ultimate self-contradiction."[102] Both direction and purpose arise when we listen to the call that emerges from the bottomless depths of our self, our true self, to be who we are and act in accordance with our deep nature.[103] Eventually, when death does overtake us, we re-enter the nothingness from which we came, but as unique expressions of the whole of which we have always been a part, offering unique perspectives together with heretofore unexperienced histories./The self that enters into eternal nothingness is historically unrepeatable, unique, and individual. There never was, nor will there ever be, a life exactly like yours. Taken together, all of the forms of existence represent different apertures from which reality is glimpsed, and by means of which it continues to thrive, evolve, and perpetuate change. Everything is said to be impermanent, and it is the identity of self-contradiction that powers change and impermanence, without end.

Nishida and Mysticism

The late George B. Burch began his lectures on mysticism with the following analysis. There are three types of experience: empirical, rational, and mystical. An example of an empirical experience would be the seeing of a house. An example of a rational experience would be recognizing the truth of the Pythagorean theorem in geometry. An example of a mystical experience is the realization of the oneness of all things. This may be stated differently in various traditions, such as union with God or with the absolute, but the experience of the oneness of all things remains the simple core of mysticism.

One who cannot see a house is blind. One who cannot grasp the truth of the Pythagorean theorem is mathematically challenged. One who does not experience the fundamental oneness of all things, is normal. Burch's delightful account makes clear that mystical experience is available only to those who, in some way, move beyond normal everyday experience, even though the experience is potentially open to all. However, the vast majority remain unaware even of the possibility.

There have been many other definitions of mysticism over the centuries, but, without rehashing these, I will adopt Burch's simple account: mystical experience is seeing, that is to say, actually experiencing the oneness of all things.[104] Experiencing the oneness of all things should be taken here to refer to the nondual awareness of enlightenment: all separate things in existence now disappear as absorbed into nothingness as a oneness. And yet, while they "disappear" they are not lost, for a return to dualistic thinking displays the many things as separate. They are simply one, from the nondual perspective, and many, from the dualistic perspective. Additional concern could arise over the nature and meaning of "seeing" and "oneness," but I will simply inquire into whether Nishida's philosophy includes awareness of the oneness of all things. Yet, it must be noted at the beginning that Nishida himself declared that his philosophy was not mystical. His denial is straightforward, although not as developed as it might have been. What he takes to be the distinguishing factor that separates his philosophy from mysticism is the fact that mystics remain within a dualistic framework of understanding—what he thinks of as operating from within "object logic"—which continues to separate God, or the absolute, from the individual. Yes, there is union, but it is a union of two: the mystic unites with a God who remains separate. At least this seems to be the case within the three main Western religious traditions. There are exceptions in all three traditions, but as a general rule it has been frowned upon to speak of the annihilation of the self or soul, where the two actually become one (for then the individual would *be* God, which, for most Western religious traditions, would be a heresy). Nevertheless, an intense oneness still is experienced in the "union" of the human and the divine. Union, however, involves viewing oneness from "the outside," where one views the two-as-one. While this is true to a large extent, it does not account for those mystics who came to ignore the admonition not to dissolve the great divide between the Creator and the created, and who described in their writings the total loss of self in the merging with God or the absolute. This is clearly a view from "inside." Meister Eckhart stands as the prime example within the Christian tradition, and his account is remarkably similar to Nishida's. Little wonder that it is Eckhart who captured the imagination of D. T. Suzuki, Nishitani, and Ueda, all of whom were significantly influenced by his writings, and to some small extent, to Nishida as well. As will be discussed shortly, it is Eckhart who pointed Ueda to a position that he calls "non-mysticism" or "de-mysticism" to explain Nishida's reluctance to be thought of as a mystical philosopher.

Nishida's position is that his philosophy is not mystical "in that the true individual must be established from the absolute's own existential negation."[105] Put simply, insofar as God empties Himself in creating us, the distinction between Creator and created vanishes: all are divine incarnations of the original creative energy. This is clearly a view from "inside." You are God, and God is you. Such a philosophical understanding does not require a "special kind of consciousness," since all that needs to be done is to realize what has been underfoot all along. However, in his early work,

Nishida does credit some forms of mysticism with being capable of viewing mysticism from the inside: as cited earlier, he writes that "the religion of India of the distant past and the mysticism that flourished in Europe in the fifteenth and sixteenth centuries sought God in intuition realized in the *inner soul,* and this I consider to be the deepest knowledge of God."[106] Borrowing an image from the sixteenth century mystic Jakob Boehme, Nishida asserts that God is to be found with a "reversed eye."[107] This is the perspective from the inside, where object logic is no longer applicable, since both subject and object have disappeared in an intuitive oneness. You perceive that you are God and that God is you.

D. T. Suzuki offers a similar argument when he states that Zen is not mystical: "mysticism in the West begins with the assumption that there is an antithesis—God and human being—that ends with 'unification or identification.' "[108] By contrast, in Zen "there is no antithesis, therefore no synthesis or unification." In Zen, it is not that union occurs, but rather that oneness has been the state of things all along. Enlightenment is simply the recognition of what is already the case.

It is Ueda Shizuteru who sheds the most light on this issue, suggesting that Nishida both is and is not a mystic—a formula that we have already encountered as the logic of *soku hi* (that something both is and is not, at one and the same time). Ueda, having written his PhD thesis on Meister Eckhart, at Marberg University, traced Eckhart's mysticism to its culmination, an understanding that was remarkably similar to Nishida's. Eckhart taught that God and humans are of the same stuff, or, in his words, shared the same "ground" ("*grund*" in German). Therefore, not only is God identical with the innermost in us (from the inside), but the culmination of the mystic's journey is to go "beyond God" to the *Godhead.* Eckhart exclaimed that "I beg of God that he makes me rid of God,"[109] for "as long as the soul has God, knows God and is aware of God, she is far from God."[110] Once rid of a concept or image of God, nothing or nothingness remains. All imaging and naming cease. The experience of the ineffable is all that is left.

Ueda's take on Zen, Nishida, and mysticism is that both Zen and Nishida include the mystical, but that they go beyond the mystical into what Ueda terms "non-mysticism."[111] Bret Davis prefers the term "de-mysticism," and he reports that "[p]rofessor Ueda agreed with my preference for this way of putting it."[112] Davis goes on to suggest that the move from mysticism to de-mysticism consists of four ingredients:

1. An ecstatic transcendence of the ego [a letting-go of the everyday self];

2. A mystical union with God or the One [seeing the oneness of all things];

3. An ecstatic breakthrough beyond God or the One into an absolute nothingness [the letting-go of the everyday ego is now echoed by the letting-go of God];

4. A return to an ecstatic/instatic engagement in the here and now [a return to the "everyday" world, but now seen as though for the first time in wondrous brilliance and color].[113]

While ingredients (1) and (2) characterize most mysticism, ingredients (3) and (4) go "beyond" mysticism. In point of fact, the third ingredient characterizes the mysticism of Eckhart, as well as that of Zen which, no doubt, is why Ueda was drawn to Eckhart's work. But it is the fourth ingredient that is distinctively Zen, including Nishida's thought.

The first ingredient is a negation of the everyday self; the third is a negation of God, and the fourth is a negation of absolute nothingness, assuring that it is not itself reified or "thing-ified," but rather it, too, is emptied and the entire universe reemerges as the ultimately real: nirvana is samsara, samsara is nirvana, or, as the *Heart Sutra* expresses it, emptiness is form, and form is emptiness. Nishida himself often refers to the form (created things) of the formless (God, nothingness), and the formlessness of form. Absolute nothingness is the emptying out of reality from the formed to the formless and is the "open expanse" that Ueda writes about as the "place" wherein we and things arise: Nishida's *basho* and *topos*. Here the self is now not-a-self, and things are not-things; they are empty. Ueda calls them "hollow." Yet, as hollow, they are what they are, and they are at the same time what they are not. They burn brilliantly as individual things, and also as self-manifestations of absolute nothingness. Everything that is, is both formed and formless. We are, in Hisamatsu's words, "formless selves."

Philosophy has now joined with poetry. To live with the ecstasy of the fourth ingredient of de- or non-mysticism is to render every moment as an eternity: one that is now outside of time—and each and every awareness becomes a pure experience. A loved one is now comprehended more fully, no longer characterized by prejudice or habit, but taken in his or her fullness, as though for the first time. The poppy in one's garden burns brightly with an orangey-red that is beyond all expectation, enough to make one weep with delight. Subsequently, one's world has changed dramatically, and even to watch the evening news on television makes one gasp in disbelief: Can they not see what wonders they are wasting, what they are doing to themselves, others, and the world? Can they not catch even a glimpse of what they are missing out on?

Every reader of Zen encounters at some point the Ten Ox-herding pictures, and Professor Ueda often makes use of them in his writing and lectures (see below, pp. 98–110). This is not the place to describe them in detail, except to note that the boy in these drawings represents the everyday self. He has heard, we are told, that there is far more to life than most people think, and that there is a deeper reality (that is a deeper self) that can be known. Already he is asking a question that most of the people featured in the news never entertain. The deeper self is represented by the Ox, and by the seventh image, it is clear that the boy has come to know that there is no Ox separate from his own self. He *is* this deep self.

Is that true?

In the eighth drawing, even the true self disappears, and one looks at an empty circle. There is absolutely nothing now, for both the boy herder and his bullish deep self have been forgotten. Yet out of this empty expanse, the ninth drawing appears and it is brilliant in its depiction of a river, trees with blossoms in full bloom, craggy rocks, all more intense than you have ever experienced before. At this point you are beyond mysticism, beyond dualism, and there are now only . . . forms. There are flowers, people, rocks, and trees, and since you have disappeared, you are them. You have become the flower, your lover, the poppy and rock in your garden, rivers and trees, birds and cicadas. You have not only seen the oneness of all things, but you are this oneness. There is not you and the other things. There are only the other things, and they are you!

This realization is beyond mysticism, but it is arrived at through mysticism. Mysticism is the path to non-mysticism, and to the experiencing of the world in its astonishing magnificent depth through the lenses of enlightened awareness.

In the chapters that follow, the legacy of Nishida's philosophy will be evident. Whether in an expansion of his position or a critique of it, "absolute nothingness," "*basho*," "the identity of self-contradiction," or "*soku hi*," all enter into the thinking of those who followed him, to some degree or other. Of these and other ideas, it was "absolute nothingness" that was central. A "school" of thinking emerged that took nothingness as its focus, and it was not nothingness in a negative sense (as the absence of being) but in a positive sense as the origin and foundation of all that exists. Nothingness was the background to all foregrounded things: the foundational unseen to all that is seeable. To speak of the unspeakable in philosophical terms was Nishida's quest and achievement. Those who followed him took up the challenge in their own unique ways, but it was Nishida who first formulated the problem and chartered a pathway toward its possible solution.

2

Tanabe Hajime
(1885–1962)

[U]nlike Nishida, he [Tanabe] did not believe that the metaphysical ground of individual self-consciousness could be intuited.) Instead of an intuition into the self-identity of absolute
contradiction, Tanabe turned instead to the religious notion
of faith as a model of authentic subjectivity. . . . "Faith" is
the metanoetic awareness that arises only after the death of
subjectivity. Thus Nishida's "action-intuition" is to be contrasted with Tanabe's "action-faith." Once again, in Tanabe's
estimation, the issue of existential transformation in the death
and resurrection of subjectivity marks the critical element of
difference between the two.

—James Fredericks, "Philosophy as Metanoetics:
An Analysis," in *The Religious Philosophy of Tanabe Hajime*

Whereas Zen Buddhism serves a relatively small population of
practitioners and is often viewed as difficult and inaccessible, Pure
Land Buddhism has by far the largest following of any religion in
Japan (consisting of more than half of the Japanese population)
and is accessible and instantly effective. Pure Land is "Buddhism
for common folk," educated and uneducated, requiring only the
speaking of the divine name with serious intent: "*Namu Amida
Butsu.*" Zen is both difficult to understand and rigorous in its
practice. Pure Land requires no philosophic sophistication, but only
faith in the efficacy of repeating Buddha's name.

It is Tanabe who grasps the significance of faith for every man and woman, turning its insights into a "philosophy that is not a philosophy." But these insights did not come easily for Tanabe. Having been a nationalist before and during some of World War II, he came to see the horror and futility of war and the suffering it engendered. In the midst of the growing carnage, the collateral damage spread to his own belief in traditional philosophy and the power of reason. He began to see that reason was not based on anything solid and lasting and was more often than not possessed of an arrogance that seemed limitless and often destructive. He found himself to be paralyzed, unable to speak out during the war, or even to become clear about what his duty was. The war taught him that even loyalty to one's country could lead to horrible results that could only be mitigated by a broader loyalty and a wholesale rejection of the reasoning that led to such and other disasters. As a result, he turned to the teachings of Shinran, the founder of the Pure Land Buddhist tradition, who taught that it was faith, not reason, that would lead to societal peace and individual "salvation." While reason spun its wheels, dredging up societal change after societal change, and as different philosophies came to the fore, faith offered an immediate release from such futility by offering instead the healing power of love and both personal and social transformation. But how did this highly successful and "rational" philosopher, this specialist in scientific philosophy, come to abandon his many achievements and be led to "repent," abandoning his support for the war and his quest for truth through philosophical reasoning? The answer is that the need to repent, to confess his "sins," and to place his faith in Other-power, seemed the only possible way forward and the only antidote to unending frustration, struggle, and grief. To admit one's finitude is to fall on one's knees and to humbly ask for help and forgiveness from a higher power.

It was from such a position of humility that Tanabe began the journey back to a philosophy that is not a philosophy and to a reason transformed by faith in a higher authority. It was as though Tanabe had to be crushed by the recognition of his own arrogance, shortcomings, and errors. Only then, in utter humility, was he able to find a way back from personal disaster to a new understanding of himself and the world. He had been "reborn," to use Christian terminology, and his past shortcomings were somehow forgiven through the very act of faith.

Life and Work

Tanabe Hajime was born in 1885. After graduating from high school in 1904, he studied at Tokyo Imperial University in the Department of Science and Mathematics, but prior to his graduation in 1908, he switched to philosophy, although his interest in science and mathematics still remained. In 1913 he was appointed lecturer in the Department of Natural Sciences at Tohoku University, where he taught German. His first book, the *Philosophy of Science,* was published in 1915, and in 1918 his *Outline of Science.* In 1919 he was invited by Nishida to assume the post of assistant professor of philosophy at Kyoto Imperial University, an invitation which he considered a great honor. Not only had Nishida—the philosopher whom Tanabe most admired—invited the young philosopher to join his department, but he also agreed to Tanabe's plans to study in Germany, combining his interests in philosophy, science, and German.

In 1922 he got his chance to study abroad, going to Berlin on a government scholarship and working under Alois Riehl, a Neo-Kantian scholar "interested in showing the relevance of Kant to scientific positivism."[1] Neo-Kantianism was a revival of Immanuel Kant's philosophy begun in German universities around 1860. It blended empiricism and rationalism and emphasized a more scientific reading of Kant. After a year, Riehl advised Tanabe to go to Heidelberg, to work with Heinrich Rickert, but instead he went to Freiburg to study under Edmund Husserl (a phenomenologist: the founder of the phenomenological method that studies phenomena as they appear in our consciousness). Husserl was impressed by Tanabe and thought that he might become a purveyor of phenomenological ideas in the East. Tanabe, for his part, had hoped that Husserl's scientifically oriented attempt to avoid the subjectivity of Neo-Kantian thought would prove to be a step forward in his development. But he soon became disenchanted with Husserl's approach, which he found to be too abstract and difficult to apply to the lived world.

Tanabe next turned to Martin Heidegger, at Marburg, whose "phenomenology of life" was more suited to his interests. Heidegger's "existentialism" was meant to apply to this world and demanded that people be authentically responsible for their actions and their choices. Heidegger overturned the assumption that "being" was understood, and demanded a reexamination of its meaning and function in the everyday world. In its own way, this reexamination was a new theology, a rethinking of what we mean when we speak of God. Tanabe and Heidegger became friends and, in addition to introducing Tanabe to his own work, Heidegger helped him considerably in his wider study of German philosophy.

James Heisig suggests that Tanabe's philosophic journey was both complex and ever changing, leading him from philosopher to philosopher, and position after position. Yet, one could argue that there are two major phases in Tanabe's philosophical career: the first, a traditional interest in the philosophy of science, Neo-Kantianism, and in phenomenology; the second, which began as World War II was grinding to a close, had its focus on faith rather than reason, and on a personal repentance for the "sin" of arrogance, of which the war served as an instance. Tanabe now saw the futility of war and called for a general acknowledgment of responsibility for it, which included himself. His cry was for a "philosophy of repentance."

In 1924, Tanabe returned to Japan, anxious to continue his work on phenomenology, but he was asked by Nishida to deliver a memorial lecture to commemorate the two hundredth anniversary of the birth of Kant. During the preparation for this lecture, Tanabe came to see the shortcomings and impracticality of Kant's idealism. In the same year, he wrote articles on various aspects of European philosophy, especially phenomenology, epistemology (theory of knowledge), and the philosophy of science and mathematics. Over the following two years, in addition to lecturing on Fichte and Schelling, his study of Hegel loomed increasingly important. Impressed by Hegel's dialectic (a dialectical logic marking progress and change in history through the movement from thesis to antithesis to synthesis, which in turn becomes the new thesis), Tanabe began to develop his own dialectical method of thinking, which proved to be "his own original contribution to Kyoto-School philosophy."[2]

Tanabe was appointed a full professor in 1927, and assumed the departmental chair in 1928 upon Nishida's retirement. His classes were extremely popular, bringing both students and faculty to his lectures. However, storm clouds were on the horizon, for although Nishida was Tanabe's mentor, the relationship between them became strained when Tanabe published an essay entitled "Revering the Teaching of Master Nishida" in 1930. This essay angered Nishida because of Tanabe's harsh criticism of his approach, and their relationship continued to deteriorate until, as James Heisig puts it, "they could hardly read each other's writings without misunderstanding."[3] This rift between the former friends seemed to provide a new direction to Tanabe's philosophy, as though he was cut free from Nishida's powerful influence. In 1935 he published his "Logic of Species" which was in direct opposition to Nishida's "Logic of Basho," which further widened the rift between them. In the same year, Tanabe published an article entitled "The Logic of Social Existence," in which the state was given precedence over the individual. This essay was eventually used to lend support to Japan's imperialistic and aggressive tendencies in Asia. In one of his lectures in 1943, Tanabe raised the nation to the status of a manifestation of God, writing that the idea that "the nation enters between God and man is a reality. Wise men can offer their lives for God and patriarchs, but we ordinary people cannot think of so doing. We do so through our nation. . . . A nation transcends the character of a particular nation and is a manifestation of God. . . . To offer one's life comes to have a concrete meaning when the nation and God are linked as one . . . that is to say, when even though God and the state are different, they are one . . . and thereby, as people offer their lives for their country, they touch God, they are united to God. . . . There is no more urgent time in which it is necessary to privilege the nation to put it above the people."[4]

With the defeat of Japan, the ideology that supported Japan's expansionist policies came under severe criticism, and some of the leading scholars of the Kyoto School were fired from their teaching positions. "Tanabe who had already retired about five months prior to the end of the war in 1945 was labeled a 'racist,' a 'Nazi,' and a 'Facist.' "[5]

With the war ended, Tanabe proclaimed a change of heart and acknowledged his weakness at not speaking up against the war, which he now deemed to be wrong. At the same time he came to realize the inadequacy of traditional philosophy, and undertook a complete overhaul of his philosophy and of philosophy generally. Having retired from Kyoto University in 1945, he moved to his cottage in the mountains. His famous *Philosophy as Metanoetics* appeared in 1946, and in 1947 he revised his "Logic of Species" which he modified by narrowing the definition of "nation" and instead emphasized moral responsibility.

In 1952, Tanabe received the Cultural Order of Merit from the government. In 1957, Heidegger recommended him for an honorary Doctor of Philosophy degree from the University of Freiburg, which he received in absentia due to ill health. Tanabe Hajime died in 1962, at the age of seventy-seven.

Metanoetics

Philosophy as Metanoetics was published in 1946. Tanabe begins this influential book by confessing that he had doubts about whether he was qualified to be a philosopher because he was unable to speak and act decisively. Caught between the desire to openly and publicly criticize Japan's political and military leaders and his fear that to do so would undermine Japan's chances for a successful outcome, he remained paralyzed. This paralysis led to his "surrendering" himself "to my own inability."[6] The result of this surrender was a life-changing insight in which his confession (his *metanoesis* [the need to go beyond reason to find a solution] or *zange* [confession and repentance]) forced him toward his "interiority," that is, forced him to look at his own honesty and integrity. He humbly accepted his weakness and, by doing so, he was led to a "philosophy that is not a philosophy." Thus, a new conception of philosophy arose from the ineffectual remains of ordinary philosophy—a study and teaching of philosophy that, in the end, had left him paralyzed. It was a non-philosophy that functions "as a reflection of what is ultimate and as a radical self-awareness."[7] Most importantly, this non-philosophy, or metanoetics (*meta*, which means "beyond," or "after") and "*noetics*" or "*noesis*" meaning "thinking," "reasoning," or "intuition" (both from the Greek), involves the giving up of any expectation that one can solve practical matters of importance through one's own efforts (*jiriki*, or "self-power"): "That power has already been abandoned in despair."[8] From this perspective, instead of using one's own limited resources to resolve issues of importance, it is necessary to humbly call on an outside, superior "Other-power" (*tariki*) to move one in the right direction and to provide solutions to ethical and other matters. *Zange* involves repentance for wrongs done, the anguish and sorrow in knowing that one cannot undo what has been done, as well as the shame and disgrace resulting from such wrongdoing, and the straightforward recognition of one's helplessness and inadequacy. Tanabe argues that such a realization itself comes from outside of oneself, for it is Other-power that takes over, working in and through the humility of *zange*, bringing about a "conversion," a new direction, and a new beginning. For him, all of this is evidence of Other-power acting in and through *zange*, that is, through the sincere acts of confession and repentance.

In Western philosophical circles there is a quip that one is born either a Platonist or an Aristotelian, representing rationalistic or empirical tendencies, respectively. Within the confines of the Kyoto School it might be said that one leans either toward self-power or Other-power, with Nishida and Tanabe being the major and foundational proponents of these two very different perspectives of philosophy. Nevertheless, one reads in both Nishida and Nishitani that these two approaches are actually complementary. Nishida concluded that "both views [self-power and Other-power] have their own distinctive features, but they are identical in essence."[9] And while self-power remains dominant in Nishida's "Zen approach," he concludes the *Inquiry* by observing that "to know and to love a thing is to discard self-power and embody the faithful heart that believes in Other-power."[10] Further developing this theme, Nishida stressed that "religion is the culmination of knowledge and love."[11] But to get there, he believed that one had to use self-power. It could likewise be argued that Tanabe used self-power in order to reach the point of ultimate despair that led to his letting-go of philosophy and any expectation that reason could supply answers to life's most vexing perplexities. Recognizing this, Tanabe writes of the paradox of *zange*: "Even though it is my own act, it cannot be my own act."[12] Prompted by a power outside of himself, but prepared for by the unsuccessful use of self-power, the "interior" ground was thus opened to conversion.

Tanabe's philosophy of Other-power represented a new direction in Kyoto School philosophizing. And because it broke out of the mold of "Nishida philosophy," it signaled the birth of the Kyoto School, a school of thought that now contained diversity, notwithstanding the many obvious similarities. Nishida and Tanabe, while working on similar themes from the common standpoint of "nothingness," diverged in their understanding of nothingness, and their use of self-power and Other-power yielded quite different methods of doing philosophy. For Tanabe, the working of Other-power represents the "absolute negation" of everything reflective—old views, old ways-of-being-in-the-world, old hopes and expectations, and old methods of philosophizing—while granting conversion and "rebirth" into a new way of life "as nothingness-qua-love."[13] And this negation of the relative by the power of nothingness must be continuous or else one will fall again into the trap of arrogance and self-reliance. The cycle of death and resurrection (rebirth) is unending.

"Metanoetics" (*zangendo*) is a transcending of traditional philosophy and its methods. Tanabe relied on *faith*, rather than reason, for reason, he believed, only led to uncountable antinomies or unresolvable paradoxes. By contrast, Nishida employed reason and "intellectual intuition" in his search for understanding, working mostly within the long tradition of Western philosophy. Nishida grounded his approach to philosophy in Zen Buddhism; Tanabe in Shin, or Pure Land Buddhism. Having already looked at Zen and its influence on Nishida in the first chapter, it is now important to understand Shin Buddhism as well, in this discussion of Tanabe's philosophy.

The founder of Shin Buddhism was Shinran (1173–1262), a student of Honen (1133–1212) who taught a similar doctrine. Shin Buddhism (in Japanese, Jōdo Shinshō, also referred to as "The Pure Land School") taught that anyone, from the most illiterate peasant to the scholar, could achieve salvation by simply calling upon the name of Amida Buddha (*Nembutsu*, or the practice of repeating the name of Amida Buddha, with the belief that through trust in Amida, one will be born in the Buddha's paradise, the "pure land") as an expression of faith. Along with Shinran, who himself came to metanoetics after experiencing the helplessness of reason, Tanabe cites Pascal and Kierkegaard, all philosophers of faith over reason. Yet Tanabe did not always "of necessity adhere to the doctrine of [Shin, or] Pure Land Buddhism."[14] Rather, while Shinran's teachings served as a guide, Tanabe's deliberations often took him well beyond Shinran, to other philosophies and religions such as Christianity. Furthermore, Tanabe applied his philosophy of metanoetics to the problems of wartime Japan and its aftermath. Shinran's approach led Tanabe to a critique of reason, which inevitably led him to *zange*, a complete letting-go of self based on the recognition of his own inadequacies and the inadequacies of reason, both of which led him to completely repent his old ways. Thus, Shinran led him to the point of new hope, for even the common man was offered salvation, a salvation that was open to everyone. In this view, following the death of the old self, there is a resurrection of the self through faith whereby a new self is given to one: one is restored by the "transformative grace of absolute nothingness" (Other-power, Buddha).[15] Reason is decidedly finite, yet pretends to be absolute; nothingness *is* absolute, as is the help that it provides. The power of nothingness is infinite and absolute. In his view, Nishida's claim of "intellectually intuiting" nothingness is a pipedream, for absolute nothingness is itself "mediated" by us, through our actions, and would otherwise be unknown. Therefore, even absolute reality is mediated, not immediate, in and through our awareness of it. Our knowledge of absolute nothingness (Buddha, God, the Absolute) comes only through the mediating power of nothingness: Other-power. This mediating power is, for us, transformative. It moves us from our fallen, evil state, to rebirth as a forgiven and saved being. Our old self dies as a result of our heartfelt repentance and admission of our sins—*zange*—and, in turn, a new "true" self replaces it through the transformative power of Other-power.

Mediation

While the term *mediation* is central in Tanabe's writings, it is never defined, and it is used in a variety of different senses. "Mediation," as ordinarily used, means to promote reconciliation between two or more disputing parties, such as a mediator as marriage counselor, or a mediator appointed to resolve salary and other employment matters in dispute. The mediator is an intervening agent attempting to bring about an accord.

"Mediation" can also signify reconciliation, often as a result of the transformation of one or more of those involved. For example, two people locked in a heated legal dispute, with no resolution in sight, might find a compromise solution if one of the disputants had a change of heart and became conciliatory, less selfishly stubborn. For Tanabe, repentance yields salvation through the transforming mediation of Other-power. Thus, a transformed human being is able to mediate between him/herself and other human beings. The transformed self can be a mediator *of* Other-power through loving or selfless action. Other-power bridges, or mediates, the opposition between self and other. The transformed self is able to express Other-power because of the mediation/intervention/facilitation of Other-power, rendering him/her a "self that loses itself." Furthermore, the absolute (absolute nothingness) and the relative (human beings) form a union through absolute mediation. / Thus, the absolute, by means of "absolute mediation," mediates between the relative and itself, but also between one relative and another, creating harmony where before there was strife.

To mediate, then, is to promote reconciliation, to transform through Other-power, to facilitate genuine agreement where disagreement previously reigned, all leading to salvation. Thus, the transforming love of Other-power moves us toward salvation in the Pure Land (ōsō-ekō, "going to"), and in the return to this world (gensō-ekō, "returning to this world") one is now able to "serve as the medium for the absolute mediation of nothingness." The transformation that makes possible our ability to love other people is what makes it possible for us to love in our lives, in this world. The mediation of transformed selves now acting through the love of Other-power is precisely that which enables nothingness to realize itself. Hopefully, this lengthy attempt at definition will become clearer as the details of Tanabe's teachings unfold.

What becomes starkly evident in Tanabe's metanoetics is his account of human nature as originally evil. / Nishida taught that human nature is intrinsically good, or at least that our deep inclinations lead us toward that which is good, at the level of Buddha-nature, although regularly corrupted by wrong desires, selfishness, and the too often warped societal teachings and normative expectations. Tanabe will have none of this: "Human sin and evil are not accidental phenomena; nor do they signify merely the evil acts of individual persons. They constitute, rather, a negative determination of our being itself that lies at the foundation of human existence in general."[16] He even adopts the Judeo-Christian notion of "original sin" to describe the "latent evil" produced by "human arrogance."[17] Our basically evil nature demands that all philosophy begin with the earnest confession that is *zange* and, therefore, all philosophy must be metanoetical. Tanabe held that our corrupt, finite nature makes it impossible to do philosophy in any other way. Immanuel Kant was correct in his insight that reason seeks answers to questions that it cannot answer: questions such as the existence and nature of God, the origin of the universe. Kant went on to settle for well-argued belief, but a corrupted and finite reason will fare no better here as the grounds for probable belief, for both the belief and its argued defense will remain human, finite, and flawed. The only possible way to move beyond our limited, finite, and evil nature is by totally renouncing our sins, together with our inadequate philosophical answers, and to call on the name of Amida Buddha for help. Then, Other-power will grant us rebirth. Proof of the existence of such power is the transformation of self which must be given to us from outside of ourselves, since the transformation of self is not the work of self-power but of Other-power. To think otherwise is still to be trapped by our own arrogance, our *hubris* (the arrogance of falsely thinking that one has the power and wisdom of a god).

According to Tanabe, then, the fact is that even *zange*, the act of confession and repentance, is itself powered by Other-power. Tanabe confirms this when he writes that "my power, by itself alone, is so ineffective, and my folly and wickedness so tenacious, that if left to myself, I could not perform even this *zange*."[18]

Mediation and Absolute Mediation

The term *mediation* has already appeared in our discussion of Tanabe's philosophy, and it appears over and over again in Tanabe's writings. However, it seems to be used in several different senses. Because it is never formally defined and because of its varied uses, we must conclude that it is not a technical term despite its obvious importance in Tanabe's writings. For example, Tanabe contends that, as acting agents in the world, having received the healing transformation of nothingness through Other-power, we become "mediators of absolute nothingness."[19] Again, we can say that absolute nothingness mediates between our old and new selves, as a legal mediator might work to resolve issues and disagreements between two parties. Or, absolute nothingness may become "manifest in the mutuality between one relative being and another," acting as a power to transform such relationships.[20] Mediation may be the required means to achieve an end or goal, as in the saving-power of Amida Buddha. Despite such a variety of uses of "mediation," perhaps it can be suggested that it is most importantly used to identify the relationship between ourselves and absolute nothingness as a thoroughly transforming act that brings (mediates) new (transformed) individuals and beings into "true" existence. Beings are transformed "under the influence of absolute nothingness which is neither the self nor an other."[21] From this it can be seen that absolute nothingness is not a thing, not an object, but an absolute power of absolute transformation. Heisig maintains that, since all reality is interrelated, then "all the events of the world are a dialectic of that interrelatedness."[22] Every person, every being, and every action performed is grounded in relationship with other individuals, beings, and actions. Thus, every individual consciousness, besides being itself, is also the *other* with which it interacts. But this applies not only to individual consciousnesses, it also includes relationships between people and physical objects, as well as "the whole range of customs, institutions and social structures in which the historical world entangles us."[23] Where Nishida had difficulty in moving from individual enlightenment back to the world of history, Tanabe plunged headlong into history from the start. Absolute nothingness is always active as a transformative power in the world and in history.

Tanabe uses the metaphor of a "net" to illustrate this all-encompassing, everywhere-present aspect of absolute nothingness. Each knot in a net is tied to other knots, and they in turn to yet other knots, giving added strength to the whole, as well as to each individual knot. In this way, each knot is related to every other knot, just as each person is in relationship with every other person and with every other thing that makes up the world. And each of us is affected by each and every action taken by anyone:

"The knots of the net can exert their role only as they are in [a] mutual relationship of joint responsibility."[24] The "net" is the absolute nothingness in which we live and breathe. Within the periphery of the net—which is absolute nothingness—every individual has the freedom to interact with other individuals. This relationship of one individual to another is neither interfered with, nor mediated by, the absolute, for if the absolute did so, then the absolute would cease to be absolute and would be just another relative being acting in this everyday world of relationships. Thus, the role of the absolute is found in the process of mediation that transforms relative beings such that each corrupted ego-self can find its true self, but without involvement in specific relationships directly.

Once true consciousness arises, then the relative completely surrenders by negating itself and affirming the absolute. Tanabe argues that without itself being mediated by relative beings through the act of absolute affirmation, the absolute would have no existence of its own. The absolute exists only as and through acts of mediation. He adds that "since the true absolute always entails an absolute mediation, it can never dispense with the relative beings but brings about their co-operation in this mediation in order to make its own nothingness real."[25] The absolute can neither get rid of relative beings, nor can relative beings oppose the absolute. The absolute only exists as a transformative power through the mediation of relative beings. Thus, "the self is not a substance, the absolute is not a thing."[26] One might say that the absolute/Other-power/nothingness is not a thing, but rather a process, an action of transformation.

Absolute mediation is "absolute" because it applies to everything. The Bodhisattva in Buddhism is one who vows not to leave this world until all sentient beings (some say all beings, sentient and nonsentient) attain salvation. All of this makes perfect sense given the Buddhist doctrine of "dependent origination." This is the understanding that anything exists only because of the existence of other things in a complex web of cause and effect. Tanabe, as we have already seen, offers the metaphor of a "net" to help explain his notion of interrelatedness. A similar, more traditional metaphor, is "Indra's Net" which symbolizes the interrelatedness of dependent origination. Indra's Net is a spider's web on which lie an infinite number of dewdrops, or jewels, and in each of these are reflected the reflections of all the other drops. Simply put, everything depends on everything else. Whether "web" or "net," our lives are fragile, and yet, because of our vast connections, we are remarkably strong. And we are mediated in this not only by each other, but also by absolute nothingness, which is the "all" in *absolute* mediation, offering us Other-power, which offers trans- formation to all. It is this sense of the availability of the grace of transformation (universal salvation) for all that the Bodhisattvas envisioned. James Heisig contends that the principle of "absolute mediation" must be taken to mean that "one must always look for the connection between two apparently unconnected things, and one can always look for an underlying connection between two apparently directly connected things."[27] Hence, "(1) there are no pure individuals; we are all related to those about us. And (2) individuals do not relate directly to universal humanity [human- kind], as unmediated instances of the 'human'; humanity reaches our individuality by way of (that is, through the mediation of) cultures, social units, languages, and all the other 'specifics' the particular groups share"[28]—that is, we are not, as individuals, sim- ply human in some abstract general sense, but we are Japanese, or English speaking, or Republicans, or Catholic human beings. But to better understand the mediation of the specific, we must turn to Tanabe's "Logic of Species" (or the "Specific"), as Heisig translates this term.

The Logic of the Specific

Heisig perceptively suggests that the "logic" in the Logic of the Spe- cific is not actually a formal or "pure" logic, but more "a method of thinking."[29] Still, Tanabe tied his "method of thinking" to Hegel's dialectical logic, which was an attempt at a "pure," new logic. Even before Hegel, logicians taught that between the universal category (the one) and the individual (part of the many), there was the category of the "particular." Tanabe took the particular to be an intermediary between the universal and the individual: the particular, or "species," grouped the many into a collection larger than the individual, yet smaller than the universal "one." The particular (species) *mediates* between the whole and its individual parts. Thus, what Tanabe took from Hegel's dialectical logic was its immediate linkage to historical reality. The dialectic of thesis-antithesis-synthesis proved to be more powerful and accurate in its grasp of unfolding history than was traditional two-valued logic (either this, or that). The historical world simply cannot be comprehended through the lens of either/or logic, which freezes states of affairs as being either this or that. Movement and transition are lost, leaving a historical world devoid of process and becoming. Dialectical logic depicts a world ever moving from what it is, to what it is not, to a new and changed "what it is." This unfolding of the new arises unceasingly, as thesis gives way to its denial—the antithesis—which gives birth to a new synthesis, which, then, becomes the new thesis, and the process begins all over again. This process never ends, just as history never ends, but it serves as a record of constant change. Buddhism teaches that the Buddha/absolute nothingness/reality is impermanence. Dialectical logic charts the flow of such impermanence. But the flow of reality "cannot be expressed, still less, described, in terms of a logic that takes the laws of identity and non-contradiction [the two fundamental laws of traditional logic] as fundamental principles. . . . Existence destroys and transcends the logic of identity."[30] The implications of dialectical logic for the Logic of the Specific are profound: "The mediation that propels history through time as an interrelated totality itself belongs to reality."[31] The flow of actual history as it develops is an expression of ultimate reality. Reality is a process.

That Tanabe's "Logic of the Specific" and his theory of absolute mediation was tied to the world as experienced stood in sharp contrast to Nishida's attempts to apply "pure experience," or even his Logic of *Basho* (place), to real events, races, nations, and world politics. Tanabe's methods were meant to be immediately applicable, and he demonstrates this by engaging his philosophy with the cultural, national, and international events leading up to World War II. The Marxists of his day criticized all philosophy that did not touch down in the real world and Tanabe was no doubt aware of their critique of Nishida for being otherworldly and irrelevant to the contemporary situation.

It was a book by the French philosopher Henri Bergson (the same philosopher who had inspired Nishida), the *Two Sources of Morality and Religion,* that served as a guide for the application of Tanabe's Logic of the Specific to contemporary society. Taking ethics as the most central aspect of philosophy, Tanabe examined Japan as his subject. Bergson had written of "open" and "closed" societies. A closed society is one that is ethnically based, a sealed clan mentality "which would prohibit it from joining the great open societies of the world."[32] Nakamura Hajime, in his monumental *Ways of Thinking of Eastern Peoples,* concurred when he wrote that "the traditional concept of honesty as loyalty to the clan and Emperor is applicable only to the conduct of man as a member of the particular and limited human nexus to which he belongs; it is not applicable to the conduct of a man as a member of human society as a whole."[33] Nakamura, who published his study in 1964, suggested that "the rapidly changing relations of Japan to the rest of the world requires a change from a strictly ethnic or national focus, to an international one."[34] Tanabe, writing long before Nakamura, believed that Japan was so deeply grounded in its own culture that it was unaware of the moral implications of the strict cultural conditioning that kept Japanese eyes on Japan and "Japaneseness," with little or no awareness of the greater world that lay beyond. He regarded Japan as a rigid, clannish, and closed society that was incapable of joining the open societies of the world. As we now know, Japan would open itself to the rest of the world amazingly quickly, but only by being forced to abandon much of its clannishness and becoming remarkably world-conscious. But prior to the allied occupation of Japan, its citizens were quite willing to accept the cultural conditioning that was imposed. Since any society is a community of individuals, any change in society requires a change in the psyches of the individuals composing it. Significant social change cannot be accomplished by simply converting the intellectuals who formed the upper strata of society. Instead, change had to involve the majority of citizens. In order for such widespread change to occur, it is necessary for there to be an increased awareness of the effect of clan obligations and loyalties on their behavior. But to accomplish this, Tanabe thought it essential to make the tribal biases of the Japanese apparent, examining them with a rational mind and replacing them with values in line with the more liberal and permissive open societies of the West. The binding-power of a limited social nexus needed to be replaced by a mind-set that was world-oriented and relatively free.

The Centrality of Ethics

It was Tanabe's long-standing belief that ethics was the central focus of philosophy. Heisig agrees, writing that, for Tanabe, "it is in morality that we find philosophy's vital immediacy."[35] Through morality-in-action we come to discover what "lay at the heart of the logic of the specific."[36] However, in order to make an application of the Logic of the Specific, Tanabe concluded that the "specific" had to be, in the case of Japan, the "closed" society. Such a description pointed to the Japanese society of his time, and the central issue emerging from this application was the need to find some way to bring about a conversion to a more "open" society.

Tanabe developed his new logic during the years 1934–1941 (although he revised it for a subsequent edition shortly after the war) a time of increased social control in aid of Japan's military adventures. It was at this time that he came to identify the *nation* as the locus of the specific, with Japan being a nation very much in need of conversion. If one accepts that "membership in the nation is the highest duty of the individual,"[37] and that it is imposed authority that binds people together as a nation, then a "closed" society is the inevitable result. But if one holds that one's membership in the nation is one's highest duty, but instead of placing authority in the hands of the few rulers at the top rung of an ethnic society it is given to the ordinary citizens who compose the nation, then power and authority shifts from the few to the many. The result is a transformation from a closed ethnicity to an open individualistic society. Such a shift moves the individual from closed specificity to open universality insofar as the individual is now freed to use reason to decide what ought to be done ethically. The decision no longer comes from an outside authority but from internal deliberation.

The nation, whether the Japan of his age or at any other time or place in history, is always a force that confines and constrains its individual citizens. It blinds them to the wider world, focuses them on their own ways as the" right ways," never encouraging them to look beyond the nation to universal humankind. But an open society is one that allows individual citizens to break down these barriers and to focus beyond the nation to a greater universal, such as humankind at large. The specific is always "nonrational," whereas the universal demands rational decision making. The specific (nation) inhibits the will to moral decision making and independent reasoning through clear restrictions against opposition to its dictates, moral and otherwise. It is rational reflection that *mediates* state-imposed authority, which is an externally imposed and therefore nonrational addition to our lives, and substitutes internally imposed ethical standards. Tanabe was not unaware of the effects of "herd morality" and group pressure. Hence, the turn to rationality is not an easy one for any individual to achieve. Difficult as it might be for an individual to be loyal to the nation, while at the same time realizing that the state negatively mediates against any attempt to oppose its authority, Tanabe held that the individual is on the side of absolute nothingness (as universal) in opposing the state. The individual, who is in line with the universal, must choose what is true and just for all humanity and not just for Japan, or any other nation or group of nations.

It may strike one as odd, however, for Tanabe to see rationality as the direct route to the open society when he is so insistent that our reason is corrupt and unable to grasp the truth or to decide on what is, or is not, ethically correct. As will be seen in the following pages, in order for our ordinary rationality, and our very being, to be transformed, wholehearted confession and repentance must occur. In Tanabe's view, until then, it seems that reason cannot be trusted, and surely this must also include that reason which comes to reject the closed for the open society.

Critique of Reason

If metanoetics is dependent on the realization that our rationality is finite and flawed, then it must be asked whether we are capable of being ethical before *zange*. Ethical action requires the ability to choose from among alternative courses of action, and for that choosing to be anything more than arbitrary, reason must be capable of deciding which course of action is better and which is worse. Yet what hope do we have of achieving this if our power of reason is both inadequate for the task and fundamentally flawed? Tanabe warns of the "original sin" of arrogance, that is, the "concealed tendency to forget one's relativity and presume to be the absolute."[38] Human freedom does not include the guarantee that its use will avoid evil and lead us to the good. Therefore, our freedom must be rooted in the "grace of the absolute": in Other-power.[39] Without the help of Other-power our freedom, whether at the hands of the officials of the state, or by our misuse of it, is a false and shriveled freedom. Thus, "it is only when we forsake ourselves and entrust our being to the grace of *tariki* (Other-power) that our existence can acquire true freedom."[40] Nor is this entrusting a one-time act, for we must practice "death [to the old self] and resurrection [rebirth as a new, true self]" over and over again. Tanabe believes that this act of "dying" is precisely what Zen refers to as the "Great Death": "Absolute critique is the equivalent of this Great Death."[41]

When one practices metanoetics, one is transformed into "being-as-nothingness." Other-power's mediation yields not only a transformation of the relationship between the finite self and absolute nothingness, but also between one relative self and another. Furthermore, as we noted, the mediation of the relative self to another relative self "brings the absolute into existence."[42] This occurs in the *topos* or place [*basho*], but not as Nishida described absolute nothingness (as a "place" that is immediately what it is and intuited), but in a "place" as species (as nation, community) where finite or relative beings interact with each other as *agents* of absolute nothingness. Relative beings now relate to each other as "elevated to the level of universal nothingness," and, in so doing, the existence of absolute nothingness itself is made possible. As products of metanoesis, such relative beings are now truly free, for they exist under the influence and guidance of Other-power. Having abandoned reason due to its inability to resolve its own questions, and having displayed all too often a basic human finiteness covered over by an arrogance that continues to believe in its infiniteness, reason is now cleansed and ready to be renewed by Other-power. In Tanabe's words, "Reason is lifted up out of the abyss and is transformed."[43] Even philosophy itself is now transformed from its previous reliance on reason, "to the standpoint of action-faith based on the Other-power."[44] His earlier frustration now gone, Tanabe emphasizes that philosophy, which he believed had been closed for him, now "finds a new beginning through self-abandonment."[45] Tanabe taught that philosophy is possible only after the abandoning of reason and self—the "Great Death." Such a rebirth of philosophy arises in the spirit of the teachings of Shinran. Not that he simply copies Shinran, but Shinran's metanoesis is *the* major influence on his own development of a metanoetic philosophy based on *faith*. A "philosophical" faith of this sort is not faith in a God of theism, for it requires mediation in the world of relatives as "action-faith-witness," (the faith and witness of "continuous resurrection" readies one for loving action, or witnessing, in the world) and not just a faith in some transcendent God. Tanabe's absolute is an immanent absolute whose very existence is dependent on the "work" of mediation in the everyday world of finite individuals. Theistic, pantheistic, or other religious beliefs are largely based on rational judgments of what is believable, but since

Tanabe held that reason cannot "provide its own foundations," ∂ such belief is merely the making of castles in the sand. Instead, the absolute is to be known only through *actions* based on the *faith* that, through Other-power, one's actions will be mediated such that love results in the *witnessing* (that is, demonstrating one's transformation through one's loving actions) embodying one's faith. Such a transformation in and through one's actions is the only way that absolute nothingness is known. Only the absolute disruption of self allows proper action and guided reason to emerge, the result of allowing Other-power to be one's guide.

Perhaps we see here a mature Tanabe who no longer expects that the freedom to reason will bring about the ethical transformation of a person, or a nation, for since reason is corrupt, one's actions will be as well. It is this abandonment of reason that is the full expression of the mediation of Other-power, and the letting-go of self. Only then can ethical action result. This working-out of the Logic of Species had begun nearly a decade before the publication of *Philosophy as Metanoetics*. It is clear that during that decade Tanabe had abandoned the pursuit of rational ethics and had fully turned away from reason as a guide to faith in Other-power.

Given that our finiteness is inescapably evil and inevitably arrogant in its pretentious claim to "absoluteness," the only possible cure that Tanabe found was in confessing our sins, abandoning our arrogance, and becoming truly humble: dying to the self, and accepting the guidance of Other-power. As a sinful being alone, "one has nothing to rely on."[46] Self-power must give way to Other-power, which is the only route to salvation and to correct ethical action.

What results from the activity of nothingness working through us is the "action of no-action." It is action "performed by a subject [a self] that has been annihilated."[47] Through "the conversion of death-and-resurrection, we come to realize that our true self is the self of nothingness whose being consists in acting as the mediator of nothingness."[48] Nothingness becomes actual only through a death-and-resurrection repeatedly realized at the "core" of relative beings "by means of a circular movement between the absolute and the relative."[49]

The Ethics of Metanoetics

No doubt, together with Nietzsche and some other existentialists (though for quite different reasons), Tanabe believed that for one who has died to worldly passions and then is resurrected by Other-power, "all is permitted."[50] Ordinary human beings, who have not confessed their selfish and sinful natures and have not invited the help and guidance of Other-power, are living lives that are *beneath* ethics, rather than *beyond* it. The ethics of "naturalness," of being who you truly are prior to repentance and resurrection, only reveals a core of unhealed, radical evil. Attempts at being ethical under these conditions are doomed to failure. Once one realizes this, then ethical and other failures will bring one to one's knees in an appeal for help from Other-power. Ethics, like freedom, is possible only through mediation, the transforming mediation that moves us from the influence and authority of the specific (species), to the status of the universal. Tanabe maintains that then, and only then, are we guided by the Other-power of absolute nothingness, now being able to follow that guidance in the activities of our lives.

The negation of the self is essential if one is to become truly ethical. Since salvation demands the self-consciousness of radical evil, which inevitably and predictably results from human arrogance, then those without the experience of having repented "have no prospect of salvation" and, hence, will be unable to eliminate either evil or arrogance from their dealings with others and, making ethical action at best a hit-and-miss endeavor. Our "natural" state is basically evil, before *zange*, and is to be distinguished from the "natural" state of one who has been resurrected through the mediation of Other-power. What regularly passes as "natural" is usually the result of our dependence on self-power, which can never move us beyond our inherent evil and irrationality. For

Tanabe, the greatest offender in this claim of "natural" ethics is Zen Buddhism.

The Zen Buddhist practitioner does exert him/herself through rigorous self-discipline and training demanding the strict following of rules and regulations. By contrast, the Shin Buddhist (Pure Land Buddhist) exerts him/herself to the utmost such that despair is eliminated, and the seemingly hopeless task of correcting one's inherently evil nature is achieved through total submission to Other-power. Shin Buddhism, therefore, requires that only the self-negation of self-power before the "Great Compassion of Other-power" is able to mediate a transformation and resurrection. Zen talks of realizing one's Buddha-nature, which is a "living as though one had died." Such a death is not a future death but a death of the self in the present. One both lives as a self and yet is dead as a self. While this is a contradiction of either/or logic, it is not for a logic of both/and: I die by living and I live by dying (words that Nishida would have totally agreed with). Tanabe, however, rejects both the logic of either/or and of both/and, and replaces it with a neither/nor logic: there is neither death nor life. Death does not follow life but is already within it, and the death of the self through repentance means that life is restored "within death and mediated by it."[51] And this death and resurrection never ceases but is reconfirmed over and over again, for one is always in need of repentance and, hopefully, resurrection. Life and death cease to oppose one another by requiring each other in the miracle of death and resurrection. Neither death, nor life, but death as giving birth to a new self every moment, and living as dying in each and every moment. Both life and death give way to a process that establishes neither death nor life, for each is always in the process of becoming the other.

Zen, on the other hand (which Tanabe straightforwardly identifies with mysticism), tries to achieve *satori* through self-power, a power that can, at best, grant an intuitive union with absolute nothingness. However, argues Tanabe, if absolute nothingness can be intuitively experienced, then it has to be a *being* and not nothingness. Absolute nothingness can only be known indirectly, through the mediative power of negating beings (by negating the old self through repentance), and through bringing about the resurrection of these same beings. This mediatory function *is* a demonstration of the existence of absolute nothingness, never as a being, but always as a nothingness known through its action: Tanabe describes this activity as action-faith-witness. Absolute nothingness *acts* upon and through us if we have the *faith* to die to our old selves, with the result that, as resurrected selves, we can *witness* this transformation through our actions as our way-of-being-in-the-world. According to this view, it is only then that we can act ethically. Ethics is dependent on religious transformation as the gift of the compassion of absolute nothingness through Other-power. However, the way ahead is far from straight and narrow, for such transformed individuals, even though they are in a state of "being[s]-in-nothingness,"[52] are still in possession of their freedom independently of nothingness. They are not merged with or unified with nothingness as in Zen and mysticism generally. Rather, as free and independent beings, they continue to contain radical evil within themselves "that urges them to proclaim their own being," thereby removing themselves from the mediation of absolute nothingness.[53] This is precisely why, for Tanabe, repentance (death) and resurrection (life) must be reaffirmed over and over again.

In Zen, one becomes a Buddha upon enlightenment, but there is no resurrection, as Tanabe sees it. The self remains itself, albeit a realized self now recognizing what was there all along. Tanabe adopts the language of French and German existentialism to make this point: the "in-itself" (*en soi* or *an sich*) refers to a self that retains its identity, even in enlightenment. Like a rock, it remains static and unchanged through it all. A self as "for-itself" (*pour soi* or *für sich*) is a self that self-negates in its mediated transformation. Self-identity is lost. The Zen "in-itself" degrades itself to the level of sentient and finite being, whereas the "for itself" is transformed to the universal, to a new self altogether. Zen is available to a few: Shin and metanoetics to all. Without transformation through repentance, one can, at most, achieve the naturalness of the "sub-ethical."[54] In a way, "metanoetics [is] positioning itself midway between the in-itself of Zen and the for others of *Nembutsu* [Shin] Buddhism."[55] It is neither the one nor the other. But in Zen, the practitioner often "slides into the in-itself mode," into "mere talk about Zen."[56] It is so easy to mistakenly believe that one is free to act as one pleases simply because one has identified with absolute nothingness through one's Buddha-nature. However, this is often accomplished without achieving a self-negating transformation. In fact, argues Tanabe, Zen often becomes a merely secular tradition in which the true absolute is lost.

Yet, while it is true that Zen practitioners, as with those in any tradition, can be lazy, even superficial in their quest for enlightenment, puffed-up as though their efforts were sufficient, it is equally true that one can "follow" the path of metanoia without actually following it deeply, never actually dying to the self, or be anything but steadfast in seeking unending renewals of repentance and confession. It is not helpful to compare the worst of one religious tradition with the best of another. Indeed, it is likely that the utter sincerity of a Tanabe is relatively rare in any tradition. Just as Zen or mysticism can be more contemplative than transformative, so metanoia can be halfhearted or entered into by a fearful ego only concerned with a future life with a robust ego intact.

Be that as it may, Tanabe is quite clear about the place and source of ethics in his philosophy: "In mediating the absolute through metanoetic confession of its own finitude and powerlessness, the relative ethical subject cooperates to make manifest the absolute nothingness of religion. Religion mediates itself to ethics through metanoesis in order to actualize an absolute mediation of the absolute-*qua*-relative. Metanoesis is both the gate through which ethics passes over into religion and the axis around which religion converts to ethics."[57] Metanoesis is a *kōan* that mediates the transformation of religion and of ethics. The *kōan* is that, as finite beings, we become "co-workers" with the absolute—we are finite as infinite, and the infinite has, at the same time, become finite.

Society Transformed

The earlier discussion of the "for itself" indicated that a transformed human being is a being *for* others and is clearly not primarily concerned with her or himself. Given the general Buddhist (and
Tanabian) understanding that "everything in this world exists cor-
relatively to everything else," then to destroy or do harm to others is
also to do harm to oneself.[58] However, "the nothingness of absolute
transformation can be achieved only through reciprocal mediation
in society."[59] An ethics of mediation is a *social ethics,* one "based
on coexistence, cooperation, and mutual instruction."[60] Absolute
nothingness is the "Great Compassion" expressed as brotherly love,
as fellowship. The result is a movement toward the "city of God,"
toward the Shin Buddhist Pure Land of community here and now.
Such a society is truly an open society, one that is continually
mediated as a specific (species) made universal by Other-power. As
well, in such a society each citizen continually renews his or her
act of *zange* such that each resurrected individual mediates other
individuals, with the ideal being the mediated community as metaphorically described by the net of jewels in which each individual
is reflected in, and is reflected by, each and every other individual,
with everyone living exemplary lives. This metanoetic society would
be a society fully mediated by a sense of social ethics granted by
absolute nothingness. For Tanabe, there is simply no other ground
for ethics. Ethics and community are not to be achieved by the
reasonings and calculations of finite and corrupted human beings.
Confession, repentance, and the gift of mediation and resurrection provided by the Other-power of absolute nothingness, is the
only route to, and ground for, a true ethics. The resultant society
would be based on loving interaction rather than on ego-driven
reasoning and law. While such a perspective may seem unrealisti-
cally utopian, it describes vividly the futility of any society based
on the strummings of ego, without the transformative influence
of Other-power, which yields a society of loving interaction. The
transformation of ego-driven reasoning and calculation yields lov-

ing interaction of each with each in a society that recognizes the inescapable interconnection of all beings. Each of us is our brother and our sister, and all people are now recognized as our kinfolk. Both Tanabe and Nishida taught that ethics arises from a deeper place within us than reason. For Tanabe, ethics is possible only when, through *zange,* the entire human ego is out of the way, since only then can one hear and obey the dictates of Other-power. For Nishida, ethics arises from the natural inclinations of the realized self that is not a self: a selfless self. For both thinkers it is the ego that corrupts us, and when it is dissolved, or placed in the background of awareness, it is then that the possibility of ethics arises. Note that, for both Tanabe and Nishida, a *transformation* of the person is required: for Tanabe, it is through repentance and recognition of one's sinful nature. For Nishida, transformation is the recovery of the "true" self that is no longer an ego-self, but is now a Buddha-self that recognizes the nonduality and interconnectedness that characterizes the real nature of reality, but that was heretofore hidden from us.

If ethical being and ethical action are, in the developed sense, the result of personal transformation and not intellectual calculation, then ethics appears to the transformed as an urge or feeling, whether externally revealed or internally revealed. Tanabe, as transformed, reaches outward to Other-power; Nishida, as transformed, dives inward to discover the depths hidden in each of us as Buddha-nature. A contemporary Western philosopher writes with great insight in describing the profound difference such transformation makes. Francisco J. Varela concludes his recent study as follows:

> How can . . . an attitude of all-encompassing, decentered, responsive, compassionate concern be fostered and embodied in our [Western] cultures? It obviously cannot be created merely through norms and rationalistic injunctions. It must be developed and embodied through *disciplines* that facilitate the letting-go of ego-centered habits and enable compassion to become spontaneous and self-sustaining. It is not that there is no need for

normative rules in the relative world—clearly such rules are a necessity in any society. It is that unless such rules are informed by the wisdom that enables them to be dissolved in the demands of responsibility to the particularity and immediacy of lived situations, the rules will become sterile, scholastic hindrances to compassionate action rather than conduits for its transformation. . . . [Such a] skillful approach to living is based on a pragmatics of transformation that demands nothing less than a moment-to-moment awareness of the virtual nature of our selves. In its full unfolding it opens up openness as authentic caring.[61]

The radical transformations which both Tanabe and Nishida argued for resulted in the opening up of just such moment-to-moment renewal and the appearance of a caring compassion that reached beyond human beings to an integrated concern for the entire cosmos. Whether Tanabe's God as nothingness, or Nishida's nothingness as God, the entire cosmos has taken on the hues of the sacred. Ethical action is now sacred action, but no less philosophical for that, if philosophy is understood in the sense of seeking the "truth" about ourselves and about our universe. Religion and philosophy do abide next to one another in these first two accounts of the Kyoto School thinkers.

3

Nishitani Keiji
(1900–1990)

In *Śūnyatā* [emptiness] things come to rest on their own root-source. It is not a standpoint that only states that the self and things are empty. The foundation of the standpoint of *Śūnyatā* lies elsewhere: not that the self is empty, but that emptiness is the self, not that things are empty, but that emptiness is things.

—Masao Abe, "Nishitani's Challenge to Philosophy and Theology," in *The Religious Philosophy of Nishitani Keiji*

When reading Nishitani, one encounters an existentialist who knew full well that he lived within the "existentialist predicament" and who struggled mightily to find his way through it. According to this perspective, the human predicament is one in which we have been thrown into a world without meaning. Furthermore, with no absolute guideposts or map to follow, given that God has been declared dead,[1] we are still somehow expected to live a meaningful and moral life. Heisig translates a passage by Nishitani which describes this kind of existential despair: "My life as a young man can be described in a single phrase: it was a period absolutely without hope. . . . My life at the time lay entirely in the grips of nihility and despair. . . . My decision, then, to study philosophy was in fact—melodramatic as it might sound—a matter of life and death."[2] A central theme of his own philosophical journey is this confrontation with nihilism. Nihilism, or what he also terms "relative nothingness," is the pointed awareness that our existence is without foundation and our laws, institutions, and religions are feeble attempts to paper over the growing abyss of meaninglessness and hopelessness. Nevertheless, we must somehow act significantly, or else, as the French writer Albert Camus wrote, all that is left is to commit either intellectual or physical suicide. Physical suicide needs no explanation, but intellectual suicide is the futile acceptance of ideas, laws, ethical stances, or religious/political ideologies, none of which are intellectually defensible. What it was that Nishitani sought was some "standpoint" from which meaning and foundational justification might emerge.

Life and Career

Nishitani Keiji was born on February 27, 1900, in a small town on the Inland Sea. After the death of his father, when Nishitani was fourteen, he and his mother moved to Tokyo. Tuberculosis, the same disease that his father had died from, caused him to delay his pre-university schooling. Sent to the northern island of Hokkaido, the rest and clean air offered a cure. He returned to Tokyo and this time was accepted into the prestigious Daiichi High School. His sojourn in Hokkaido left him time to read the novels of Sōseki Natsume, whose mention of the Zen state of mind led Nishitani to the Zen writings of D. T. Suzuki.

In high school he read widely, studying the works of Dostoevsky and Nietzsche, which began his foray into existentialism, as well as the Bible and St. Francis of Assisi. But it was Nishida's *Thought and Experience* that turned his attention more toward philosophy as a potential field of interest. Heisig suggests that Nishitani had three choices before him as graduation from high school approached: to become a Zen monk, to join a utopian community called "New Town," or to select philosophy as his life's work.[3] He decided on the latter, studying philosophy at the University of Kyoto, where he studied under Nishida and Tanabe. His graduation thesis was on the German philosopher, Schelling (1775–1854).

Having graduated from university at the age of twenty-four, he taught philosophy in high school for the next eight years. In 1928 he was appointed to an adjunct lectureship at Otani University in Kyoto, continuing there until 1935. He published essays during that time and, in 1932, was made a lecturer at Kyoto University. His continuing interest in mystical thought was evident in the publishing of a book on the history of mysticism that same year. This interest was unusual among Western philosophers, where mysticism had not played a significant role in their thinking, and yet most of the philosophers of the Kyoto School took mysticism very seriously. Nishitani and Ueda all wrestled with the writings of Meister Eckhart (1260–1328), the thirteenth-century German mystic, as did Martin Heidegger, with whom Nishitani and Ueda studied.

In 1936, his earlier interest in Zen broke through once again, and he began his Zen practice, which continued for the next twenty-four years at Shokoku-ji, under master Yamazaki. His dual interest in philosophy and Zen, as Heisig recounts, "was a matter, as he liked to say, of a balance between reason and letting go of reason, of 'thinking and sitting, sitting and then thinking.'"[4] The name given to him by his master was Keisei ("voice of the valley stream").

When he was thirty-seven he was awarded a scholarship from the Ministry of Education to study under the famous French philosopher, Henri Bergson (1859–1941). However, Bergson's ill health made this impossible, so he was allowed to switch to Martin Heidegger, now at Heidelberg University. At that time, Heidegger was lecturing on Nietzsche, and, during his stay, Nishitani himself delivered a lecture comparing Nietzsche's *Zarathustra* to Meister Eckhart's writings.

At the age of forty-three, Nishitani, like many other Japanese academics, incurred difficulties with the wartime Ministry of Education. Both Nishida and Tanabe encouraged him to speak out against the irrational ideology of the time, which appeared to be leading Japan to war, but he was unable to do so, unable to be decisive enough to act on their urgings. He was appointed to the "chair" of the department of religion that same year, and was awarded a doctorate, with the help and assistance of Nishida, two years later. His doctoral thesis was titled "Prolegomenon to a Philosophy of Religion."

Nishitani received a severe blow in December 1946, after the defeat of Japan, when the occupation authorities deemed him unsuitable for teaching. Not only could he not teach any longer, but he was also barred from holding any public office. The charge against him was that he had supported the wartime government. Needless to say, he was crushed by this decision, but he found his support in Zen, as well as in his wife. Heisig writes that "it was a difficult time for him, and his wife, who would watch him spending whole afternoons watching lizards in the yard, was afraid he would crack under the pain."[5] Nonetheless, during these years of academic exile, he wrote *A Study of Aristotle,* and *God And Absolute Nothingness,* and *Nihilism,* all of which Tanabe hailed as "masterpieces."[6]

Reflecting back to the war years, Nishitani observed that during the war he was criticized for not supporting Japan's turn toward militarism and rightist ideology and immediately after the war for having supported it in some way.[7] He was damned if he did support the war, and damned if he did not. Nevertheless, he was eventually reappointed to the position he was forced to leave behind, just five years later in 1952. His final collected output consisted of twenty-six volumes, which only began appearing, in Japanese, in 1986.

In his written "message" to the participants of a conference on his book *Religion and Nothingness,* which was held at Smith and Amherst Colleges in 1984, he stated that his "central concern has been to *think* the problem of nothingness."[8] Furthermore, he points out that, since Western thought has come to influence every aspect of Japanese culture, it is now necessary to "re-think" the long tradition of Eastern "thought and philosophy with the help of what we learned from Western philosophy."[9] Throughout this rethinking, Nishitani maintained a Zen position, but in the light of existential thought, that also demanded that "reality" be found in the living of everyday life and not in some theoretical account of reality. Reality is underfoot, but it requires a good deal of digging and sweeping to find it. What Nishitani offers is a standpoint that has resulted from his digging and sweeping and from which the ordinary world may be perceived in an extraordinary way, a way that has been available all along for anyone looking at it from the standpoint of nothingness/emptiness/*Śūnyatā*. It is the ordinary world as extraordinary, the extraordinary as ordinary.

Nietzsche and Nihilism

Nishitani not only researched the topic of "nihilism," but, as a young man, he had lived it, eventually wrestling it to the ground and then finding a pathway through it and beyond. The malady he had experienced was "European nihilism," as he called it, which arose due to the "rapid collapse" within him (and throughout Europe) of traditional metaphysical philosophy and "the death of God," as announced by Nietzsche. What had happened was that the worldview that had nourished and supported the spiritual life of Europe for more than two thousand years was all at once thrown into question: the foundation of European life had not just cracked but had collapsed altogether. Philosophy and religion were now seen to have been human-made, mere constructions. An abyss opened, casting all forms of meaning, security, and hope into radical doubt. As a result of this, a great despair swept through Europe, at least among the intelligentsia, and the only way beyond it was to shift the assurances of religious faith and metaphysical reasoning to that of the self. The courage to face this yawning abyss, then, required living without assurances, and, yet, living a passionate life grounded on one's own choices. The disclosure of "nothingness" or nihility at the core of existence demanded an "overcoming" of this nihilism by sheer determination to create and chart one's own historical destination. Nihilism was overcome by first admitting the truth of nihility and then choosing to live in the face of it. The old values arose from outside of the individual. The new Nietzschean values came from human beings, empowering and emboldening each person to create values for him/herself. This brings forth a "will to power." We would no longer be held down by the gravity of past traditions-old values that kept us from creating values for ourselves and fanciful threats of eternal damnation and divine punishment.

Nishitani argued that the only way to defeat nihilism is "through nihilism."[10] His guide in this was Friedrich Nietzsche whose *Thus Spoke Zarathustra* was based on the idea that nihilism could only be overcome by a reframing of our understanding of nihilism. Perhaps the best route for understanding Nietzsche's brand of nihilism is to use Nishitani's own analysis in his *The Self Overcoming of Nihilism*.[11] Once Nietzsche had announced that "God is dead," (that is, now that, for many, God is no longer believed to exist) it became necessary to investigate what constituted the life of Christianity and then the slow implications of its demise resulting in the need for new values. Nishitani points out that with the collapse of Christianity, "the ground of received ideals and values has become hollow."[12] For centuries, Christian values had themselves protected its followers from despair at the meaninglessness of human existence. The way this was accomplished was that Christianity "granted the human absolute *value*" as the "image of God" on earth. Furthermore, Christianity countered the actual existence of evil and suffering in the world by positing a divine plan, which gave meaning to evil and suffering. Moreover, Christian teachings guaranteed a God-given morality, rendering the inclination toward physical suicide far less of a threat due to a feeling of hopelessness.

However, with God's death, all of these assurances were taken away, leaving the potential for a yawning abyss of hopelessness. What emerged was a second look at that which Christianity had promoted, now that its "truth" was no longer unassailable. Christian morality had taught that human beings were weak ("the meek shall inherit the earth"; Psalms 25:8) and that the world is filled with suffering and evil. The beliefs in Heaven and Judgment Day were a denial of this world as good, leading naturally to a "hatred of the natural," a justification for the preference of the weak over the strong and culminating in the denial of the passions. So Christianity was born as an antidote to the nihilism of the time, yet it produced another nihilism: "European nihilism." The breakdown of Christianity yielded a fresh look at what, for Nietzsche, was a world-denying philosophy. This new nihilism, at its very depths, gave rise to a new overcoming of nihilism, the "will to power." In place of God is the love of self and the world just as they are, argued Nietzsche. The self-loathing of humans as lustful, erotic beings gave way to a view of humans as proud, powerful erotic beings who loved life and were capable of creating meaning and values for themselves. Pleasure is not intrinsically evil but actually is a sign of the fullness of life and the establishment of life-affirming values. One fictional example of one who lives in this positive and life affirming way is Nietzsche's "overman" (*übermensch*), who says "yes" to the world and to his/her own existence. Such a one displays the power and strength to give meaning to a meaningless world. Indeed, Nietzsche taught that one must love the world that you helped to shape to such an extent that you would be willing to accept its worth even if you were committed to reliving it just as it is over and over again throughout eternity. The "myth of eternal recurrence" is a test of the worth of the life you have created. Can you will its existence without end, or is your created existence less than worthy of your continued existence? This was Nietzsche's self-overcoming of the nihilism that was left exposed after the imposed values of Christianity had begun to crumble. The abyss became evident, and the way out was through "yea-saying." To Nietzsche, we must make our meaning by affirming that we ourselves have the power to make meaning and to create values worthy of us.[13] "Nihility," writes Nishitani, "refers to that which renders meaninglessness the meaning of life."[14] Religion arises when meaning, including the point of our own existence, is in doubt or is even absent. When we question the significance of our own existence, the door to religion is opened: "A gaping abyss opens up at the very ground on which we stand."[15] Indeed, the abyss is always present, "always just underfoot." Everything that we love, treasure, and find meaning from is intrinsically fragile and perishable.

Nishitani defines religion as the "*real* self-awareness of reality."[16] Reality actualizes itself in and through us, and this Buddhist way of understanding infuses meaning back into existence.

Nishitani echoes Nishida here, for he envisions "creation" as the self-manifestation of nothingness (or God), with the result that our perspective has changed from individual ego to a cosmic one. Thus, each of us is part of divinity and, as such, share in the purpose and exploratory nature of the absolute.[17] As a result, each of us, as well as the cosmos as a whole, is once again filled with meaning and purpose. The flatland of meaninglessness and despair gives way to a robust landscape of hope and intrinsic worth.

The Ten Ox-herding Pictures

As a guide to Nishitani's complex and detailed analysis of his position, it may prove helpful to recall in detail the famous Ten Ox-herding pictures, which were briefly mentioned at the end of chapter 1, to help in charting a course somewhat akin to Nishitani's more philosophical path. Nishitani did not offer or provide this sequence of steps and pictures that lead one toward hope and understanding of the path to enlightenment, although he knew of them. The author of the pictures and their poetic commentary was a twelfth-century Zen master in Sung Dynasty China, (960–1279), named Kaku-an Shi-en. These ten watercolors (line drawings in this book) trace the journey from ordinary, everyday consciousness to enlightenment. The first picture, entitled "Searching for the Ox," begins with a young herder who heeds rumors that there is a deeper self than the everyday ego self, one that grants fullness of meaning and purpose. In asking, "Who am I?" and "What is the meaning of my life?" as his initial curiosity suggests, he is taking the first and vital step away from ordinary understanding toward enlightenment. As with Plato in ancient Athens, this initial questioning is a crucial step in pursuing the path—the "way"—to a deeper realization of self. To know that you do not know is crucial to the search, for if you think that you already know, or if you have never given any thought to who you are, then searching never begins. Awareness of ignorance (knowing that you don't know) is the first step toward knowledge and, in this instance, towards "self" knowledge and enlightenment.

5

6

7

8

9

10

What makes it so difficult to begin the journey toward enlightenment is the fact that one has absolutely no evidence to support the view that there is such a thing as a "deeper" self that exists beneath the everyday self that now questions. A few have told the ox herder that an enlightened awareness can be achieved and that a truer sense of who you are is a genuine possibility. But what drives him to take the first step is his own inner dissatisfaction with the state he finds himself in. If we overlay Nishitani's understanding of nihilism (or meaninglessness), then this young herder despairs over his life and its limitations; he has a sense that there has to be something more, something more satisfying than the noise and bustle of ordinary existence. This is the "existential predicament" that he finds himself in. Confronting the abyss of meaninglessness, he takes a first step toward finding the "ox"—the metaphor for the deep, enlightened self. As Nishitani argues, it is nihilism itself that must lead to an overcoming of nihilism, and the overcoming begins with this first step. Our own awareness of the meaninglessness of existence is the goad that spurs us on to search for something more. Nihilism, like the Socratic "gadfly" of ancient Athens, bites beneath the saddle of complacency spurring us on to seek something better. Like a still small voice at the back of our ordinary consciousness, we are prodded to look further in an attempt to move from meaninglessness to meaning, from ordinary ego-consciousness to an awareness that seems to transcend the limits of the ordinary and everyday.

The first picture is followed by the second, entitled "Seeing the Traces." Following the metaphor, the herder sees only faint footprints, faint tracks left behind by the supposed "ox." What the metaphor suggests is that these tracks, or traces, are hints that the boy herder finds in his reading of the scriptures, or perhaps from his early attempts at meditation, or from lectures or sermons. These whispers give some hope that others have genuinely found what he is now looking for. The hoofprints of the ox provide some slight evidence that there may be a path to deeper understanding that will satisfy. Still, it could be a myth that there is anything better: a crutch used to superficially and temporarily sooth the masses.

The third stage ("Seeing," or "Catching a Glimpse of the Ox") of the herder's development consists in actually seeing a portion of the retreating ox. As D. T. Suzuki writes, "He finds his way through the sound [noise]; he sees into the origin of things."[18] His "true" self is now present, at least at the background of consciousness, which involves seeing "into the origin of things" insofar as enlightenment is a seeing into the oneness of all things. The deep self is aware of this unity, revealing that the herder is actually one with ultimate reality itself. Like salt in water, both the deep self and nothingness are already present in the background of consciousness, while remaining unseen.

It is now that the hard work begins. There is no longer any doubt that the deeper self exists (the ox), but awareness of it fades in and out of consciousness, like a hologram on a credit card, which appears and disappears as one slightly adjusts the angle of view. Habits need to be acquired to keep the ox present, to prevent it from slipping away. The everyday consciousness continues to override the deeper self. In the fourth picture, entitled "Catching the Ox," a rope is attached to the ox and the herder struggles to control it. When he meditates, his mind chatters away, or wanders from fantasy to fantasy, limiting the effectiveness of meditation. His passions and fears, longings and memories continually come to the forefront of his awareness, leaving him disordered and frustrated. The taming of the deep self (or is it, first, the taming of the shallow self?) demands focused concentration and diligent training. Indeed, all of the Japanese arts, from meditation to the martial arts, demand rigorous and sustained training if one is to develop as a practitioner. Only sustained practice and severe self-discipline will keep the ox from receding from awareness and returning to the quiet pastures of the unconscious.

The fifth frame, entitled "Herding the Ox," is the stage of *consistent* self-discipline. The herder is now almost free of the many conceptualizations that filter out the right-now, right-before-him experience, which Nishida referred to as "pure experience." It requires simply being fully aware, fully present, as experience unfolds before him. There is no thinking, no conceptualizing, no representing of something through words, or by comparison with something else not present. The ox has become his partner and they walk together along the path.

The sixth picture is entitled "Coming Home on the Ox's Back," showing the herder and the ox to be in perfect harmony. The joy and serenity of this new state of awareness is symbolized by the music the herder plays on a bamboo flute while riding along upon the ox. "The struggle is over," and he is no longer distracted by the noise of the world; he and his ox are as one. He now experiences joy in the flow of things, awestruck by the exquisiteness of each unique moment; he is living in the "now." At last able to live fully in the world, he realizes the he *is* his own deep self and that somehow it is within him that the birds sing, the brook gurgles, and the sun shines. He is finally at home, in his own home-ground, as Nishitani would have it.

The realization of the seventh drawing, entitled "The Ox Forgotten; Leaving the Man Alone" is that there never really was an ox separate from him. The ox was only symbolically separate. Now the herder sits all alone, fully at peace in the universe.

The eighth stage, entitled "The Ox and the Man Both Gone out of Sight," is the realization of nothingness, or emptiness. Both the ox and the herder have disappeared. Nor are there trees, or birds, or anything else. There is nothing! The empty circle, or zero, is a total negation. Because he no longer sees himself as he once did, the chains of the empirical or everyday self are now broken. All things have collapsed, have disappeared, and with it any further possibility of *substance* thinking. Buddhism teaches that the central cause of suffering is the false belief in permanency: of self or soul, of mountains and waterfalls, or wealth and reputation. All is impermanent, and the realization that nothing has substance and that all things are empty is central to seeing that all is nothing. More importantly still is the fact that the empty circle announces that nondual consciousness has been fully established. There is no herder, no ox, no world, but only the oneness of all things—the formula that describes enlightenment. Speaking technically, there is no herder, no world, only *awareness*: the flowing of water, the crash of thunder, the buzzing of insects; better still, there is only flowing, crashing, and buzzing. Each of us flows, crashes, and buzzes. When the English philosopher John Locke (1632–1704) tried to explain what the "substance" was that he assumed, he could only say that it was a "something I know not what." Locke was followed by David Hume (1711–1776), the third of the three great British empiricists (Locke, Berkeley, and Hume), who added that there was no evidence that a substantial self existed, but instead pointed to a "theatre" of awareness where sounds and flowing occurred. There is really no empirical evidence either for the existence of substance, or of a continuing self. Instead, we simply assume that there are such. Zen tells us to still the mind, forego concepts, presuppositions, and language, and just take in the flowing, the crashing, and the buzzing; just *be* the buzzing. It is now that we are on our own home-ground, according to Nishitani, at the same time on the home-ground of every other thing. The deep self buzzes; the buzzing is the deep self. We are home at last. In any event, the eighth picture represents what Nishitani calls the *field of Śūnyatā*. It is on this field that "things" arise in their suchness; as buzzings. In itself, the field of nothingness, like a light table (which must be assumed to be formless, except that it is not possible for such to exist in the ordinary space/time world) used to display photographic slides, illuminates the buzzings and other things that now arise in a new light, as will become evident with picture nine.

It may be that pictures nine and ten were added at a later date, but whether part of the original collection or not, they are essential in explaining how one reenters the ordinary world after having bathed in the fullness of absolute nothingness. The ninth picture is entitled "Returning to the Origin, Back to the Source," and it is rich, lush, radiant with the incomparable beauty of the world of nature. Trees, flowers, birds singing, a flowing river have all reappeared, but are seen now as never before. Now, out of emptiness comes the rich many. The "emptying" of all things in picture eight is now overcome in the ninth frame as things now return with a fullness that is so bright that one is dazzled. The mountains and "buzzings" that disappeared in the eighth stage of awareness have reappeared with an incredible brightness, newness, and richness because we, as aware observers, have been freed of our old ways of dualistic understanding which, by necessity, placed objects "out there," at a distance from us. Now, we have become those objects insofar as the seer and the seen have become one. Furthermore, all that exists is now "backlit," as it were, because they are now lined with nothingness, the background to all the foreground appearances of things. Everything now shimmers in its suchness, its thusness, for things now appear in their own home-ground, just as they are in themselves.

Ueda Shizuteru suggests that figures eight and nine should not be taken in succession, but rather as co-related. They should be viewed as "oscillating back and forth." The two should be taken together, "like two sides of a single sheet of paper, a paper without thickness."[19] Each stage infiltrates the other so that eight implies nine, and nine implies eight. The enlightened man or woman sees both at once, stereoscopically. Everything perceived exists in its suchness on the field of *Śūnyatā*, as Nishitani understands this. The field of *Śūnyatā* is figure eight, upon which the things of picture nine now exist. Imagine drawings eight and nine on clear transparencies projected on a screen. First eight is projected, and then nine, except that eight is not removed but nine is placed on top of it. Both drawings are present, but nine now rests on eight. If we could add to this metaphor some way of making nine brighter because of eight, then this putting together of the two would be an apt metaphor depicting an enlightened awareness of how things are in their "suchness." Furthermore, now that it can be seen that all rest on the field of *Śūnyatā*, nothingness, then each thing is related to the others as kindred manifestations of nothingness, arising out of it and resting upon it. Nothingness, *Śūnyatā*, allows each thing to be in its own home-ground while simultaneously being in the home-ground of everything else, for they share the very same lining, the same place and origin of being.

The correlation of pictures eight and nine captures nicely the notion of the self-contradictory identity that Nishida struggled to describe in more precise philosophical terms. The contradictions infiltrate each other while maintaining their "otherness" as separate and distinct. The world of things (the many) is also nothingness (the One), and nothingness is the world of things: "Form is emptiness, emptiness is form; nirvana is samsara, samsara is nirvana."[20] Form (things) as formless (nothingness), or the formless as form, are two distinct perspectives on reality, but both are required if one is to have an adequate grasp of the world. The seeing thus described is a kind of double vision, but whether taken separately or together, a perspective is given that is far clearer and focused than ever before. One is now fully in and of the universe, and this provides a sense of belonging that utterly dispels any threat from nihilism or meaninglessness. To be a part of the ongoing flow of the universe itself is the ultimate in meaning. Having reached this point by having gone through nihilism only makes the arrival all the sweeter. As with Ueda's "non-mysticism" in the chapter on Nishida, the insight gained plunges one back into the everyday world with a new intensity.

The tenth picture, entitled "Entering the City with Bliss-bestowing Hands" implies that the herder, now an old man, has hands that can transform another. The commentary tells us that one would never know that he was enlightened, for he is found in the company of "wine-bibbers and butchers, [and] he and they are all converted into Buddhas."[21] The drawing has him encountering a young boy, and we might imagine that the boy is asking him whether there is such a thing as an ox. A reflection of someone young who is where he once was, he answers that he would teach the boy what he has learned about the existence of the ox. We can then imagine them sharing a cup of tea and a piece of bread while the enlightened old man starts the boy on his journey to enlightenment.

The first of the ox-herding pictures corresponds roughly to this awareness of the emptiness of ordinary understanding. The nihilism at this stage is the simple recognition of the unsatisfactory nature of our existence, and with it the dim aspiration that there ought to be something more. The underlying abyss is ever-present for one who thinks deeply, for death always looms, ethical demands change from generation to generation, wars continue to break out, and neither religion nor the existing philosophies are able to eliminate our awareness of a dis-ease based on a radical uncertainty.

It was Nietzsche who alerted Europe to the existence of the abyss that undermined traditional values, the belief in the existence of God, and the stability of so-called rational choices. Nietzsche's successes were real, but what he achieved, as Nishitani understood him, was a new nihilism within what Nishitani terms the "field of consciousness." The dualism of self and world remained, but the "power" of the self was now engaged in a historical battle between an inner self and outer things. Yet neither self nor things could be known except from a distance, that is, representationally. Representational knowing is knowing by means of concepts, words, or propositions. All of these are at least once removed from the actual experience that they seek to identify, describe, or represent. Such knowledge is *mediated* (by concepts, words, or propositions) and not direct or *immediate*. To know self or things in the outside world is to know them as represented, and not as they might be apart from consciousness. Neither the self-in-itself nor things-in-themselves can be grasped directly, but only as an image within consciousness. The security of divine knowledge now gives way to the nihility of subjective awareness. The price for human power, it turns out, is the relativity of a total subjectivism: that is to say, it is a "knowledge" without guarantee reduced to a matter of taste or majority opinion. Even science itself is rendered subjective, a series of value judgments, for the data of science is subjective appearance, mere phenomena-in-consciousness. The religious and metaphysical guarantees of reality itself have been lost and, instead, there is only existential choice, a choice to be made without an abiding map or even an innate sense of direction. Real or unreal, good or bad, beautiful or ugly have become matters of subjective taste or of the "reality" of the moment.

The Meaning of "Nothingness"

Before turning to Nishitani's creative response to the nihilistic challenge, it must be remarked that for Kyoto School philosophers, "nothingness" is said in many ways (to paraphrase Aristotle on "being"). What Aristotle said was that "there are many senses in which a thing may be said to 'be,' but all that 'is' is related to one central point, one kind of thing, and is not said 'to be' by a mere ambiguity."[22] Similarly, a variety of meanings came to be attached to "nothingness" by the Kyoto School thinkers. Nevertheless, "nothingness," in spite of differences in meaning, was held to refer to the same foundational or originary reality that is the basis of Kyoto School philosophy.

Ueda Shizuteru, Nishitani's best-known student and later colleague, suggests that Nishida's characterization of the West as cultures of "being," and the East as cultures of "nothingness," does not take into account philosophers in the West such as Eckhart and Nietzsche who do explore "nothingness" in considerable depth; nor does it do justice to the variations in meaning given the notion of "nothingness" by Eastern thinkers, including later members of the Kyoto School. Nevertheless, Ueda concludes that "it does after all seem that in European philosophy, that which is foundational and originary is ultimately grasped in terms of "being." That is to say that "in the west nothingness is understood as non-being, that is, as the negation of being, and in this sense is based on being."[23] Nothingness is thought of merely as the negation of some being of some kind. By contrast, the Kyoto School philosophers thought of "nothingness" as referring to that which was originary, ultimate, or absolute. However they each gave very different *meanings* to this notion.

Both Nishida and Tanabe rested their philosophies on the notion of "absolute nothingness" (*zettai-mu*). Yet, there were important differences: "While Nishida's [philosophy] conceived of it in terms of 'place' (*basho*), Tanabe's conceived of it in terms of 'praxis' (*jissen*)," or the working of absolute nothingness in history, through love.[24]

In contrast to both of these views, Nishitani chose the Mahāyāna Buddhist term *emptiness* (*Śūnyatā*) as the better designation for nothingness because of "the significant role that the arrival of nihilism played in his thought, a problem that had not been an issue for Nishida."[25]

Ueda argues that given that the problem of nihilism remained front and center in Nishitani's writing, "the idea of 'absolute nothingness' could not help but be impacted."[26] The "death of God" made the use of the language of absolutes an unlikely choice, if not an impossible one. "Because of the collapse of the absolute, the loss of the horizon of ontology, and the endless nihilization of nihility, 'absolute nothingness,' which would accommodate within itself even absolute being, could no longer be the basic category of thought in a world horizon."[27] Terms such as "absolute" and "God" now "rang hollow," and a new term was needed—still to refer to the central notion of "nothingness," but with none of the baggage of "absolute nothingness." Nishitani found such a term in classical Mahāyāna Buddhist thought, one that had not been discredited by the nihilism of the modern age. "Emptiness" (*Śūnyatā*) was such a term, although Nishitani admitted that he used it "rather freely," adopting a position that attempted to "stand at once within and outside of tradition."[28] If God was dead, then absolutes died with him. Nishitani emphasized that finding an alternative term for nothingness was, in fact, "demanded by the problem of nihilism."[29] What he tries to show with this term is "the breaking free of nihility, and the positivity of the freedom that emerges from that break."[30] Ueda contends that the literal meaning of "emptiness" conjures up a variety of nuances such as the image of a vast blue sky with its limitless possibilities, or of the wind, perhaps because it can circulate anywhere and is invisible yet sensible. Nishitani chose to rethink Kyoto School philosophy from the ground up while yet retaining the core of Kyoto School philosophy. The overriding philosophical problem was no longer the bridging of Eastern and Western philosophical traditions through the adoption of Western terminology and method, but the overcoming of a growing sense of meaningless, depression, and despair that now extended more or less around the world.

A Way Out

Nishitani offered a way out of this nihilism of the field of consciousness, which leaves us forever trapped within our own subjective consciousness. He does this by substituting "the field of *Śūnyatā*" for the field of consciousness. The path to this second field is already present in the first. The realization that both the self and things are mere objects for and in consciousness means that the self and everything else is without foundation, empty, and utterly impermanent. Everything will perish, scientific theories will follow, one upon another, and death looms before each of us as inevitable. No longer is complete nihility covered over, for now everything is unreal, that is, impermanent. In Nishitani's words, "What I am talking about is the point at which the nihility that lies hidden as a reality at the ground of the self and all things makes itself present as a reality to the self in such a way that self-existence, together with the being of all things, turns into a single doubt."[31] No longer is there a distinction between the doubter and what is doubted, and the entire field of consciousness gives way to the Great Doubt of Zen. The self becomes the Great Doubt, a doubt at a far greater level than theoretical doubt. Such Doubt is lived, not theorized, and one is left with nothing.

Nishitani's mention of a "path" corresponds to pictures two through six of the ox-herding series. The Great Doubt brings us to our emotional and intellectual knees, for nothing that we know will dispel our awareness of meaninglessness. But thinking, studying, listening to the wisdom of the testimony of others who have seen the "ox," constitute the path forward. It is hard work, and for much of the journey there is still no confirmed evidence that the path is not a blind one.

The everyday self now seems to be a myth. Stage seven is the realization that the herder and the ox have always been one, never separated from one another, but it took courage and a steadfast resolve to come to realize this. Now, in peace and contentment, the boy herder relaxes under a tree, finally aware of the unity of the self. Yet, as we know from the pictures and their description, the boy has not yet reached the end of his quest. The oneness of the everyday self and the deeper self—or, perhaps better, when the everyday self simply disappears—leads to the recognition that all things are one, for the nothingness of the everyday self now spreads to the nothingness of everything. There is no ox, no herder, just absolute nothingness.

Somehow, out of this realization of "absolute nothingness," when it seems that the situation we find ourselves in is "beyond all solution," "then demand arises for a transpersonal field to open up."[32] This field is the Buddhist standpoint of *Śūnyatā*. For Nishitani, this represents a birth of the self: not the old self but the self "in its original countenance," to wit, that of absolute nothingness. The result is a nihilism that stands on the experience of nihilism as the foundation of everything, including ourselves. *Śūnyatā* is an emptiness that even empties itself, a nihilism which empties nihilism. In doing so, nihilism itself is transcended, and self and the world reappear in their suchness, in their true depth. Nishitani's phrase for this is the "*real* self-realization of reality," which serves also as his definition of religion. This account of "reality" affirms a nondualistic perspective: it involves "both our becoming aware of reality, and, at the same time, the reality realizing itself in our awareness."[33] Such awareness is nondualistic insofar as the distinction between the knower and that which is known vanishes. With the ego-self gone, one is able to experience a level deeper than in the field of normal consciousness. The field of consciousness inescapably separates the knower from the known. But on the field of emptiness, which is *Śūnyatā,* one becomes aware of reality more deeply, without the intervention of the self on the field of consciousness, allowing reality to "speak" on its own and in its own way. Of course, there is still awareness, but it is now nondual awareness without a distinction between the knower and the known. All the issues relating to reality as subject, or substance, or whether the mind automatically adds to what is "out there," the forms and perceptions of time and space, together with the categories of causality, and so on, can now be passed over as not applicable to awareness on the field of *Śūnyatā.* Whereas on the field of ordinary consciousness things can only be known via their representation in and for consciousness, which renders the knowing of anything in-itself impossible, on the field of *Śūnyatā* all knowledge is direct, rather than mediated by and through representations. Reality is no longer apprehended by means of concepts (such as "chair," "round," "flower") but directly, in its suchness.

Nondual awareness, represented by the empty circle, is difficult for most of us living in the West to grasp, and probably for most Japanese as well. However, Japanese culture is a meditative culture, and, as such, talk of nondual awareness is in the cultural environment much of the time. Traditionally, and, to a lesser extent, even today, many Japanese children are exposed to one or more of the meditative disciplines—flower arranging, landscape gardening, the tea ceremony, the martial arts—all of which are meditative paths to enlightenment.[34] Businesses often send their employees to workshops on haiku poetry, or to learn the swordsmanship of *kendō*. The suffix *"dō"* at the end of *kendō, chadō, aikidō,* for example, translates as "way" or "path," ways meant to lead to enlightenment.

Enlightenment

As you may recall from the chapter on Nishida, all enlightenment experiences are pure experiences, although not all pure experiences are enlightenment experiences. Pure experience occurs prior to the subject/object split and prior to any and all judgments or other activities of ordinary consciousness. The claim is that, as a result, reality is now able to speak directly to our awareness, as it is in-itself. Of course, it remains true that nondual awareness is distinctly different from regular conscious experience, and is much richer. Such experience is not concept-bound, nor is it a representational abstraction. Now reality speaks directly, seemingly as it is, in its "suchness" (as it is in itself). This is the "real self-realization of reality" speaking directly to us. Having confronted the emptiness of all things, and having faced our inevitable death head on, rather than becoming shrouded in despair, an aperture of awareness leads from the Great Doubt to the field of *Śūnyatā*. It is then, because of the background of impermanence and emptiness, that the impermanence and emptiness of all things now take on a shimmering freshness and brilliance for us as though we are seeing things for the first time. All awareness is now fresh awareness, and each instance manifests a depth and richness that is inspiring. Each and every awareness now arises from its "home-ground," its original "place."

Relative and Absolute Nothingness

Unno Taitetsu comments on the implications of such a perspective: "In absolute nothingness life becomes very clear—what is truly of value and what is not. That which is to be cherished as having ultimate value is the here and now, each moment, each encounter, each thing before us: the flower I see, the star in the heavens, my pet dog, my father, my mother. Each of the realities realizes itself through my awareness, and my awareness is deepened and expanded through each reality thus realized."[35] Such knowing is a "knowing of non-knowing" (that is, not known in the more usual inferential or mediated way) where immediate presence itself is granted.[36]

Furthermore, *Śūnyatā* is not some thing, but, rather, simply an absolute emptiness that is emptied even of the representation of emptiness. This non-knowing reveals that absolute emptiness "appears as one with being."[37] That is to say, insofar as things appear in their suchness, in absolute emptiness and on their own home-ground, then in this nondual awareness of things in their home-ground in absolute emptiness, absolute emptiness and things are one: emptiness is being, and being is emptiness. Nishitani elaborates: "Emptiness might be called the field of 'be-ification' . . . in contrast to nihility which is 'the field of 'nullification.' "[38] Things are absolutely empty on the field of emptiness, *and yet* precisely because they are empty, they are fully realized as what they really are in their suchness. This realization can only be expressed as a paradox: "It is *not* this thing or that, therefore, it is this thing or that."[39] It is a realization beyond concepts or representations ("this or that"), and only appears as a "this" or a "that" directly in its suchness. Thus, all things are empty, and therefore all emptiness is things (forms): form is emptiness, emptiness is form: *samsara* (the things of ordinary consciousness) is *nirvana* (emptiness) and *nirvana* is *samsara*. This is what appears on the field of absolute nothingness.

Relative nothingness, or nihility on the field of consciousness, is relative because, negating the being of things, it is still understood in relation to being, and, therefore, cannot be absolute nothingness. Furthermore, when we think about nihility, we still represent it in our consciousness as being something. It is still understood as being outside of the self,[40] as something distinct from and external to the self. Moreover, nihility itself is purely negative in that all things, from the standpoint of nihilism, are thrown into question. The awareness of nihility at the base of each and every thing casts the being of each and every thing into doubt. Thus, an abyss opens up at the root of everything.

By contrast, *absolute nothingness* is beyond nihility, or else *Śūnyatā* as a new form of nihilism would be a viewpoint still trapped within being. Absolute nothingness, or *Śūnyatā,* must take us beyond all conceptualization and representation, both positive and negative. *Śūnyatā* is not some "thing," nor is it emptiness represented as some thing outside of being. All that can be said, or if saying anything at all is impossible, then all that can be pointed to is an empty nothing, stripped bare of the representations of emptiness. In this sense, *Śūnyatā* empties itself completely and must now be seen as a place where beings "be." As such, absolute emptiness, which is not a thing, is synonymous with *being* as things. Things are now *Śūnyatā,* and *Śūnyatā* is now beings. The standpoint of *Śūnyatā* requires a double negation: there nihility, and a negation of the negativity of nihility, and this double negation yields a positive, an affirmation. This affirmation of an empty nothing reinstates all things, but now as what they are in themselves, each on its own home-ground.

The standpoint of *Śūnyatā* is not a "thing." Rather, it is that non-thing that allows things to present themselves as things. Things reappear in their "non-substantial substance," in their true suchness, on the field of emptiness. Using a series of analogies, Nishitani tries to explain what he means when he says that things appear on the field of nothingness in their own home-ground: fire does not burn fire; the sword does not cut the sword; the eye does not see the eye; water does not wash water.[41] Fire burns firewood, but it cannot burn itself; the eye sees all things, but it cannot see itself. Were the eye to see itself, then it could only see itself and nothing else, for seeing would be blocked by the eye seeing itself alone. The eye functions precisely because it does not see itself, and precisely because fire does not burn itself, it is able to burn other things. Only where fire does not burn itself is it truly fire, on its own home-ground. Only where the eye does not see itself is it on its own home-ground. In not seeing itself, yet seeing, the eye is what it is in itself. Abe Masao summarizes Nishitani's position as follows: "Nishitani's notion of 'in-itself' denotes the self-identity of things which points directly to the thing itself in its original mode of being."[42] The activity of fire is to burn things, but fire itself—in-itself—burns without burning itself. The true nature of fire is maintained as non-burning, even while it burns other things. Therefore, it burns without burning, put paradoxically.

To know fire on its home-ground is to know it as it is in itself. What results from such examples is a "completely distinct concept of existence."[43] The poet Bashō, whom Nishitani quotes, hints at this kind of existence and the difference entailed in knowing it:

> From the pine tree
> learn of the pine tree,
> And from the bamboo
> Of the bamboo.

We come to know a thing not by scientific analysis, or by philosophical analysis, but by entering into "the mode of being where the pine tree is the pine tree in itself, and the bamboo is the bamboo itself, and from there to look at the pine tree and the bamboo. He calls on us to take ourselves to the dimension where things become manifest in their suchness, to attune ourselves to the self-

ness of the pine tree and the selfness of the bamboo."[44] Having left
our ego-selves behind, we can now see with an undistorted eye the
pine tree before us, on its own home-ground, from the standpoint
of *Śūnyatā*. It is as though we see *as* the pine tree, from the inside
rather than the outside. Here philosophy and poetry coalesce, for
by seeing fully from the inside of the pine tree, we become the
pine tree in this instant of immediacy, fully in the right-here-now.
It is not a knowing that comes by comparison with other things
(taller, prettier, to the left of) but from the thing in-itself directly.
Thus, each thing affirms itself on the field of *Śūnyatā*.

This way of knowing renders each thing unique. The pine
tree is not viewed as a member of a species, but rather as this
utterly unique thing before me. It is at the center of the universe,
as is every other thing. It is the master of all things, *and yet* it
is the servant of all things. It is master because of its centrality
and absolute uniqueness. It is servant because it is related to all
other things: "Being one and all are gathered into one."[45] This
relationship of utter uniqueness, yet interconnected to all other
things, Nishitani calls "circuminsessional interpenetration."[46] Each
thing is a "constitutive element" in every other thing: the universe
is significantly interdependent, as the Buddhist notion of dependent (or interdependent) origination makes plain.[47] Everything
in the universe is linked together. Things come into being linked
with each and every other thing, *and yet*, each thing is individual
and uniquely what it is. Each thing, therefore, while on its own
home-ground is, at the same time, on the home-ground of each
and every other thing, and each and every other thing is on the
home-ground of this unique individual thing. Like a giant web,
each thing is enmeshed with every other thing; and this circum-
stantial relationship "is the most essential of all relationships, one
that is closer to the ground of things than any other relationship
ever conceived on the fields of sensation and reason by science,
myth, or philosophy."[48] The system of mutual interpenetration
Nishitani likens to a "field of force," a unifying force that makes
the world a world, and not a hodgepodge of random, chaotic
events.

The voice of Nishida might be heard in the above account: the One becomes many, and the whole is linked by a unifying force: "a field of force by virtue of which all things as they are in themselves gather themselves together into one."[49] Nishitani's reframing of Nishida's account is a step forward into eternity and an antidote to existential nihilism.

The freshness of perceiving each and every thing in its uniqueness, on its own home-ground, is represented by picture nine of the ox-herding pictures. Furthermore, as Ueda suggests, the total interconnection of things is represented by the superimposition of picture nine onto picture eight: things in their unique suchness are, at the same time, lined with nothingness. It is on the field of *Śūnyatā* that things shine forth in their interconnected individuality—each thing on its home-ground, and yet, each thing on the home-ground of every other thing, on the field of nothingness. Every thing is fresh and new; and yet, at its core, every thing is no-thing, empty. On the field of *Śūnyatā* every thing dissolves into a nondifferentiated nothingness. There remains only what the eighth picture exemplifies through an empty circle. And yet, out of this field every thing arises, in its suchness, and dazzles the beholder with its vividness. Pictures eight and nine describe this double vision well, when superimposed. One might speculate that the enlightened person is able to access the contents of both depictions at one and the same time. Each entity is also a nonentity: every thing is nothing, *and yet* nothing is every vivid thing. In Nishida's words, the formed is formless, and the formless is (each and every) form.

The Self

Our ordinary sense of self pales in comparison with becoming "truly ourselves" on the field of *Śūnyatā*. On the field of ordinary consciousness we try, in vain, to grasp ourselves, and we have similar difficulty in representationally trying to grasp things in the world objectively. On the field of *Śūnyatā,* the "original self in itself" opens up on its own home-ground. Here, our self, like all other things, is emptied, and at the base of ordinary consciousness is found to be non-consciousness. Non-consciousness is known through not-knowing, meaning that it is nonreflective knowing. Nishitani drives home this difficult account of the real self by returning to the eye and fire analogies: "Just as the essential function of the eye, to see things, is possible by virtue of the selfness of the eye itself; and just as the fact that fire burns things is possible by virtue of the selfness of fire, whereby the fire does not burn itself; so, too, the knowing of the subject is rendered possible by the not-knowing of the self in itself."[50] Try to catch the self "selfing," and you come up emptyhanded. To catch the self as objectified is easy, but to catch the self directly, as pure subjectivity, is impossible. Try this experiment: think of your self; now try to catch that which thinks of your self (now as an object of thought); now try to catch a glimpse of the self that just objectified the self. As soon as you try to do so, self becomes objectified—and so on to infinity. The "observing" self can never be caught as subjectivity, for any attempt to do so is to objectify the self once again, which is precisely to lose the subjectivity sought. The self of pure subjectivity is known in a not-knowing: we know it is there, but we simply cannot capture it in ordinary consciousness whose only way of knowing is to objectify things with concepts. The self that we are searching for is not a self in the ordinary sense: it is a self that is not a self, or "that which is self in not being self."[51] The self is now free of self-centeredness since, on the field of *Śūnyatā*, it interpenetrates the home-ground of every other thing, everything merges into a oneness, and yet, at one and the same time, each remains distinct. Being everything else (all the things that we come to know, we know in consciousness), the self really is not a self, because it is no longer an isolated, closed-off individual self; it is a non-selfing self. To be a true self is to be open to all things, to be able to *become* the pine tree or the bamboo from the inside, from the home-ground of the other. All things are said to advance now to one's own true self, for all things are now also in the home-ground of the self. I am the pine tree, or my neighbor. Such knowing by becoming is what Nishitani calls the "natural light."[52] It is the light of things coming to us, with the result that "hills and rivers, the earth, plants and trees, tiles and stones, all of these are the self's own original part." One's being and the being of all things is nothingness, so even the self is nothing and nothing is the self. The self "resists all explanation"; it is one with emptiness and, therefore, one with all that exists.

Returning to the ox herder once more, he is now free of self-centeredness, no longer controlled by the ego-self, the herder (in picture ten) is now a mature man who is ready to greet another with the compassionate knowledge that the other is himself. He extends a hand in friendship, and one can imagine the boy asking for advice and somehow sensing the incredible depth in the walk and the smile on the face of the mature herder. The boy asks if it is true that there is a state of enlightenment, that there is a deeper sense of self and whether through its realization a profound sense of meaning arises that sweeps away doubts, psychological pain, and confusion. The older herder, we imagine, invites the boy to share with him a pot of tea, and they sit as the older herder talks, pointing out the path that the boy will need to embark upon. It will be a long journey, but there is no doubt that it leads to the desired goal. The boy listens intently and, for the first time, begins to discern the faint tracks of the ox in the manner and wisdom of the herder's account. Just this glimpse of the tracks seen in the stability and joy of the herder's body and mind are enough to give the boy the courage to begin his own journey. In truth, he is already on the path, thanks to this remarkable encounter, for this connection with an enlightened man is already the completion of the first picture, and the energy resulting from this encounter with the old herder has moved him to the second stage in his journey. Enlightenment is contagious for one who is open to it.

Selfless Ethics

While ethics was not a focus in Nishitani's writings, it is worth noting that he closed his monumental work *Religion and Noth-*

ingness with a discussion of ethics on the field of *Śūnyatā*. His deliberations, there and elsewhere, make plain how very differently he thought ethics was understood in the context of Japanese Buddhism. What he describes may help to explain why the analysis of ethical terms such as "good," "right," "ought," and "intention," has little or no place in the history of Japanese philosophy and religion. In general, the Japanese come at ethics from a radically different standpoint.

In an essay on "The I Thou Relation in Zen Buddhism,"[53] Nishitani begins by citing an encounter between two "Zen men" recorded in the *Blue Cliff Records*.[54] In the form of a *kōan* (or puzzle), entitled "Kyōzan roars with laughter," we read:

> Kyōzan Ejaku asked Sanshō Enen, "What is your name?"
> Sanshō said "Ejaku!"
> "Ejaku!" replied Kyōzan, "that's my name."
> "Well then," said Sanshō, "my name is Enen."
> Kyōzan roared with laughter.[55]

Sanshō was a great Zen Master, and his response to Kyōzan's query must be taken as instructional. Sanshō took Kyōzan's name and, in so doing, collapsed the difference between them. Looked at from the standpoint of *Śūnyatā*, Sanshō *is* Kyōzan. As a master, Sanshō suggests that a genuine encounter with another should begin by "becoming" the other, or, as we might say, by standing in the other's shoes. But further clarification is needed, for it is not enough to stand in another's shoes simply as oneself—as Sanshō— one must stand in another's shoes, in this case, as Kyōzan. In such an encounter, the two become one, *and yet* each remains distinctively Sanshō and Kyōzan. Furthermore, if Kyōzan has "caught" this life lesson, then he should respond by saying, "And I am Sanshō." The one is the other and the other is the one. We are meant to believe that Kyōzan understood this, since the *insight* caused him to roar with laughter and delight at this surprise instruction. The I is the Thou, and the Thou is the I. Nishitani states that they have become "non-differentiated," resulting in genuine compassion and revealing the true meaning of loving another as oneself. One actually experiences the *being* of the other as all discriminatory differences have vanished. Sanshō has "emptied" himself and has put Kyōzan "in his (Sanshō's) place." Stated simply, "where the other is at the center of the individual, and where the existence of each one is 'other-centered,' absolute harmony reigns. This might be called 'love,' in the religious sense."[56] As such, non-self meets non-self in this extraordinary encounter, *and yet* self and other are neither one nor two, "for each self retains its absoluteness while still being relative, and in this relativity the two are never for a moment separated."[57] The maintaining of individuality is possible in that each has become the other with nothing sacrificed, *and yet,* because each is in the other's home-ground, they share the same home-ground.

The ethical import of this reported encounter is enormous. With the emphasis on the transformation of the individual "on the inside," there is no need to analyze terms or evaluate lists of pros and cons to determine the right way to meet another or invoke rational principles such as Kant's "Never treat a person as a means (alone), but always as an end (in him or herself)." It is not that doing so would be somehow wrong, just that it is unnecessary for one who meets the other *as* the other. In breaking the hold of the everyday selfish self, that is, the self's own obsession with itself, one is now able to return to the home-ground of the other, and, indeed, with all other beings.[58] The self can no longer be referred to as an end in itself, as Kant argued, for the self is now empty and potentially filled with all other things that are, each of them, ends in themselves for the newly emptied self. Thus, the self is no longer an end for him/herself, even though s/he is now an end for all of the other things. The self is now a "nothingness." This is the ethical import of circumincessional interpenetration, where each thing *is* all of the others and all of the others *are* this thing: everything interpenetrates the home-ground of every other thing and, in so doing, has discovered its own home-ground.

Love or compassion demands a putting aside of self-love: the ordinary self must be emptied of its own fixations to make room for other things. Moreover, this love or compassion embraces the other just as s/he/it is, "so that every other is loved just as it is: loving him as a sinner if he be a sinner, or as an enemy if he be an enemy."[59] Such a perspective opens up "a field in the self . . . to love one's neighbor as oneself with the non-differentiating love that makes one 'like unto God.' "[60]

Nishitani's understanding of selfless love extends not just to encounters with other people but with anything: "This must be a standpoint where one sees one's self in all things, in living things, in hills and rivers, towns and hamlets, tiles and stones, and loves all these things 'as oneself.' "[61] Just as St. Francis encountered wind and rain, fire and heat as "brothers and sisters," so we, too, will come to grasp that "every single thing actually *was* a brother or a sister, since each had been created, together with himself, by God."[62] The result is a cosmic love that is available to anyone who has emptied her or his self. It is an ongoing encounter, or experience, and not an obligation, rule, or command. It comes about when attachment to the self has been extinguished, allowing other-directedness to emerge from the nothingness of the non-self self. The non-self self is now boundlessly open, without restriction and, as a result, the entire universe is now able to manifest within it. Sanshō and Kyōzan, you and I, the artist and the flower, the tea master and the tea-guest, the landscape gardener and his rocks and trees all have become one with the other. This is a formula for great discovery, great art, and the deepest love and friendship. And for Nishitani, all of this can, and does, take place on the field of *Śūnyatā*. It is a place much deeper than the demands of ethics, deeper than reason, deeper than calculation, and is open to everyone and anyone who wishes to make the effort. It is already available, right underfoot.

For those who have not yet made the move toward "enlightenment," ordinary systems of ethics and our reasoning will still be required to steer them through the complexities of encounters with other people and other things. But the greatest ethical insights have been given by those who were aware of the true origin of, and interconnection with all that exists. Ordinary ethics is merely an attempt to codify the main thrusts of such insights into a system of rights and wrongs, do's and don'ts. Such systems are, however, always much less than the insights on which they are based: they rarely carry the same passion, compassion, or deep conviction. For the enlightened person, these last three elements are an essential part of the transformation that results from viewing the cosmos from the standpoint of *Śūnyatā*. To be truly ethical is now to be who one really is, that is to say, a non-self that now "selfs" by spontaneously and effortlessly loving each being as a manifested form of the formless, for s/he *is* each and every form. Fire burns without burning (itself), the eye sees without seeing (itself), water washes without washing (itself), and the enlightened person acts compassionately by being a self that is not a self. Ethics of this kind arises when one's own home-ground is the home-ground of everything and everyone.

4

Watsuji Tetsurō
(1889–1960)

Whether what we call "the West" has always been incorrigibly tilted towards a prioritizing of the individual and a neglect of what Watsuji called "betweenness" (*aidagara*) is, I think, an important question. . . . During the recent centuries of their intellectual and social life, Europe and America have placed a stress on the individual to such an extent that intellectuals in certain Asian contexts have come to view that emphasis as an imbalance needing to be challenged. Watsuji was arguably the best read and the most sharply articulate among the Asian thinkers who addressed this problem. And the *Ethics* is where he best demonstrated that point of view and the challenge to thought implicit within it.

—William R. LaFleur, "Foreword,"
in *Watsuji Tetsuro's Rinrigaku: Ethics in Japan*

Life and Career

Watsuji serves as a vital contrast to the other Kyoto School thinkers, for whereas Nishida's focus was on metaphysics and epistemology and logic, and both Tanabe and Nishitani took religion as their focus, Watsuji emphasized ethics and culture. And like Japan itself, after its forced opening to non-Japanese in 1854, he was conflicted by what seemed to be the superiority of Western cultures. Yet, it was anything but clear what gave Western cultures supremacy in military arms and industry, and for a time the Japanese speculated that perhaps it was the result of Christianity. Some even urged the Emperor to renounce Shintō and convert to Christianity. Such a step was deemed unacceptable to most Japanese, but the example serves to illustrate just how humbled Japan was by this early encounter of unequals. A glorification of anything Western and a rejection of things Japanese began to take hold. Japan was in shock, and it took time and much thought to recover both balance and pride.

The young Watsuji had little interest in things Japanese, for his passion was for Western literature, especially the poetry of Byron. He wished to emulate Byron, hoping to be a poet himself. But he was also taken with Nietzsche's philosophy. It was the emphasis on individuality that enthralled him, a way of life so different from the Japanese emphasis on the importance of the group. But by the time he reached his late teens and early twenties he began to reject much that he had gleaned from his studies of the West and began to plumb the depths of Japanese and Eastern cultures generally. He was a major force in Japan's rediscovery of its past, including its cultural achievements such as architecture, poetry, and its remarkable social solidarity.

Born the son of a physician in 1889, in the village of Nibuno (now part of Himeji City), he eventually moved from literature as a central focus, to philosophy. He attended Tokyo Imperial University (then called the First Higher School), and as his graduation thesis he decided to write on Nietzsche. One can speculate why Nietzsche was rejected as a suitable subject for a graduate thesis in philosophy, but it likely had to do with the fact that Nietzsche was a poet-philosopher. Indeed, until quite recently in the West, Nietzsche was studied in departments of literature and not in departments of philosophy. However that may be, at the very last minute he was forced to write a second thesis, and he chose to write on Arthur Schopenhauer. His thesis was entitled "Schopenhauer's Pessimism and Theory of Salvation." Presented just in time, the thesis was accepted, enabling him to graduate. Significantly, his *Nietzschean Studies* was later published.

As his career developed, he published studies of Schopenhauer and Kierkegaard, as he continued to search out ideas from Western thinkers. However, while at university, he would often stand just outside the classroom window where the well-known novelist Sōseki Natsumi was lecturing. He never met Sōseki while at university, but shortly afterward he became a member of a study group that gathered in Sōseki`s home. Both Watsuji and Sōseki were beginning to reevaluate Western cultural ideas and their critical focus fell on the idea of individualism. Individualism often led to a lack of social cohesion and a rampant selfishness, in their eyes. Sōseki died three years later, in 1917, and Watsuji published a lengthy reminiscence of Sōseki in 1918. In this piece it was apparent that Watsuji was now a critic of the West and had turned his gaze toward Japanese and other Eastern cultures. He researched widely, rediscovering the ideals and achievements of an earlier Japan. He published such works as *Ancient Japanese Culture* (begun in 1917, with successive volumes in 1926 and 1934), and *Pilgrimage to Ancient Temples,* in which he traced the Buddhist influence on Japanese culture (1920). In the course of this research, he read the writings of the Sōtō Zen Master, Dōgen, whom he found to be a truly great, but utterly forgotten, thinker. Watsuji singlehandedly conveyed Dōgen`s importance to Japan and to the world, presenting Dōgen as a thinker of the highest order, perhaps Japan`s first great philosopher. Watsuji's account of Dōgen's importance as the founder of Sōtō Zen and as a philosopher has recently been translated by Steve Bein and is entitled *Purifying Zen: Watsuji Tetsuro's Shamon Dōgen.*[1] The scope of Watsuji's scholarship was remarkable: he researched the ideas of Socrates, Plato, Aristotle, Descartes, Kant, Hegel, Brentano, Scheler, Schiller, Dilthey, Durkheim (perhaps his favorite thinker), Bergson, Husserl, Heidegger, and others. His reading in Eastern philosophy and religion was equally impressive. The result was an East/West dialogue of high quality.

In 1925, Nishida and Hatano Seiichi invited Watsuji Tetsurō to teach ethics in the philosophy department at the Kyoto Imperial University. He continued to teach at Kyoto University (and also at Ryukoku University from 1929) until his appointment as professor at Tokyo Imperial University in 1934. Thus, except for the eighteen months he spent studying and traveling in Europe (March 1927–Summer 1928), he was a full member of the Kyoto Philosophy Department for nine years, teaching alongside Nishida and Tanabe. If one reads only his *Climate and Culture,* and particularly his *Ethics,* one would have to conclude that he had little or no interest in religion. However, a quick glance at his prodigious scholarly output includes book-length studies of *Primitive Christianity, Primitive Buddhism, Confucius,* and the *Spiritual Development of the Japanese People.* Since none of these works have been translated into English, the English-speaking reader has a limited view of Watsuji's philosophical interests. Nevertheless, it is true that, unlike Nishida, Tanabe, and Nishitani, he did not place religion at the center of his philosophical work. His emphasis was on ethics and the understanding of culture. At least in this sense, *Climate and Culture* and *Ethics (Rinrigaku)* do provide an accurate sense of his scholarly focus.

Climate and Culture

Without a doubt, the most startling of Watsuji's works is *Climate and Culture.* In it he attempts to demonstrate that a broad understanding of "climate" can show that a person raised in one of the three main climate types—monsoon, meadow, and desert—will display a perspective on the world in line with his or her climate type, and quite distinct from perspectives characteristic of either of the other two. In chapter 1, he recalls Kant's critique of Herder, who had "attempted a 'Climatic Study of the Human Spirit,' " concluding that the attempt was "not so much the labor of the scholar as the product of the poet's imagination."[2] Certainly it would be a stretch for the contemporary reader to conclude with Watsuji that it is "humidity" that has been a central force in shaping the Japanese mind-set. And yet, his detailing of the central characteristics of monsoon, meadow, and desert people is remarkably convincing and accurate. *Climate and Culture* is well worth the read even if one discounts the validity of taking climatic forces as key ingredients in the shaping of individual and cultural patterns of psychological and social formation. What he presents is tantalizingly perceptive and pragmatically helpful. Even if the work of a philosopher-poet's imagination, his three-culture analysis is, at times, truly brilliant and always insightful.

Climate, or *fūdo,* which literally means "Wind and Earth," Watsuji tells us, is "a general term for the natural environment of a given land."[3] Watsuji's expanded notion of climate, however, includes far more than a people's natural environment, for he includes not only weather patterns and climatic conditions such as humidity, heat, cold, and rainfall, but also types of clothing worn, agricultural patterns, house styles and architecture, social and even recreational activities, food, cooking styles, and so on. Using "cold" as an example of just how much is to be included in his view of what constitutes climate, he observes that coldness is *our* experience of actually finding ourselves *out* in the cold: we feel the coldness. Coldness is always an encounter that by necessity includes our own experience of it. Furthermore, we experience coldness along with others who feel the cold. Already climate is social, and, as such, it is also historical since we deal with the cold in ways similar to that of our ancestors: heavy clothing, in-house heating sources, house architecture that best contends with harsh winters, winter food choices that fortify us and utilize foodstuffs available during cold winters.[4] Whether considering heat or cold, humidity or dryness, rain, snow or wind, topography, vegetation, flora and fauna—any of these will impact on the way we live individually and socially. All of these, taken together, is what Watsuji means by climate.

Geoffrey Bownes, who translated *Climate and Culture,* writes that "all inquiries into the culture of Japan must in their final reduction go back to the study of her nature."[5] In the case of Japan, there is a fusion of heat and humidity which, while difficult to tolerate, is also "nature's gift" to humans, for it brings about lush growth and an abundance of plant life. There is no need to struggle against nature, for there is little that one can do to offset the heat or the high humidity, or to diminish the monsoon rains of the rainy season or the power of typhoon winds. In any case, the rains, heat, and humidity bring life to Japan in abundance such that resignation rather than resistance is the correct response. In desert climates, one must resist the external heat and dryness in order to survive. But in Japan, one is more likely to be submissive, receptive, and passive rather than to actively resist the irresistible which returns again and again, year after year.

There are also abrupt seasonal changes. In central Japan, winter becomes spring almost overnight, and spring becomes summer in the blink of an eye. Change is perceived to be a part of the way things are, and sudden change is equally inevitable. The samurai swordsmen combined sudden, violent change with quiet meditation. They were resigned to die if need be: they did not cling to life, but accepted death as a part of life. Like the cherry blossoms that bloom for a day or a week and then are gone, the warrior lives fully day by day, and accepts death when it comes. Watsuji explains that "it is of deep significance and highly appropriate that . . . the Japanese should be symbolized by the cherry blossoms, for they flower abruptly, showily and almost in indecent haste; but the blooms have no tenacity—they fall as abruptly and disinterestedly as they flowered."[6]

Violence and meditative calm is akin to the violent monsoon winds, followed by a calm and rewarding growing season. One loves passionately, and yet calmly, and the example of love-suicide (such as our Romeo and Juliet) crystallizes the passion and quiet acceptance that life in a changeable world demands. Watsuji suggests that "calm love" is hidden "behind a violence of passion."[7] Such love has a "typhoon savagery," with suicide as "selfless resignation" serving as a "clear and concrete" example of this. What one has here is "an exaltation of love rather than a yearning for life."[8] Typhoons and earthquakes, let alone the activities of the samurai, require that life give way to love, beauty, and honor. And love, for the Japanese, is always "of the flesh," that is, it is embodied in space as well as existing in time; "Love is never a union of spirit only."[9] Love, gardening, and the loyalty of the samurai all display a selflessness that is characteristically Japanese. There is a fusion of self and other both in intense love and in the loyalty of the samurai.[10] But love and loyalty are always embodied: we are unities of body and mind; except in death, there is never one without the other. The home and family display this fusion of self and other most dramatically. The value of the home is always more than that of the individuals in it.[11] The family is the bedrock of values. Families live in houses, and the house encloses a community. The entryway, where shoes are left behind, together with the gate and/ or door, mark the "inside" community from the "outside" world. The distinction between individuals all but disappears in the family-community. Rooms are without locks and keys, and sliding door-panels indicate a fluidity of possible living arrangements. The front door is locked as an indicator that this is where the division between inside and outside begins. Many locks are largely symbolic, given that the door or doors simply rest on hinge pins that allow the entire door system to be removed by lifting upward, lock and all. Sliding screens within indicate "division within unity," based on the mutual trust and the lack of a strong need for division.[12] Japanese "gods," or *kami,* are heads of the greater household or Japanese family, and the emperor is head of the Imperial House, and a direct descendent of the *kami,* the head of the Japanese family household. The Japanese people as a whole are united as one big family. The filial piety of the family (honoring the head) becomes loyalty to the emperor, for there is an affinity between the Japanese people and the *kami,* as they all are of the same blood.[13] It is worth remarking that in the indigenous Japanese martial art of *aikidō,* for example, there are no "opponents," only "partners." There is no enemy, only partners from whom one can always learn. Watsuji writes of "brothers" (and "sisters"), and the virtues illustrated are those of nobility rather than meanness, cowardice, baseness, or servility.[14] Nietzsche's *Beyond Good and Evil* points to a similar distinction between the noble and the mean-spirited.

In the Japanese home, one does not feel the need for protection, "nor [is there] any distinction between himself and others."[15] From this springs a spirit of cooperation arising from a "natural affection so strong that it would readily call forth a spirit of complete self-sacrifice."[16] Sympathy, consideration, and affection are the states that propel obligations. As a result, one feels a spontaneous duty to others in the home.

Just as the home brings forth qualities such as affection and a spirit of cooperation, the Japanese garden, too, elicits positive social attitudes. The garden seems to urge us to reflect on nature as something of great inherent value: "Nature was treated not as something that is to be mastered, but as the repository of infinite depth."[17] The lushness of the Japanese garden is made possible by the high humidity of the Japanese climate, but the garden itself is a spiritual achievement, an "idealization of natural beauty."[18] Indeed, the garden may well express the enlightenment experience of the architect. As such, it can be an embodiment of enlightenment values. Furthermore, as a kind of spiritual "teacher," the garden encourages spiritual growth in the viewer. The garden is also a place of great calm, a perfect place of meditation.

In summary, Watsuji recapitulates that what he means by "humidity" is "not simply a meteorological phenomenon but rather a principle governing man's spiritual make-up . . . [yielding a] lightly emotional and contemplative attitude to life . . . which created the belief that all life is one."[19] This sense of the interconnectedness of things, together with the strong family ties of the home and nation, forms the basis of Watsuji's understanding of ethics in Japan. However, before leaving *Climate and Culture,* it is worth noting that Watsuji's early reading of Martin Heidegger's *Being and Time* while in Germany caused him to object to Heidegger's emphasis on time (and the individual) to the neglect of space (and community). Watsuji's insight and argument is that it is not enough to consider the individual-in-time in one's philosophizing given that everyone also lives in spatially connected groups and communities. Indeed, human history itself arises only in time *and* space, and climate is the entire interconnected network of influences that together create a peoples' attitudes. One of Watsuji's most famous students, the late Yuasa Yasuo, wrote that "history and nature, like man's mind and body, are in an inseparable relationship."[20] History and nature, and mind (in time but not in space) and body (in space and in time) cannot be correctly understood in isolation. Yuasa remarks that Watsuji took Heidegger to task not only for neglecting the importance of spatial concerns in his analysis of human beings (*Dasein*), but even more so for not giving more emphasis to space than to time. To exist in space "is the primordial fact, the primary significance, of being human" [21] These issues are given more definite shape in his studies of ethics.

Ethics as the Study of Man

There are many who consider Watsuji's work in Japanese ethics to be the definitive study. His *Ethics as the Study of Man* appeared in three volumes, the first published in 1937, the second in 1942, and the last in 1949. Previously, in 1931, he published a book entitled *Ethics,* and in 1952 *The History of Japanese Ethical Thought.* But it was his three-volume work that proved to be the richest. Surprisingly, it is as much anthropological and sociological as it is philosophical. Rather than concerning himself with whether the Japanese people think and act ethically, he simply analyzes in great depth how they do think and act. Furthermore, he traces these ethical characteristics back to ancient times in order to illustrate the depth of certain stances taken toward others and their various adaptations over a considerable span of time. Instead of attempting to evaluate or justify ethical positions, he is content to describe what they are in some detail and what historical influences led to thinking and acting in such a way. Perhaps the title of his major study—"ethics as the study of man"—should have been enough to alert us to the fact that his is a study of what is, and not necessarily of what ought to be. Nonetheless, his account of what is and what has been is philosophically rich and rewarding precisely because he deftly unpacks the most salient characteristics of the Japanese mind.

Watsuji begins with a critique of the modern "misconception" that ethics is a "problem of individualistic consciousness only."[22] Such a view arises from a perspective that gives a central position to an individualistic conception of a human being: this is the "standpoint of the isolated ego."[23] In his late teens and early twenties Watsuji, like so many Japanese intellectuals, had tried to emulate Western thinkers. Central to most Western thinking was an emphasis on individualism. It seemed apparent to the Japanese that Japan had fallen behind the nations of the West because of its feudal, collectivistic social structure. Dynamic economic and industrial advances seemed unlikely given Japan's emphasis on the group with its rigid cultural uniformity. By his mid-twenties, Watsuji began to rethink the successes and failures of both Western individualism and the cultural values of the Japanese. Increasingly, he came to see individualism as only one aspect of what it means to be human, while other equally important qualities were left unexplored. Individualism was as much an exaggeration as was group solidarity, when considered alone. Individualism loses touch with the vast network of interconnections that serves to make us what we are; individuals inescapably immersed in the space/time of a world, together with others. Moreover, without taking into consideration this network of social interconnections, ethics is impossible. Individual persons, if conceived of in isolation from their many social contexts, do not and cannot exist except as abstractions. If you think of a person in a strictly temporal way, wrapped up in his/her thoughts, one can be misled into thinking that a solitary individual can and must decide his or her own fate, charting ethical decisions in the isolation of one's mind. But this is much more difficult to do when one thinks of an individual spatially as well as temporally, for then we see that we move in a common field of possibilities and interactions.

From this perspective, ethics is the study of our interactions with others. The Japanese understanding of this is encompassed in the word they use for "ethics." The Japanese word for ethics is *rinri*. *Rin* means "fellows," "company," or *nakama*, which refers to a system of relations guiding human association with, and attitudes toward, others. *Ri* means "principle," referring to the rational ordering of human relations. *Rinri*, then, is the rational ordering of relations with our fellow human beings. However, it is the uniquely

Japanese definition of "human being" as encompassed in the word
"*ningen*" that really begins the study of ethics in Japan for Watsuji.[24]

Ningen encompasses two seemingly contradictory meanings,
and then adds a third. *Ningen* is composed of two characters, the
first, *nin*, meaning "human being" or "person," carrying with it
the dual-nature of individual and social. *Gen* means "space" or
"between," as in the space or betweenness between human beings.
We are both individual and social beings, and the space between is
where we interact with others: it both separates and joins us. This
space is a place of interactive potential, a space where community
happens. As human beings, we are enmeshed in a vast network of
relationships. As individuals, we cannot be separated from social
relationships except for the one-sided purposes of abstract thinking,
for we share a common language, walk along common footpaths
or travel common roads, eat food grown and prepared by others
using tools common to us all, in a climate that shapes us in so
many ways. We enter the world already within a network of relationships, expectations, and obligations not unlike the network of
roads, railways, and communication facilities that we share. We are,
at one time or another, children and parents, cousins and friends,
students and teachers, consumers and merchants, laborers and care
givers. However onerous the network of social relationships and
obligations may seem, we remain individuals, nonetheless, within
the midst of social responsibilities. One must view the dual-nature
of a human being as in constant tension—as individual, yet as a
social being; as social being yet as individual—in a way that is
reminiscent of Nishida's identity of self-contradiction. Indeed, to
affirm one side of this duality at the expense of the other is to
present a partial view, and to ignore the tension that continually
exists between them is to deny change. The Buddhists tell us that
Buddha, or reality, is impermanence, and to ignore change is to
foster the suffering that results from not seeing things as they really
are. What we often mistake as an excessive group mentality is, to
the Japanese, an integral part of being human.

In simple terms, *ningen* identifies persons as being both
individuals and as social beings in a myriad of social relations.

Furthermore, *ningen* also refers to a "betweenness" between human beings, a subjective space that can shrink or expand depending on the nature of the ensuing relationship. Thus, *ningen* refers to the "public" or social orientation of a human being, *and also* to the individuality of a person. Human beings are viewed as having a dual-structure, and this dual-nature is dialectical. One becomes an individual by *negating* the social group or by rebelling against various social expectations or requirements. All the while, one remains a member of various social groups such as family, peer group, and, of course, the Japanese family as a nation. Watsuji refers to this dialectical relationship of a human being as a "double negation." Over the course of a lifetime, there is a rather constant flow where individuality at one time, or group membership at another, becomes the dominant emphasis.

Double Negation

Like a seesaw, one can easily swing the balance from an emphasis on individuality to an emphasis on membership in one or more groups: that is to say, in one or more relationships. While it might seem bad logic, an instance of either/or thinking, what Watsuji is describing is a dialectical both/and relationship. One is always and inescapably an individual. Likewise, one is always and inevitably a member of one or more groups. He writes that "an individual is an individual only in a whole, and the whole is a whole only in individuals. . . . In other words, an individual is an individual in its connection with multiplicity and totality, and the whole is a whole in its connection with multiplicity and individuality."[25] However, at any given time, the heavy emphasis might be on one's individuality, as one struggles to break away from parental control, a repressive regime, or a rigid curriculum. At another time, one might need to abandon stress on one's individuality in order to become a full and active member of an organization such as a political party, church, or even a marriage relationship. The dialectical component is that throughout one's life and from situation to situation, one will inevitably swing from one emphasis to another, and in varying degrees. And the dynamism between the two poles never ends: we are always in process, each of us: "Human beings possess this dynamic structure of reciprocal transformation."[26]

Ningen, it must be remembered, is not a thing, but a description of a subjective tension that exists whenever (Japanese) human beings act, or contemplate taking action. Since we are both individuals, and yet inescapably involved in social relationships, then we become individuals by *negating* our social involvement or group connection, or we overemphasize our group membership at the expense of our individuality. But while individuality requires a distancing from group affiliation, and while group membership demands giving up at least some independence as an individual, there is an additional negation that occurs; a "negation of negation."[27] And this is where the third aspect of *ningen* comes into play. This further negation occurs when, and if, one becomes a truly ethical human being by abandoning individual independence from others, or from groups: one abandons one's own self. True morality is the forgetting of the self, as Dōgen urged, resulting in a "selfless morality."[28] The ultimate ethical negation is the annihilation of the separate self such that one is now identified with others in a nondualistic merging of self and other. Both self and other disappear as separate entities, and enter an intimacy of oneness. The true fact of *ningen* is that of benevolence and compassion as a result of this nondual oneness.[29] The distance between self and other has disappeared and emptiness or nothingness is what becomes of betweenness as a result of this merging. Yet it is in the betweenness that this is accomplished, where the betweenness shrinks to nothing.

It must be remembered that for Watsuji, neither individuality nor social relations is superior to the other: they are co-equals. This initial dual-nature vanishes in the selflessness of compassion, for now a nondualism of merged self and other has taken over, and yet, both the individual and the other person remains in tact, as does their relationship to each other as individuals. Again, as with Nishida, a both/and logic pertains, for duality gives way to nonduality, and nonduality to duality again.

The Importance of Relationships

In Japan, nothing is more important than relationships. One needs to understand this when dealing with the Japanese. Interpersonal relationships are not to be taken lightly. The practice of gift giving, while often little more than a reflex, is meant to reinforce the ongoing importance of relationships. For example, a student's gratefulness for a teacher's instruction often continues to the end of the teacher's life. It is one's responsibility (*on*) to show gratefulness through periodic gift giving long after one has completed one's schooling. To do less is to be less than human.

Perhaps the Japanese perspective can be better understood if we attend to the third meaning of *Ningen*. The third meaning is "betweenness," a concept borrowed from Sōseki Natsume (1867–1916: Japanese novelist), but brilliantly amplified by Watsuji.

So, to be human is to be in a rather wide array of relationships, and ethics is concerned with those problems that arise between persons. *Rinri* (ethics) refers to a system of relations guiding human association, including some sense of the appropriate attitudes to embody in one's dealing with others. These rules and principles are required for people to live in community in a friendly and nourishing manner. Given this heavy emphasis on relationships, it is little wonder that Confucianism is the starting point for ethics in Japan. Watsuji himself refers to Confucianism when describing the "principles" of human relationships. The precise ordering of relations between "parent and child, lord and vassal, husband and wife, young and old, friend and friend, and so forth."[30] For the most part, these are the ordering principles which give sense to social relations, and on which Watsuji bases his description of an ethical Japanese person.

The Confucian Background

While Watsuji's goal was to give an account of the patterns of Japanese ethical action, he knew that in doing so he was including the influences of Confucianism, as well as Daoism and Chinese Buddhism. Of these, it is Confucianism that is most important for ethics. Recall the slogan that in Japan one is born into Shintōism, lives as a Confucian, and dies a Buddhist. One lives as a Confucian by following the strictures of Confucianism. The major influence of Confucianism began in 404 CE, when it first entered Japan, but it took another two centuries for its influence to gain strength. Confucius and his followers taught that the "way" of proper social interaction was to order one's life in accordance with the "laws of Heaven." The hope was that the microcosm of human relationships would perfectly reiterate the order of the macrocosm of Heaven. The "wise men" of ancient China believed that they had discerned these laws in much the same way that ancient Chinese healers had found the laws of health and disease: through long years of observation and practice.

The "five obligations" of Confucian ethics are spelled out as between sovereign and subjects, father and son, husband and wife, elder brother and younger, and the obligations of friendship, plus the three virtues of wisdom, compassion, and courage, which are the ideal moral qualities that people are to strive to embody.[31] These relational rules and virtues were the "oil" of social and political harmony, and the pathway to personal self-development. The virtues, or characteristics of a *developed* Confucian, included respect, reverence, loyalty, and sincerity (which included the notions of integrity, honesty, truthfulness, and trustworthiness). *Ch'eng,* or sincerity, is "the Way of Heaven" itself, for "to think how to be sincere is the Way of man. He who is sincere is one who hits upon what is right without effort and apprehends without thinking."[32]

Confucianism provided precisely what early Shintō lacked: specificity of behavioral patterns in an organized and written form. Confucianism was not thought of as a new religion to be taken in, but rather was understood to be a systematic account, and perhaps a deepening, of what was already common practice in Japan: a profound belief in the importance of showing respect for one's ancestors, one's family members, and one's benefactors, including the *kami*; a sense of the vital importance of filial piety;

an existing practice of rituals and ceremonies; and a codification of an acute ethical sensitivity.[33] Confucianism was adopted as a constituent element in Japanese culture because its teachings were so compatible with the existing sensibilities of the Japanese. The two virtues that the Japanese took to be the most important were loyalty and filial piety. These virtues are essential virtues of the family and of the political realm. Watsuji writes that "the virtue that is called filial piety from the aspect of the household becomes loyalty from the standpoint of the state. So filial piety and loyalty are essentially identical, the virtue prescribing the individual in accordance with the interests of the whole."[34] Filial piety is shown through one's respect for the imperial family, but insofar as Japan is thought of as one big household or family, then filial piety was to be evidenced in one's relations with others as well. Whoever has power over others is responsible for their well-being. Thus, it is the family that is the central image of proper human relationships, and it extends even into the political realm (the emperor as father of the country; the royal family), and into business (the boss/owner/ father takes responsibility for his workers' [children's] well-being and even for the social contribution which his company's products make to society at large).

What is distinctively Japanese in this Confucian adoption is the emphasis on the notion of family "writ large," extending all the way to the emperor and the imperial family. In addition, filial piety was increasingly taken to mean "loyalty," and not just respect for those above one in position and/or power. It was this strong sense of loyalty for which the samurai were willing to give their lives, through a sense of betweenness that included whoever was to be defended, and excluded all others, or at least placed them at the farther reaches of the continuum.

In the Betweenness

Yuasa Yasuo suggests that we might think of betweenness as the field or place (*basho*) in which we live. It "consists of the various human relationships of our life-world. To put it simply, it is the network [of relationships] which provides humanity with a social meaning, for example, one's being an inhabitant of this or that town or a member of a certain business firm. To live as a person means . . . to exist in such betweenness."[35] In this "network" of relationships, the family is the primary model.

The influence of the family model may be discerned in many, if not most, of the values which the Japanese hold dear. It matters greatly that harmony (*wa*) reign within both the domestic nuclear family, as well as in the various larger "families" such as communities, corporations, and even the nation. Social relations occur in the betweenness (*aidagara*) between us. Betweenness opens up far more than Confucian principled interaction, for this space or place between us is already etched with the possibilities of genuine encounter, with expectation, good will, reverence, open-heartedness, fellow-feeling, sincerity, availability, and the desire for consensus. One who lacks some or most of these attitudes is at least poorly brought up, or at most, considerably less than human. This cluster of "virtues," or attitudinal values, is already subtly present in the cultural climate that all Japanese are born into; is to be "Japanese." To take a single example, while law in much of the West is based on the adversarial system of justice, law, in Japan, as well as everyday social practice, is based on the consensus system or model. The adversarial model is black and white: there is a winner and a loser. In Japan, after hearing the evidence, a judge will often delay a decision for several days or weeks, instructing both sides to come to a decision that they can both accept and to which they will be committed. Otherwise, the judge will impose a judgment. Not to be able to reach a consensus is deemed by Japanese society to indicate a psychological and social shortcoming with respect to one, or both, parties. When a consensus is finally reached it usually means that neither party in a dispute has achieved all that they had hoped for. Instead, a compromise is reached which both parties can live with. Animosity between the parties is lessened as a result, since no winner can laud it over a loser. But such an approach is possible only in a society that is already predisposed to finding a way to work through disputes with the least amount of resultant harm. In other words, there is a predisposition to settle for a compromise in order to do as much as possible to save the good relations between the disputants, rather than hold to a single-minded sense of there being only one right answer that constitutes justice. That we "live" in the same betweenness helps to ensure that when we come into conflict, we possess the same desire to reach a compromise solution.

Kokoro and Aidagara

A key personal and cultural trait in Japan is having *kokoro*. *Kokoro* translates as "mind and heart," suggesting that one's reason should be compassionate and that one's feelings in general, should be reasonable. To further this point, when asked where the mind is, a Japanese will likely point to the chest (heart), not to the head (brain). When told that a Westerner would more likely point to the head, a moment of disbelief usually results, followed by a curiosity about why one would come to think something as outlandish as the mind being located in the head. *Kokoro* implies that the body and mind are a unity, and one who "has" or displays *kokoro* is a trustworthy, even exemplary person, with whom one can freely enter into a relationship. One who has *kokoro* is seen as speaking and acting from the heart with no selfish or utilitarian motive in the background. Such a person is expected to be compassion-ate, possessed of both personal integrity and a robust amount of fellow-feeling. Not every Japanese has *kokoro*, of course, but it is an ideal that is inevitably in the cultural air. There ought to be *kokoro* in the betweenness between us, as a cultural ideal to which we aspire in our attempt to creatively and humanely close the distance between us. It is to be found in the formal polite greeting, *hajime mashite, dozo yoroshiku onegaishimasu*: "please smile favorably upon me" at this first meeting, so as to occasion future meetings between us. It is a "pleased to meet you" which carries with it a hope that the relationship will develop in a mutually beneficial manner.

Thus, it can be seen that *Aidagara*—betweeness—is not just empty space in which we meet, but an apparent empty space that is deeply etched by cultural tradition. We do not come into the world as blank slate (*tabula rasa*), for we have already been influenced by climate and culture in the womb, and will certainly be directly influenced as we encounter mother, father, siblings, temperature, clothing, food, and a host of other cultural forms and practices. Through exposure, one will learn how to make the most of relationships, drawing on the centuries of experience and tradition that are inevitably a part of the betweenness in which positive relationships come to be made. To be pointedly aware of the betweenness between us opens relational possibilities for resolving issues with others as they arise. A shared and already etched-upon betweenness provides a desire to resolve disputes without a passion for winning at all cost. That we are in this betweenness together is already an expectation of positive resolution.

Watsuji and Nothingness

One of the telltale signs of Kyoto school thinking is the important role that the notion of *nothingness* plays. It was Nishida who brought this notion to the fore, and it continued to be a notion of importance in Watsuji's thinking. Recall that *ningen* has at least a dual-structure: human beings are individuals, and yet they are also members of social groups. What is in play here is a "double negation" whereby the individual aspect is negated by the group aspect of self, and the group aspect, in turn, is negated by the individual aspect. However, neither negation obliterates that which is negated. As with Nishida's "identity of self-contradiction," the contradictories are both preserved, as is the unity. There is no blending of the contradictories in a new synthesis, for the original two are required in giving a full(er) account of *ningen* as actually experienced. To try to smooth away the contradictory tension between opposites is to abandon actual experience in favor of an abstract construct. Furthermore, both the individual and social aspects of a human being are taken to rest on an even deeper ground, which, itself, is neither individual nor social but is that greater context prior to all distinctions out of which both arise. Like Nishida's "pure experience," Watsuji presses his analysis beyond foundational distinctions (individual and social) to the nothingness out of which they are carved. Nothingness is that deep profundity, the indistinct and indefinite, that is beyond all characterization and without ordinary qualities or characteristics. Like the silence out of which sound emerges, or the monochromatic sand out of which the fifteen rocks at Ryoan-ji arise, nothingness is the underlying matrix that grounds and surrounds all distinctions. It is the background to all foregrounds. Ethically speaking, it is the betweenness in which we meet and to which we bring our cultural attitudes and expectations. The emptiness between us is itself empty, yet it makes possible all of the delights, hopes, horrors, and failures in human relationships. Nothingness, as betweenness, serves as the context in which all good and evil may arise.

For Watsuji, nothingness also signifies the ethical importance of the annihilation of the self, which "constitutes the basis of every selfless morality since ancient times."[36] The losing of self is a returning to one's authenticity, to one's "home-ground" (a phrase used by Nishitani, you may recall). It is only then that ethics becomes a matter of spontaneous compassion, a spontaneous caring and concern for the whole of existence.

True ethics, then, is a return to an authentic unity through an initial contradiction within the self, and between the self and the "other" in the betweenness. The negation of "otherness" reestablishes the betweenness as a nondualistic connection between the self and others that negates any trace of opposition: a negation of a negation. One is now aware of the interconnection of all things, ultimately eliminating any sense of a separate self and other (from within a nondualistic perspective). Dualistically comprehended, both the self and the other are preserved. And, of course, there is the betweenness itself in which our human actions occur. We may speculate that a "master" of ethics, a truly wise person, would "see" both the nondualistic and the dualistic perspectives simultaneously. Like stereoscopic or three-dimensional films, the ordinary "flat" presentation is enhanced by the third depth dimension but without annihilating the first two dimensions. All three dimensions are preserved, and yet one can remove the glasses and see in two dimensions only. Such a person is a selfless self, a formless self, but still a self, who is intrinsically good, generous, and compassionate precisely because his or her self is a no-self, thus able to identify with the joys and sorrows of others because she/he has "become" the other. This self, as a no-self is, like the "eye" of Nishitani, able to see all things precisely because it does not see itself. The truly compassionate person loves all things "as him or herself" because she or he *is* the other: the ordinary self is gone, and what appears now is a no-self self. And betweenness is the place where such compassion arises and is acted out spontaneously and selflessly in the spatiotemporal theatre of the everyday world. Recalling the Ten Ox-herding pictures, it is the realization that pictures eight and nine together describe the enlightened experience of reality, and the compassionate actions and the beatific smile on the face of the mature herder (in picture ten) encapsulate this realization in action, in the everyday world.

Back to the Everyday World

Needless to say, there is a real difference between the ideal of betweenness as nothingness and the everyday world where we need some guidance in finding a morality that effectively assists us in living our lives well. Watsuji reflects extensively upon the critical importance of truth and trust as foundational for all positive ethical human relationships. For him, it is *makoto*, the virtue "sincerity," that serves as the root of truthfulness, honesty, and trustworthiness. To be sincere means that you will do what you say you will do, that you can be counted on to be true to your word, and it further connotes a recognition of one's intrinsic or innate spiritual purity that one strives to express in all of one's actions. *Makoto*, collectively understood, reveals a cultural attitude of mutual trust

as an important aspect of what is already etched in the betweenness. But a word of clarification is needed here: if betweenness is
nothingness, then how can anything at all be etched upon it? The
answer must be twofold. First, as nothingness, nothing at all is
etched upon it. It is a place (like Nishida's *basho* or *topos*), which
is pure potentiality, pure empty space open to any and all impositions. It is but the locus of possible events. However, as we meet
another in the betweenness, not as sages but as ordinary people,
we will employ whatever we have learned about relationships, from
nursing at our mother's breast to the most recent learning event. It
is as though all of this personal, social, and cultural instruction is
already built into our encounter, because it is built into us. And if
the other party is also Japanese, the chances are good that a similar
imprinting will have occurred. These two individuals now meet in
the betweenness with a similar politeness and with similar expectations. The betweenness is already heavily choreographed, which
is all to the good, except that situations are rarely the same and
that times and mores change and cultural uniformity itself waxes
and wanes. Hence, the balm that the etchings were supposed to
produce, from time to time, turn to vinegar or even gall. Still,
most of the time it works effectively.

When relational encounters do not flow smoothly, thinking
is required to solve the problem at another level. A new strategy,
including alterations in body language and so forth, might help.
Ultimately, however, a sage will be required to put the matter in
a radically different perspective. If all things are manifestations of
the whole, the One, then you and the other are divine creations
from this ultimate source: an empty-self meets another empty-self
in the emptiness of nothingness. Now there are no selves to be
offended, or, at least, the sage is a non-offendable no-self. S/he is
the peacemaker, the light-bringer who guides others through their
relational difficulties to a point of acceptable consensus. The sage
has nothing to win or lose: s/he is simply a dispassionate mediator seeking a solution and minimizing ruffled feathers. That the
"sage" is but an ideal, and only rarely encountered, however, takes
nothing away from the importance of the ideal. While compas-

sion-as-oneness is the end point of ethical development for Watsuji, for most of us there are, at best, only glimpses of this achievement available. Instead, we live in the betweenness, sometimes shrinking the distance between ourselves and another, at other times resting quite content with the distance well established. Nevertheless, the ethical ideal remains to find another with whom it is the distance between us that needs collapsing, yielding a relationship of true friendship or love through genuine compassion.

This same attitudinal stance can be found in the martial art indigenous to Japan (as well as in some other martial arts): *aikidō*. Very early on one learns that one will never face an opponent in *aikidō*: there are only "partners." The goal of practice is for each "partner" to lift the other up to a higher level of performance and understanding. Competitions of the usual sort are not a part of *aikidō*, for competitive fighting places the accent on winning and on individual pride. Partnering places the emphasis on assisting the other to grow and on humility and other-directedness. Should a trained *aikidōka* (a student of *aikidō*), then, be in a situation where a knife or a gun, or a physical attack is directed his or her way, s/he is still obliged to adopt this "partnering" stance: s/he should seek a nonviolent solution, or use the least amount of force to disarm or deflect the other's blows. Also, the gun, knife, or sword that has been taken should not be pointed at the downed and disarmed attacker, for to do so would only replay the violence from the other side. Instead, one hides the weapon behind one's back, simply offering a verbal warning that it would be fruitless to join in battle once more. At this point, it would be far better to walk away or call the police to protect others from additional attacks. Many officers in police forces in Japan and Hawai'i are trained in nonviolent disarming skills by *aikidō* masters.

Whether *makoto* is in the betweenness or is carried there by all those who meet there, it is a vital part of such meetings in Japanese culture. This sincerity leads to *wa*, or group harmony. "*Wa*" implies a solidarity of community feeling that manifests as peacefulness, good will, and happiness. Trust and truth are not mere intellectual demands made from a purely theoretical interest, but are to be found in the actual actions through and by which they are connected to one another. Even those who act in such a way as to seemingly reject truthfulness or trustworthiness in their relations with others—those who lie and cheat, break promises, and do harm to persons and property—nevertheless rely on the expectation that others will act truthfully and in a loyal and trustworthy manner in order to be able to carry out their nefarious deeds. The very fabric of social interaction of any civilization is based on that network of trusting relationships without which our lives together would be "nasty, brutish, and short." So there is no state of nature, as Thomas Hobbes presupposed, from which we emerged as individuals slowly making our way to a contractual society for the first time. There never was a time, nor could there have been, when we were not first immersed in a network of social interconnections. And all such social interconnection must inescapably be based on some sense of trustworthiness and the expectation that one be sincere. A state of nature is but an abstraction, crafted by the imagination, that will not pass serious examination as an actual state of being.

Shintō is another major source of those attitudes which con-stitute the Japanese spirit. Shintō, the indigenous religion of Japan, has no founder, no scripture, no revelation, and no systematic moral code. The "climate" of Shintō is so unconsciously "caught," rather than taught, that one is hardly aware that one has become part of a tradition that reaches back to the wellsprings of Japan. Shintō emphasizes directly experiencing one's kinship with the world around one, including the sacred realms, and with purify-ing oneself in order to experience once more the divinity of one's own inner depths. In so doing, one subtly learns of a cluster of attitudes (or values) that, together, serve one well in living a happy, and relationally fruitful life. In addition to sincerity (which includes truthfulness, honesty, trustworthiness, and, as Sallie King suggests, "genuineness, spiritual purity, and the completion and perfection of the individual,")[36] there are other attitudes of importance which Shintō communicates to its followers, including harmony, commu-nity or fellow-feeling, a spirit of thankfulness, peacefulness, good will, happiness, sincere effort, hard work, and steadfastness. All of these together, ideally, should flow spontaneously, arising from the heart for no extrinsic or calculated reason. Between human beings, the most appropriate relationship is that of benevolence. To be significantly less than this in one's attitudinal stance is to risk being shamed not only to oneself but to all of those around you, including your larger community. Everyone shares in the disappointment and failure, at least to some degree. The shame is in not being better, in not fulfilling one's potential as a son or daughter of the divine (*kami*). In a letter to me regarding Watsuji and Shintō, the late Yuasa Yasuo wrote that "it seems to me that Watsuji supported the Imperial system precisely because he saw it as integral to the set of cultural and religious beliefs that the Japanese people had embraced for many centuries."[37]

A striking example of the Japanese emphasis on community can be found in the "corporate philosophy" of Ricoh Company, Ltd., a large producer of copiers and other office equipment, such as facsimile devices and digital imaging systems. The former CEO, now retired, is Hamada Hiroshi, the author of several books on leadership. He writes that at Ricoh, "I am concerned with creating an environment of consensus in which people can work harmoniously together."[38] He explains that at the heart of his business philosophy is the concept of *oyakudachi,* which he prefers not to translate but which means roughly "helping others," "being of mutual assistance," "doing what is useful for others," and "putting yourself in the other's shoes."[39] Reminiscent of Watsuji, Hamada analyzes *ningen,* noting that the term is composed of two characters meaning "person" and "between." He adds that "we human beings live by forming groups, and these groups together make up society, which is based on the relations between one person and others."[40] Summarizing, he writes that "all our interactions with other human beings are based on the amount of help or service that we provide for one another. In that sense we are bound whether we like it or not by a network of *oyakudachi.* . . . I want to think of ourselves as providing not copiers, but *oyakudachi.*"[41] For Hamada, work is "conscious *oyakudachi behavior.*" Furthermore, "when I suggest that Ricoh employees should find self-fulfillment by providing *oyakudachi* to others, I'm not suggesting a life of self-sacrifice."[42] To the contrary, he suggests that by living every day to the fullest, purpose and happiness will result, but only if we work in order to contribute to others something of genuine worth. The emphasis here is on shrinking the distance between workers, as in a well-ordered family and even extending this intimacy-as-concern to the nation and to Ricoh's customers. The spirit of *oyakudachi* now applies to the vastly wider Ricoh family, which includes the nation and all others in contact with Ricoh and its products. It is a spirit designed to move people closer to the nondual ideal of a selflessness which reduces the space between oneself and others, to *nothing*. Watsuji argues for just such a spirit leading to selfless compassion.

The Importance of the Body

Watsuji affirms that "bodily connections are always visible wherever betweenness prevails, even though the manner of connection may differ."[43] This emphasis harkens back to his earlier encounter with Heidegger's *Sein und Zeit*, whose emphasis on temporality, at the expense of spatiality, allowed relationships to be between mind and mind, with scant reference to the body. Watsuji demanded a fuller account of relationships between body-minds and body-minds. A recent study, which integrates contemporary feminism and Watsuji's ethics, written by Erin McCarthy and entitled *Embodied Ethics*, argues convincingly that "body is from the beginning an epistemological site for Watsuji—an essential element in attaining knowledge and identity—one that cannot be separated from self as *ningen*. Rather than limit knowledge, the body is an intimate part of the self's way of knowing."[44] Thus, we not only meet in the betweenness as individual selves, but we do so as "body-minds." Japan has long recognized that the body is not only a knowledge site, but has an essential role in the attainment of nondual awareness. All of the practices refined by the Japanese—the way of tea, of flowers, the martial arts, and so on—reach us through the body as well as through the mind. They are direct routes to the body-mind. As body-minds, we eliminate one hindrance to nonduality; the false separation of body and mind. Only then can we meet the other person as a real, embodied self, and not just another ethereal soul. By meeting body-mind to body-mind, we learn of our relationship with each other, and with all other, material things that exist—the oneness of all things. Through that knowledge we become aware of this oneness, for it is not just a thought, but a full-blooded body-mind experience. Human beings exist as both flesh and blood in *space* and not just as thinking beings (that is, we exist in both space and time as bodies and minds).

Conclusion

William LaFleur writes convincingly that "it was [in] the Buddhist notion of emptiness that Watsuji found *the* principle that gives his system . . . coherence."[45] He also argues that Watsuji's understanding of Japanese ethics included religion, but as a cultural phenomenon, like communication and transportation, the arts, and such, whereas for Nishida, religion transcended culture. For Watsuji, religion was but a part of the network of human interaction. While the pivotal notion of emptiness or nothingness came from Buddhism, he treated religion as a social phenomenon. Insights gained from Confucianism and Shintōism were treated in a similar fashion. Religion was more an ethical humanism for Watsuji and not the underlying factor in all knowledge that it was for Nishida.

Nonetheless, in his work on Dōgen, he shows himself to be an able interpreter of religion in his lengthy comparisons of Dōgen and Shinran. Readers will remember the emphasis on *faith* in Tanabe's work, a follower of Shinran, but Watsuji points out that faith is also a central concept and concern for Dōgen as well, but rather than a faith in the unending compassion of Other-power, it is a faith in human culture: "[H]e [Dōgen] gave sufficient importance to the efforts of human beings to try to seize the ultimate ideal (the Dharma) [i.e., truth or enlightenment] with the entirety of their own personalities. By doing so, life on this shore will be affirmed. Unceasing diligence gives life meaning, as opposed to the worship of Amida, which ignored diligence and considered cultural developments meaningless, Dōgen's diligence clearly restores faith in human culture. We can see 'prostrating to the attainment of the marrow' as an important chance at making it possible for culture to elevate itself."[46] While Watsuji treats both Shinran and Dōgen fairly, it seems apparent that his philosophical heart is with Dōgen: always the cultural historian and interpreter, Watsuji emphasizes the "this worldly" achievements toward the elevation of culture as being all-important. He adds that salvation lies in "making the self a buddha. The Dharma is something we embody in ourselves."[47]

Watsuji's emphasis on the state as the culmination of ethics and human culture, and on the importance of loyalty to the emperor, caused him to be branded as a right-wing totalitarian by some, particularly after World War II.[48] His patriotic nationalism was cause for concern, but, in the context of a nation attempting to rediscover itself after defeat in war, it is really not surprising that he might overemphasize the Japanese legacy, or highlight the importance of the emperor as the secular and religious head of the greater Japanese family. His emphasis on the state as the culmination of ethics may be the major issue, for such emphasis seems to privilege the social over the individual. Having so brilliantly shown that the dual-nature of human beings is an ongoing and dynamic interplay between the individual and social nature of self, one in which the tension between the two persists in self-contradictory harmony, it would be a disappointment for this important analysis to collapse into a porridge-like state that simply engulfed the individuals it incorporated. My assessment is that, while the power of the state over individuals remains a real issue in his writings, the thrust of his work on ethics lies with *ningen,* which encompasses both the individual and the social, on nothingness as the betweenness between us, and on the positive attitudes which the Japanese bring to, or find in, their remarkably fruitful encounters in the betweenness.

5

Conclusion

The Kyoto-school philosophers give the west a way into the east like none other. Theirs is not an eastern thought diluted for foreign consumption, nor is it a simple transference that assumes a background in the history of oriental ideas. It makes an unsolicited contribution to world philosophy that both respects the traditions of philosophy and expands them. . . . Never has the west produced an intellectual movement whose contributions to the east can compare with what these three thinkers [Nishida, Tanabe, and Nishitani] offer the west.

—James W. Heisig, *The Philosophers of Nothingness*

Nishida and Tanabe

A difficulty with any introductory text is that it must leave out a great deal if it is to truly serve as an introduction. To take the reader through the four stages of Nishida's philosophy would deserve a book by itself, if not several books, and the complexity required would likely cause a reader to look elsewhere. Each philosopher included in this exploration produced many volumes of work: the collected works of Nishida comprise nineteen volumes in Japanese; Tanabe fifteen volumes; Nishitani twenty-six volumes; and Watsuji twenty volumes. But the aim of the present study is to *introduce* each thinker and to tie that account to a major, readily accessible, text. Nevertheless, while Nishida is here classed primarily as a self-power thinker, and Tanabe as a primarily Other-power thinker, both of them in their later writings sought to minimize the apparent differences and to bridge the two perspectives. Tanabe did not reject Zen Buddhism, nor did Nishida reject the Pure Land tradition, a tradition for which he had increasing admiration.

Clearly, any conclusions reached here must be tempered by the study of the complete works of each philosopher. However, since most of these writings have yet to be translated into English, no introduction can detail the subtle and not-so-subtle changes in thinking that transpired over years of thinking and rethinking, to the tune of seventy collected volumes that were produced by these four in total, let alone the dozens and dozens of volumes produced by other members of the Kyoto School. What is offered here is a glimpse of the excitement and originality that characterizes Kyoto School philosophy. Therefore, the conclusions which I offer here are to be held tentatively, lightly, knowing full well that a more comprehensive exploration might well make each conclusion less strident and apparently clear. If the late American jurist, Roscoe Pound, was correct in his insight that the art of teaching is the art of lying and then progressively qualifying that lie, then I can only hope that this "lie" is sound enough to lead the reader to further qualifications of that lie.

Perhaps the most striking differences in emphasis between Nishida and Tanabe are the following: first, Nishida's assumption that our "true" self is inherently good contrasts with Tanabe's insistence that human beings are born in "original sin" and, through inherent arrogance, are inclined toward evil. The second striking difference is Nishida's reliance on reason, while Tanabe adopted the standpoint of faith, although these claims must be qualified. For Nishida wrote of the importance of faith, and Tanabe of the importance of reason, once granted the assistance of Other-power. A third important difference, already qualified above, can be found in Nishida's reliance on self-power, whereas Tanabe adopted the standpoint of Other-power; and yet Tanabe did not reject the self-power position, nor did Nishida reject the Other-power position. In fact, both thinkers attempted to combine the two, although in different ways. Both men did grant the importance of the other position, and Nishida, even in the *Inquiry*, wrote that the two positions might actually be identical. More on these points shortly.

Tanabe's Critique of Nishida

To begin, the distance between these two approaches can be lessened somewhat if we look closely at some of Tanabe's criticisms of Nishida. Beginning with "absolute nothingness," the central and defining characteristic of the Kyoto School philosophers, is Tanabe correct in concluding that Nishida's grasp of absolute nothingness through "intellectual intuition" renders it an instance of *being*, rather than of nothingness? The issue is complex, made even more so given that Tanabe does not mention Nishida even once in his *Philosophy as Metanoetics*. However, it is quite clear that he groups Nishida together with Eckhart and mysticism, as well as with Zen Buddhism. It is worth noting here that Nishida did not study Eckhart's work, although he does occasionally refer to him. Nishida argues that absolute nothingness is neither being, nor not-being (relative nothingness), but rather that emptiness out of which both arise. Furthermore, absolute nothingness cannot be apprehended directly, but only indirectly as the unseen "lining" of all things. He maintains that at the foundation of all things there is a "reality" that is not seen, heard, or perceived in any way. Unless we look through things in the everyday world, feeling the lining at their depths, absolute nothingness is simply unknowable. Absolute nothingness is never itself a form, a being, but is always formless and known only through the formed beings that are manifestations of it. The formless remains forever unknowable and yet can be intuited in pure experience.

Yet, even granted this Nishidan analysis, Tanabe's criticism cannot be easily disposed of. If the formless is, in any way, an *experience,* that is, a pure experience, then it has to be experienced by a self's consciousness, and all the contents of consciousness have being, in one sense or another. The unicorn is an experience, and though its status is that of a fictional being, it has being precisely as fictional, and can be drawn and otherwise imitated. The mystical experience, however, is totally un-representational. You cannot draw it, or even speak it—it is ineffable, or unspeakable. Mystics throughout the ages, and in diverse cultures, have claimed that it is a knowledge of the heart and not of the mind. It is more a feeling than a thought, and yet it is claimed to have noetic value—that is, value as a kind of knowledge. It strikes me that Tanabe would have difficulty understanding this because of his religion-as-faith perspective. Traditional religious thinkers in the West have repeatedly condemned mysticism because it is not directly confirmable through ordinary sense perception, and particularly because it often challenges the teachings of the orthodox religions. If anything is clear about Tanabe's position, it is that he is not a mystic, nor was he in any way likely to be so inclined. Nishida, on the other hand, while denying that he is a mystic in any straightforward sense, has in common with the mystics what he calls the "principle" of unity as the unity of all things, or absolute nothingness. It is such that "we cannot see it as an object of consciousness," although "we can become it and function in accordance with it."[1] As noted earlier, Nishitani cites a wonderful passage from Dōgen, taken from Yüeh-shan Wei-yen (745–828), who, when asked how we can think of that which "lies beyond the reach of thinking," responds, "We do not think it."[2] Kasulis calls this "without thinking," and it may best be understood as something arising in the act of meditation. Put aside all thinking, and do not try not to think, for that, too, is a thinking of not thinking. Just meditate, without thinking, and an awareness of the unity of things, of reality, of absolute nothingness, may arise. Recall the image of the "reversed eye" as a metaphor for "seeing" that which is within us. To look at the unity within us is to see God, to see absolute nothingness, because "our spirit is simply a small part" of reality as spirit.[3] One intuits, or feels, that this deep unity within is the same unity that is in the cosmos as a whole: it is a "cosmic consciousness." This "feeling" is no more communicable to others than is attempting to describe what coffee tastes like to someone who has never tasted it. For another who has had the experience, one need only point to one's awareness, and the communication is immediately made. Even terms such as "one," "unity," or even "the formless," are but *markers* pointing to a possible shared experience, like a finger pointing to the moon. Look at the moon, not the finger, except that, in this case, the moon of reality is invisible. One can only point, thereby encouraging others to look for this same realization.

Tanabe argues that it is impossible to perceive such a "whole," as is implied by the metaphors of the net, or the web. He writes that "it is by no means possible to intuit such a totality. What can be intuited is superficial being, not the reverse aspect of nothingness."[4] Yet this is precisely what non-mystics have claimed over the centuries: what the mystics claim is not verifiable in any ordinary way, except through one's own personal experience. So it is that the argument continues, even today. Nishida's final words in the *Inquiry* are worth repeating: "Vedantic teachings in India, Neo-Platonism, and Gateway of the Holy Path-type of Buddhism [the self-power traditions of Zen, Tendai, Shingon, and the Kegon sects] refer to knowing God, whereas Christianity and Pure Land Buddhism refer to loving and relying on God. Both views have their own distinctive features, but they are identical in essence." The final sentence closes the distance between faith and reason even further: "We can know God only through love, through the intuition of faith. So it is that those who love and believe in God without knowing God are the ones who best know God."[5] It is Nishida that brings the two approaches together in this final passage, because love is the mystics' approach to knowledge, and the love of God is central to faith-oriented traditions. The culminating insight for both is the centrality of loving the absolute in order to experience the absolute. Nishida's open-mindedness encourages both paths to the absolute. Some will journey along the path of faith, and they will be in the majority; others, along the path of reason and experience, and they will be much fewer in number. Yet over the centuries, untold numbers of individuals, in every religious tradition and even outside of any religious tradition, have had mystical experiences, while only a few have recorded what they "saw."

On a different issue, Tanabe also takes exception to Nishida's concept of "action intuition," as well as to his claims for "intellectual intuition." In attempting to be clear about the meaning of intellectual intuition, Nishida states that it "is nothing more than a further enlargement and deepening of our state of pure experience," and what results from this deepening is a "disclosure of a great unity."[6] For the scholar there comes "a new insight," for the moralist "a new motive," for an artist "a new imagination," and for a religious person "a new awakening." Intellectual intuition is an ever-deepening path to enlightenment, and it is "intellectual" in that it is a form of knowledge, although not knowledge through either mere sense experience or reason.

"Acting intuition" refers to *action* based on *intuition*. In ordinary or everyday action, there is a clear distinction between acting by means of the body and the knowledge that guides that action. We intuit the situation (knowledge), and then we act on that knowledge. Such ordinary intuition is passive in relation to the world, simply "reading" what is there in preparation for deciding how to act. (It is important to note here that "Intuition" is used here in the Kantian sense as information gained through the senses; empirical knowledge.) For example, in looking both left and right before stepping off the sidewalk onto a roadway, one gathers information on the basis of which one then decides to walk or to continue standing in place. Action is the active function, for it acts in and on the world, on the basis of what intuition reveals. However, nonordinary or *enlightened intuition* is not passive, but active, in that it "becomes a thing and exhausts it." Nishida writes that to become a thing "means . . . that the mind (*kokoro*) becomes one with the thing and it strikes to the heart (*kokoro*) of the thing."[7] In order to become a thing, one must have let go of one's ego, so that, in a state of pure experience, the distinction between body and mind, knowing and willing, is not present. Intuition is now "creative" intuition, the "skillful knack" that Nishida mentions, such that the body moves with the mind as one, as body-mind (a central teaching in the various practices, or *dō* ["ways"] in Japan). One acts as a "self without a self," effortlessly and spontaneously, as the "master" of any art does. After prolonged training, the once inert and heavy body becomes light, alive, and completely responsive to the biddings of intuition. This self without a self now acts in the world by "becoming" the thing that it acts with or upon. The body is no longer separate from the mind, nor is the body-mind somehow separate from the world. In Western culture we might refer to this state of affairs as "being in the zone," as with Michael Jordan in basketball, or the gymnast who performs with incredible ease and accuracy; the body and mind functioning seamlessly together at every step of the way. Again, it is not uncommon for a driver to think about something other than driving. One often hears of an experienced driver driving for miles but paying no apparent attention to the road, the functioning of the auto, the landscape, or the other vehicles on the road. We say that our mind was somewhere else. And yet, the driving was safe driving and because of years of diligent practice, a kind of automatic driving has occurred. One is no less aware of what one needs to take in, in order to drive safely; it is just not at the forefront of our conscious awareness. We arrive (action completed) and have seen (intuition) what we needed to see in driving safely. Should an emergency have occurred, our now single-minded consciousness would have attended to the situation fully, and we would have slammed on the brakes without deliberation, at one and the same instant that we saw the danger, and acted to avoid it. In effect, this example affords two instances of action intuition.

Tanabe criticizes this analysis of action intuition, for he interprets the "action" in Nishida's "action intuition" to refer to the functioning of self-power. For Tanabe, such action has nothing at all to do with action based on the Other-power of absolute nothingness. He writes that "action intuition" is not "a transformation based on the Other-power of transcendent nothingness, which is absolutely inaccessible to intuition and even negates it."[8] As with intellectual intuition, active intuition, "if it remains intuition, it is being but not nothingness."[9] Curiously, part of his argument is that active intuition has the effect of continually extending the self, but it does not negate the self.[10] As previously explained, the self is negated in "becoming the thing" in order to act in the world seamlessly. For Nishida, in the deepened awareness of action intuition, it is intuition that is active, and action that is passive. Intuition is active because, in the enlightened state, the function of intuition is to act in the world, not merely to know it. The samurai does not wrinkle his brow in thinking about what his opponent with a sword might do, he just acts. As a master swordsman, he both intuits what his opponent will do and acts his part instantly and deftly. Through all of this, there is no self, no samurai to worry about his future, his ability, or whether he is reading the situation correctly. Body and mind are one, and intuiting and acting come together. This can only happen if the self is no longer a self in the usual sense. The action arises out of our unconscious, not out of intellect. The action is anything but self-power; it is selfless-power, which arises out of the depths of one's own nothingness, which is part of the total nothingness of all existence. Perhaps it is in the unconscious where our separate being merges with nothingness. Action intuition transcends "contemplative and speculative philosophy," a characteristic that Tanabe insists is the exclusive trademark of metanoetics. In any case, both philosophers reach a point where the self is let go, reason is beside the point, and an altered state of awareness results: for Tanabe, it is being in the thrall of Other-power, for Nishida, it is the ecstatic state of being a self without a self that acts with a oneness of body-mind, as a oneness with the unifying activity that is nothingness. Both hold to the reality of something beyond the ordinary bounds of self and reason. Nishida's intuition is not ordinary intuition but the intuition of the mystic, and Tanabe's experience is that of the overtaking power of faith. In the final pages of the *Inquiry*, Nishida speaks often of the importance of faith, and he concludes by affirming that Zen and Pure Land traditions are "identical in essence."[11] Surely this narrows the difference between them. Neither did Tanabe reject the self-power position. Nevertheless, the emphasis was different for each of them.

The nothingness that both philosophers talk about at length is central to their respective positions, yet the content is very different. Like Nishida, Tanabe held that absolute nothingness could only be known indirectly through the actions of those transformed by Other-power. Indeed, absolute nothingness only exists because of its mediation and transformative power. It is not a thing to be somehow seen apart from the activities of Other-power. Nishida argued that absolute nothingness neither exists nor does not exist, for it is that out of which existence and nonexistence (that is, being and relative nothingness) arise. It cannot be known directly, only indirectly insofar as all beings arise from the formless absolute nothingness. The mere fact that he describes it as formless makes it evident that it is not a thing to be known directly, nor can it be spoken of in "being" language, the only language human beings can speak.

On Original Goodness

Returning to the question concerning humankind's innate goodness, there is no clear-cut way to demonstrate that we are either innately good or innately evil. Both claims have been argued over and over again through the centuries and in virtually every culture and tradition. Clearly, Tanabe (and Shin Buddhism) and Nishida (and perhaps Zen Buddhism and the mystical traditions) are equally convinced of their positions, although one could easily show that Zen Buddhists have taken both of these stances, and on occasion simultaneously. All in all, the generous and/or honest reader will conclude that human beings have the potential to be either good or bad. To take any other position would require evidence not presently available. But the pedagogical implications, either way, are important. To take the position that human beings are by nature evil will not necessarily lead to honest soul searching leading to repentance, as described by Tanabe's own journey. Instead, it may lead either to the paralysis of hopelessness or to giving in to what it is that we are by nature: evil. On the other side, the simple affirmation that we are by nature good could result in an arrogant acceptance of our goodness, without need for further introspection or the humble development of good habits. Neither position is credible if disconnected from the requirements of a system of understanding that demands such integrity and introspection.

Let us take one final look at Nishida's position on humankind's inherent nature. The late Chinese philosopher Fung yu-lan recorded that the earliest characters in the Chinese language discovered by archaeologists read that "all men are by nature good."[12] Fung adds that this sentence was probably the first sentence to be learned by school children, much like our "run Spot run." They offer encouragement to the student, empowering him or her to do his or her best, and to be compassionate, which is our "natural" way of acting. It was the Confucian scholar Mencius (372–289 BCE) who most fervently maintained that we are naturally good and compassionate. The empowerment resulting, however, was a boost to self-power. It must be admitted, however, that Nishida nowhere aligns himself with this Confucian and Neo-Confucian position. My assumption throughout this study has been, however, that Nishida holds a view that is at least akin to it. To be precise, what he does argue is that the "good is the actualization of personality," and that this actualization is achieved "in the mutual forgetting of self and others and the merging of subject and object."[13] Given that "the self and the universe share the same foundation; or rather are the same thing," then it follows that the "truth, beauty, and good of reality are the truth, beauty, and good of the self." [14] Hence, "morality . . . is simply the discovery of something within the self."[15] A good or moral self is united "with the good of humankind," and will "fuse with the essence of the universe and unite with the will of God." [16]

Rather than affirming that we are by nature good, Nishida maintained that our "real" or "true" self is motivated by those deep internal demands of consciousness.[17] The goal of realization is to display who we really are—*kenshō* is the experience of seeing who one truly is—"just as a bamboo plant or a pine tree fully displays its nature."[18] It is our real nature to be good, and the only standard for this is to be found deep within us.

By contrast, Tanabe argued that insisting that we are intrinsically good is an indication of a human arrogance that leads directly to the very evil and sin that he warned against. To claim that we are fundamentally evil leads to humility, and an awareness of our corrupted nature. Since arrogance is our greatest weakness, to declare that we are fundamentally good simply encourages arrogance rather than the needed caution due to being fundamentally flawed. To Tanabe's way of thinking, self-empowerment is the last thing that we need more of; he concludes that Other-power is the solution.

These are two opposite ways of looking at human nature, and the distance between them is another indication of the strong contrast at the beginning of the Kyoto School that provided the material for continued debate. Perhaps the best conclusion resulting from the depiction of these two views is that some combination of them is closer to the truth; human beings have the potential to be good and the potential to be evil, and history is replete with instances supporting both views. But for Nishida, the seeds of human goodness are, in some sense, inborn, while for Tanabe, sin and evil are present at birth. For Tanabe, the ability to be good comes from beyond us, while for Nishida such goodness comes from within. Not unlike Plato's "theory of recollection" in the dialogue the *Meno,* the claim is made that one could never know what is truly good unless the standard of goodness is already within us. To know the good is to recollect the good. Otherwise, whatever is judged to be good is either arbitrary, or decreed by a God (as with the Ten Commandments). Reason will be unable to find an unchanging standard, for different things at different times and in different cultures have been deemed good. Goodness, then, must be that toward which we are naturally inclined, unless culture, coercion, or selfishness serves to override our natural inclinations. Of course, it could be argued that selfishness, too, is a natural inclination, even the most prevalent inclination. Yet, when selfishness is overcome, a different and deeper inclination rises to the fore: that of selfless compassion and a profound sense of the interconnectedness of all things.

Nishitani

Nishitani Keiji was a student of both Nishida and Tanabe, but it was Nishida's path that he choose to follow and to develop further. He was influenced by his reading of Nietzsche and other European existentialists, and particularly by Heidegger (with whom he studied). Nishitani employed the insights of existentialist philosophy to set the stage for his own philosophical approach. Like Tanabe, he depicted the human predicament as being a lack of belief in God and traditional values together with a desperate attempt to somehow find a bridge that would span the abyss of meaninglessness and despair that was evident in many modern societies. That bridge could only be reached by going down into the abyss of despair that characterized Nietzsche's thought. As he expressed it, on the field of ordinary or everyday consciousness, nothing is permanent, nothing is guaranteed by a God or divine overseer, for God is dead. Like Tanabe, Nishitani brings us to the point of ultimate despair and radical doubt: the "Great Doubt" of Zen. Nevertheless, it is precisely at this lowest point that the field of Śūnyatā opens up for the serious, searching individual. What arises from this despair—again, as with Tanabe—is the death of the old self and the birth of a new, true self. Unlike Tanabe, however, this new self is the reclaiming of our original countenance, our Buddha-self, and it is not a sudden gift from Other-power. It is through nihilism itself that nihilism is negated, and, precisely at this extreme point, a new self arises in its "suchness," able to see others and the world at large in their suchness. This new self is a selfless self, and, therefore, it is able to view the world apart from the imposition of the usual expectations and distortions imposed by the ordinary self. Such awareness is a nondual awareness, where self and other, knower and known, subject and object, coalesce and become one; self and other are experienced as indistinguishable, from one another, and yet as distinct. Experience of the world is now achieved directly and not through concepts. One is now able to see the flower in its suchness and on its own "home-ground." One no longer apprehends things on the field of ordinary consciousness but, rather, on the field of *Śūnyatā*.

This *Śūnyatā* (emptiness, absolute nothingness) is, once again, not to be conceived of as a thing. It is not an object and is beyond all representation, and yet *Śūnyatā* is the "field" on which, or from which, all beings "be." It is the field of "be-ification," where things are now seen in their "original mode of being," prior to our subjective impositions and distortions: it is experience akin to Nishida's "pure experience," except that, for Nishitani, such awareness includes judgment, albeit a judgment without judging. Each thing is now perceived as being uniquely what it is. As with the metaphor of the net (where each jewel imbedded in the net reflects every other jewel in the net), while every thing is precisely and uniquely what it is, on the field of *Śūnyatā* it is clearly evident that every thing is related to all other existent things, and they to it. Agreeing with Nishida, Nishitani understands that all things are inextricably linked together. Whether individual, world, or cosmos, all things are held together by some unifying force that is similar to, if not identical with, the "unifying power" at the base of everything that was so central to Nishida's thinking.

Thus, the self, for Nishitani, loses its ordinary ego-self, becomes free of self-centeredness, and is then able to appreciate the suchness of every other thing as a result. It is just as Dōgen had taught; once the ego-self is out of the way, all things will advance as they are in themselves, including one's self, but now as a no-self: to study the self is to forget the self, and to forget the self is to be enlightened by all things. One can no longer just view the flower, for one can "become" the flower, since all obstructions have been removed. From one's home-ground as a selfless self, it is now possible to see other things from their own home-ground. And because of the disappearance of the selfish self, *ethics* is now possible. The *kōan* featuring Kyōzan and Sanshō, in chapter 3, was meant to illustrate how the distance and differences between two individuals can shrink to zero on the field of *Śūnyatā*. Kyōzan *is* Sanshō: an encounter that is not just between two separate individuals but which models human encounters as ideally beginning with first "becoming" the other. Nishitani refers to this ethics of becoming the other as the true meaning of compassion and love. For two people who engage each other from an ethics of love, each of them is "other-centered." Being in the home-ground of the other (and of all other things) is clearly the result of the self having become empty; become nothingness. Nishitani calls this state of being "circumincessional interpenetration," where each is the other. Such interconnection is evidence of having discovered one's true self as a no-self. Furthermore, if one understands this interpenetration to be not only between human beings, but between all things, then the foundation for an environmental ethics has been achieved as well. The result of such awareness is ethics as a spontaneous expression of who one truly is: a nothingness acting in the world through love and compassion.

Nishitani's ethics is an ethics arising out of self-power and, yet, is the result of transforming itself into an ethics arising out of nothingness and acting as nothingness. At this point, it might well be asked just how different Nishitani's position really is from Tanabe's: both demand the recognition of our hopeless situation as human beings, and both end with the selfless activity of nothingness by means of a selfless self. It is true that their orientations are quite distinct, and their take on the nature of nothingness differs as well. Nevertheless, all three philosophers—Nishida, Nishitani, and Tanabe—conclude with a selfless self acting out of the power and wisdom of absolute nothingness.

Watsuji

Some scholars of the Kyoto School will object to my inclusion of Watsuji in this volume. Certainly he was not part of what is sometimes referred to as the "inner circle," which includes Nishida, Tanabe, and Nishitani. Nonetheless, I side with Bret W. Davis, who, in his entry on the "Kyoto School" in the *Stanford on-line Encyclopedia of Philosophy* (2.2 and 2.3), grants Watsuji "associate membership." Certainly it is true that Watsuji's philosophical approach is very different from those of Nishida, Tanabe, and Nishitani, yet, in his own way, he does emphasize the importance of nothingness, and his views do seem to have arisen in line with a Buddhist perspective, even though religion is anything but the driving force in his philosophy. He was also hired by Nishida himself, and did spend several years teaching beside Nishida at Kyoto University. It is true that his own philosophical writing must be seen as having taken a path very different from the other Kyoto School thinkers, yet, it is also true that he was influenced by Nishida's writing. But my point is not to establish Watsuji as a member of the inner circle of the School, but only to expand our understanding of the reach of the School's influence in its own day. Moreover, Watsuji adds a dimension to this volume that enriches its scope: his analysis of Japanese culture and ethics allows a rich and distinctive vantage point from which to further understand the Japanese.

Drawing on insights gained from his depiction of the Japanese monsoon climate, Watsuji concludes that the Japanese personality is heavily influenced by the qualities of heat, humidity, and abrupt seasonal changes that characterize the monsoon climate. The experience of abrupt climatic change coincides with the Buddhist teachings that change and impermanence are the reality of existence, the Buddhist notion of *anicca* (from the Pali, or *mujō* in Japanese) teaches that all is impermanent, that all existence is in a constant state of flux. The samurai, whose life and death occurred in the midst of rapid change, usually employed some form of meditation as a means to achieve equanimity and acceptance in the midst of rapid change.

A study of the Japanese home reveals a fusion of self and other. Mutual trust is a cardinal virtue cultivated in living quarters that offer little privacy. Members of the household feel a duty toward other members of the household to exhibit the qualities of compassion, affection, sympathy, and consideration. The view that all things are one and interconnected Watsuji attributes to the experience of close living in the home, and to the extreme humidity in Japan's climate that fosters both emotion and a contemplative attitude. During a period of high humidity, one is forced to simply wait for a climate change, with the thinking of "cool" thoughts the only slight escape. It was a time to withdraw somewhat, and to contemplate, if not to meditate. Families, communities, and entire regions had to quietly endure the humid season and gain both strength and comfort from each other.

It was Watsuji's studies of Japanese ethics that still stand as his major achievements. The approach that he takes describes how the Japanese do act, with little consideration given to how they *ought* to act. For him, *Ningen,* or the human person, is born into a complex network of human social connections, and this network expands over a lifetime. Japanese ethics—*rinri*—refers to the way to interact fruitfully with others in a social network. *Ningen,* therefore, refers not only to the human person as an individual but also as a social being. Furthermore, *Ningen* carries the meaning of "betweenness," referring to the neutral space between us as individuals in some actual or potential relationship. "Betweenness" suggests distance, a distance to be maintained, entrenched, or overcome. Since relationships are of central importance in Japanese society, it is essential to know how to have and to sustain ones that are meaningful and appropriate. What is "appropriate" is taught indirectly rather than theoretically: attitudes are "caught, not taught." Both Shintōism and Buddhism instill attitudes such as trustworthiness, sincerity, humility, cheerfulness, compassion, honesty, steadfastness, and so on. Hopefully, such attitudes taken together and practiced will reveal a person with *kokoro*: an authentic person with no hidden agenda, who is up front and who displays a unity of body and mind, feeling and reason—in other words, a person of steadfast quality with whom one would gladly enter into an intimate relationship. To have *kokoro* is to possess a strong "fellow-feeling," with an empathy that verges on selflessness.

In a sense, the ethics of a mature individual has already been worked out by a society that embraces individuals as members of the larger societal family. Clearly the moral "is" of Japanese society, as it is on the whole, also describes what most Japanese take to be the ethical "ought." One is ethical who behaves the way society has taught one to behave, leaving the peace and harmony of Japanese social existence unscathed.

But Watsuji has more to say on the subject of Japanese ethics. *Ningen,* as both individual and social person, must be viewed as having arisen out of a deeper background which is neither individual nor societal: something of the widest context possible that is prior to all distinctions. Here we encounter "nothingness" once more, a deep profundity, both indistinct and indefinite, having no characteristics or identifying markers. It is the background to all foregrounds, and in our everyday lives, it is represented by the betweenness between us, an empty space in which both good and evil are possibilities.

Nothingness also signifies the importance of our becoming *empty,* for Watsuji, where we leave the ego-self behind and enter into a relationship with much, or all, of our psychological baggage excluded. From this state we may now enter the nothingness between us as an empty vessel, and if the other is also empty (of their prejudice, habits, and fears), then a genuine relationship is highly likely. Both parties are who they present themselves as being *and,* at the same time, are cultured or socialized enough to greet each other in the time-honored manner of first encounters. One brings one's socialization into the nothingness of betweenness in order to eliminate any clumsiness, allowing an in-depth relationship to develop. The encounter can now be authentic, spontaneous, caring, and wide-reaching in its embrace. True ethics requires a return to one's deep authenticity by leaving the ego-self behind, a demand evident in all four of the philosophers considered in this study. And for Nishida, Nishitani, and Watsuji, the "formless" self emerges from the leaving behind of the "formed," old self. Such a non-self sees all things as though for the first time, as they are, and in their original brightness and fullness.

There is one major difference between Watsuji and the other three thinkers. Unlike Nishida, Tanabe, and Nishitani, Watsuji does not give religion a central role in his philosophy. Watsuji understood religion to be just another cultural or social phenomenon to be studied. His approach to religion was more like an ethical humanism, even though his emphasis on nothingness, or emptiness, was taken from Buddhist teachings. His approach to religion was more like that of a philosophical anthropologist or sociologist, and even his use of "nothingness" showed few religious linkages. Perhaps he represents those who think of Buddhism as being not so much a religion of worship and rituals as a way of thinking about and walking in the everyday world; as a way of life. It was the Buddha, after all, who taught people not to take what he taught as definitive, but to try out his teachings, accepting them if they worked, or rejecting them if they did not. He offered advice, such as an eightfold path, but the responsibility for charting one's own life always rested with the individual. What Watsuji does is to look past the ecclesiastical complexities in order to focus on Buddhism as an active contributor to the Japanese worldview as it has emerged. Yet, he does insist on the unique importance of nothingness in the Japanese understanding of what it means to be a fully actualized human being. For him, it is only with nothingness as one's guide, the realization that we, too, are made of the same "non-stuff" in our depths, that we can come to be fully human. Were we not "of" nothingness at our core, we would only have the "is" of the ethical development of a person to guide us. But with nothingness at our depths, and also beyond us as the foundation of the entire cosmos, an ethical "ought" appears beyond the "is" of convention.

Nishida, Tanabe, Nishitani, and Watsuji were as one in insisting that we could become who we truly are. The route to achieving this true, selfless, non-self varied, but that we are all capable of being far, far more than most of us are was strikingly evident in all that they wrote. Perhaps it is in this sense that it can be claimed that human beings are inherently good: we all are capable of becoming truly, humbly, compassionately, spontaneously, and lovingly good. We need only to become who we truly are, in our depths. Nishida wrote that our selves are infinitely deep. The task of philosophy and religion is to plumb that depth and, thereby, help us to discover our linkage, our connection to the magnificent, mysterious, and majestic whole of which we are all a part. Ultimately, the task of both philosophy and religion is to encourage each of us to live up to our potential, a job usually given exclusively to religion, and definitely not to be found in most modern Western philosophy. In Japan, however, where the dividing line between philosophy and religion is blurred, at best, and more often nonexistent, both philosophy and religion teach of higher things, and of the potential for self-actualization. Thus, the point of philosophy, as of religion, is personal self-transformation. Without this expectation, both philosophy and religion would be rendered meaningless and empty.

The influence of the Kyoto School thinkers, as well as those on the periphery of this tradition, continues to be not only of interest to people the world over, but is becoming increasingly important both in Japan and beyond. The fact that seven new books and more than a hundred articles have recently appeared, thanks to the Nanzan Institute for [the Study of Japanese] Religion and Culture, and that a *Sourcebook* of translations of Japanese philosophy has just appeared (with many sources never before translated), is evidence of the continuing energy of the Kyoto School and Japanese philosophy. Furthermore, a history of Japanese philosophy is currently being written by Thomas P. Kasulis. The mere fact that all of this is happening right now allows me to say that the East/West connections arising from such achievements will go a great distance in fostering understanding among people from very different cultural backgrounds. I think of the Kyoto School in particular as having built a unique bridge of understanding between peoples. It may well be the best of its kind yet available, for it deftly mixes Eastern and Western thinking of the highest quality in its search for an understanding that rises above any cultural, philosophical, or religious constraints. It encourages systematic thinking in whatever direction it leads, a view of philosophic inquiry that takes seriously the Socratic/Platonic adage that "the unexamined life is not worth living." In a shrinking world where electronic connections are almost universally available, it is incumbent on philosophy to be no less aware and no less universal.

Philosophy, by its very nature, needs to explore wisdom in any and all cultural traditions in its attempt to provide the best account of who we are as human beings and what we are capable of becoming. It remains an open-ended inquiry, as it always has been when at its best, for the various paths to understanding are never complete or final. The attempt of the Kyoto School philosophers to explore both Eastern and Western philosophy and religion may well be the best example we have of an attempt to do philosophy without firm cultural boundaries or a rigid canon. It is a courageous attempt to think from a broad world perspective. Furthermore, if the only true "closure" that we have in this world is "tentative closure," that is, a closure based on the best evidence available at the time, then at the very least it can be claimed that the influence of the Kyoto School philosophers has already done much to enrich the tentative closure of understanding that we have. They have reached out to Western thinkers and ways of thought in an attempt to become clear about their own assumptions and insights. That the West is increasingly aware of the Kyoto School philosophers proffers a healthy and continuing dialogue between the various "Easts" and the various "Wests." As with the spread of technology internationally, it is to be hoped that philosophy, too, has gone global.

Glossary

absolute nothingness: Nishida distinguished "absolute" nothingness from "relative" nothingness. It is the final, enveloping, universal or *basho*; an absolute that is beyond, or prior to, distinctions such as subject and object, self and other. Tanabe used the term to refer to that to which we surrender, but that cannot become an object of consciousness. Absolute nothingness is Other-power, a power that mediates through love.

action-faith-witness: a complex term coined by Tanabe to explain that one who has repented and has received the saving grace of Other-power is able to act with compassion, thereby giving witness to the Other-power of absolute nothingness.

action intuition: Nishida's use of this term refers to a state of body/mind when knowing and acting occur at one and the same time, without separation. An artist "becoming" the flower, or a swordsman acting spontaneously and without thinking, display action intuition.

aidagara: the space where people are located; the space between people.

aikidō: an indigenous Japanese martial art founded by Ueshiba Morihei (1883–1969).

aikidōka: students of *aikidō*.

Amida Buddha: the Buddha of "infinite light" dwelling not on earth, but in the Pure Land.

an sich: "in-itself." See *en soi*.

basho: "place." Absolute nothingness is the last "place" for all that exists.

betweenness: the space or opening between persons, that can be lessened through developing a relationship or widened. See *aidagara*.

Bodhisattva: an enlightened being who forgoes *nirvana* in order to bring others to enlightenment. A model of compassion.

busshō: the Zen notion of buddha-nature, true self, or one's natural state of Buddhahood.

chadō: the "way" of tea (the "tea ceremony"); a meditational pathway to enlightenment.

circumincessional interpenetration: Nishitani's term describing the interconnectedness of all things. Each of us penetrates, and is penetrated by, the home-ground of all things. See **dependent origination**.

climate: (See *fūdo*). Watsuji's term describing not only the weather and geography of a region, but also its cultural, social, and artistic reactions to that weather and geography. There are three basic climates; monsoon, desert, and meadow.

Confucianism: a Chinese philosophical/ethical tradition founded by Confucius (551–479 BCE).

Daoism: a Chinese religious and philosophical tradition founded by Lao Tse (604–531 BCE).

Dasein: a term employed by Heidegger, among others, to describe the human person as being-in-the-world rather than as a discrete substance.

de-mysticism: a term to describe Zen as going beyond, but built on, mysticism.

dependent origination: the Buddhist view that all things exist interdependently. For something to exist, many other things must also exist, perhaps even all other things. We exist not as independent beings but as one knot in an interconnected "net of existence."

dialectic: dialectic existed as far back as ancient Greece, but the German philosopher G. W. F. Hegel (1770–1831) developed dialectical logic, that describes events as a thesis, a reaction (an antithesis), and the resolution of the thesis and antithesis (a synthesis).

dō: "way" or "path," as in the way of tea, or the way of flower arranging.

duration: the French philosopher Henri Bergson (1859–1941) contrasted clock time with duration, a flowing movement that carries the past with it, as well as anticipating the future.

élan vital: "vital impulse" or "vital force." Bergson used this term to suggest that evolution was not just random, but the result of a life force within organisms themselves.

emptiness: Nishitani usually wrote of emptiness, rather than of nothingness. *Śūnyatā* is defined as "emptiness." That in which all that is existent lives, itself devoid of characteristics. Emptiness is the home-ground of being.

en-soi: "in-itself." A rock is static, without possibilities. A person, too, can simply live by habit and within the expectations of others. Such a person does not utilize his/her freedom and is seemingly without possibilities.

energetism: inner, innate demands that move us until these demands are satisfied. These innate demands move us toward our own self-realization.

enlightenment: discovering one's own true nature (*kenshō*), and thereby realizing the oneness of all things. It is a change from a dualistic to a nondualistic perspective.

eudaimonia: Aristotle used this term to describe human "happiness," but he added that we can only be happy if we live the life of virtue. A happy person is a good person.

fūdo: a Japanese term for "climate": literally "wind and earth."

Fung yu-lan (1895–1990): a modern Chinese philosopher.

für sich: the German for "for itself." Unlike a stone, a human being has the potential to become many things even though habit and social convention often limit or freeze possibility.

gen: space, between.

gensō-ekō: "returning to the world," after the transformation granted by Other-power.

Godhead (*Gottheit*): Meister Eckhart (1260–1328), the German mystic and theologian, taught that a greater reality lay behind God; namely the Godhead, or nothingness.

Great Death: Zen Buddhism teaches that one's old self and one's old worldview must perish if one is to achieve enlightenment.

ground: Meister Eckhart (1260–1328) taught that ultimate reality and the human being are both composed of similar "stuff."

grund: the German word for "ground." See "**ground.**"

haiku: a seventeen-syllable Japanese poem.

home-ground: the non-objectifiable mode of things as they are in themselves. There is a depth beneath the surface nature of things. As interconnected, each thing is in the home-ground of every other thing.

ikebana: the Japanese art of flower arranging; a meditational pathway to enlightenment.

immanent: from the Latin, "to remain within." Divine presence manifesting in all aspects of existence. The idea that the divine is both within us and "underfoot."

intellectual intuition: the inspiration of artists, the "revelations" within religious traditions. Akin to ordinary perception but far richer and more profound. A "grasp of life" as in intuiting the underlying unity of things. A uniting of subject and object, a sense of the whole of things.

intuition: a direct seeing, a seeing into the depths of things; not just surface or superficial knowing. For Immanuel Kant, "intuition" means "sense-perception," but our sense-perceptions consist of both the *material* and the *forms* of perception (space and time) that are contributed by us (*a priori*), yet come to be known only in experience (*a posteriori*).

Jewel Net of Indra: a metaphor, developed by third-century Mahāyāna Buddhists, to illustrate what is meant by "emptiness," "nothingness," and "dependent origination."

jiriki: self-power; seeking enlightenment or salvation through one's own efforts. (See *tariki*).

kami: the Japanese term for "divine," or "god." More literally, the "awesome," the "miraculous," the "uncanny."

Kegon: a Buddhist religious philosophy introduced into Japan from China (known there as *Huayan*) in the eighth century. Its main doctrine is the interdependence of all things.

kendō: the "way" of swordsmanship: a meditative pathway to enlightenment, yet, to most today, just a sport.

kimono: a traditional form of dress in Japan; worn by both sexes, although the women's *kimono* is far more elaborate and decorative.

kōan: a Zen puzzle or paradoxical saying or story inaccessible to reason. *Kōan* practice is designed to shut down the reasoning mind, allowing direct experience or intuition becomes the focus of attention, yielding a state of mindfulness. "What is the sound of one hand clapping," is a famous example.

kokoro: "mind," "heart;" this double meaning is indicative of the lack of any firm distinction between reason and feeling, mind and body. One who has "*kokoro*" engages another with no hidden agenda, without deceit, as in speaking from the "heart."

logos: a Greek term meaning "word," "speech," "account," "reason," "principle."

makoto: sincerity, integrity, truthfulness, trustworthiness, honesty.

mediation: to reconcile, to act as an intermediary, to bring about transformation. Tanabe writes of Other-power as an intermediary between absolute nothingness and ourselves.

Meiji era (1868–1912): the reign of the Meiji Emperor began in 1868 with the "Meiji Restoration," which marked the end of the rule of the *Shōgun* who had been the hereditary military commanders of the nation.

Mencius (372–289 BCE): a famous Chinese Confucian philosopher who asserted that human beings were innately good but corruptible by society's influence.

meta: a prefix, from the Greek meaning "beyond," or "after."

metanoesis (Japanese *zangendo*): the need to go beyond reason and intuition, as well as traditional metaphysical speculation.

metaphysics: a branch of philosophy that investigates matters that transcend physics or any of the sciences.

morotomo: to be together with; a relational indicator.

mysticism: a religious path found in nearly every religious tradition which claims an extra-rational ability to grasp the oneness of all things experientially or intuitively.

nakama: a system of relations guiding human association.

Nembutsu: the Shin Buddhist practice of faithfully repeating the name "Amida Buddha."

Neo-Platonism: a mystical and religious school of philosophy that developed in the third century CE. Plotinus, the founder, reinterpreted the teachings of Plato.

nihilism: the position that there are no universal truths, that existence is meaningless, and that moral terms are without foundation.

nihility: the state of nonexistence; relative nothingness; the void; the abyss.

nin: human being or person.

ningen: human being as both individual and social being, including the betweenness between persons.

nirvana: perfect peace and lucidity; the state of mind free of craving or grasping. Literally, the "blowing out" of the fires of greed, hatred, and delusion.

no-mindedness (*mushin*): a psychological state not occupied by thought or emotion; a state in which the ego-self, the ordinary everyday mind, gives way to a "mind of no mind" that is open to everything, but not dominated by anything.

noesis: thinking, reasoning, intuition.

nondualism: the view that reality is actually one (not composed of separate entities), that the usual dualisms of mind/body, good/evil, self/other, active/passive are superficial judgments of convenience. Nondual reality is emptiness, nothingness.

non-mysticism: Zen and Nishida share many of the characteristics of mysticism, yet they claim not to be examples of mysticism. Non-mysticism (a term coined by Ueda Shizuteru) is the position that both Zen and Nishida go beyond mysticism while still carrying elements of mysticism in this "going beyond."

nothingness: absolute nothingness is beyond all description, open to pure experience for some, and yet, while it is distinctionless, it is that from which all distinctions arise. It is the undifferentiated origin of all things. Relative nothingness is nihility.

on: obligation, e.g., to one's teacher.

oneness: Nishida and the mystics share a common belief in, and experience of, the oneness of all things.

ōsō-ekō: "going to" the Pure Land.

overman (German: *übermensch*): Friedrich Nietzsche (1844–1900) posited a "superman" who overcomes the superstitions, beliefs, and values of tradition, while creating new values to live by.

oyakudachi: being of mutual assistance, doing what is useful for others, putting yourself in the other's shoes, doing work of value to others.

panentheism: the view that God is both the world as experienced and, at one and the same time, transcendent of it. The idea that the divine interpenetrates every part of existence and yet is transcendent of it.

pantheism: literally, "all is God;" the view that God is the totality of existence.

phenomenology: a philosophy founded by Edmund Husserl (1859–1938); a systematic reflection on the structures of consciousness and the *phenomena* that are present to it.

pour-soi (French): describes beings that have feelings and the freedom of choice; unlike rocks, for example, which simply are what they are.

Pure Land Buddhism (or **Pure Land School**): See **Shin Buddhism**.

radical empiricism: a philosophical position put forward by the pragmatist William James (1842–1910). Only things that are discernable through sensory experience are worthy of examination.

repetition: a notion found in the writings of S. Kierkegaard (1813–1855) and F. Nietzsche (1844–1900.) Nietzsche asked if what one has done and is doing in one's life would be worthwhile if every detail of one's life were to be repeated an infinite number of times. It is a test of the worth of one's life and activities.

ri: reason, principle; the principle for the rational ordering of human relations.

rin: fellows, company.

rinri: ethics.

rinrigaku: ethics, moral philosophy; the principles that allow us to live in a friendly community.

Rinzai: possibly the best known school of Zen Buddhism in the west. The primary training tool is meditation on a *kōan* (teaching stories that appear to be unsolvable puzzles), and the emphasis tends to be on sudden enlightenment.

sakoku: locked or chained country.

samsara: this ordinary world, as contrasted with *nirvāna* or seeing the world through enlightened eyes. It designates the empirical, phenomenal world; in Buddhist terms, the cycle of birth and death.

satori: illumination, enlightenment.

self-contradictory: Nishida held that a fuller account of some aspect of human awareness leads to an "identity of self-contradiction": for example, human life is not just living, for it is also the case that we die (a little) each day—we move one step closer to death. Similarly, we die by living each day. We perceive reality self-contradictorily, and yet also as one ("the identity of self-contradiction").

sesshin: "a gathering of the mind;" a period of intensive Zen meditation, typically lasting one to seven days.

Shingon: a major school of Japanese (esoteric) Buddhism developed by Kōkai (774–835), emphasizing direct experience of enlightenment and Buddhahood; a mystical tradition.

Shinran (1173–1262): founder of Shin Buddhism (Jōdo Shinshō in Japanese).

Shintōism: the indigenous religion of Japan; contributes significantly to the uniqueness of the Japanese culture," with its emphasis on appropriate behavior and personal values.

soku hi: "is and is not." "*Hi*" is a negative particle; one affirms by negating. Joins contradictories, e.g., *nirvana* is *samsara, samsara* is *nirvana*.

Sōtō: a Zen school typically focusing on *zazen* or seated meditation as its primary teaching method. *Sōtō* Zen teaches that the purpose of meditation is not some distant *satori*, but rather that *satori* is the very act of meditating, as are all other acts undertaken mindfully. Enlightenment is not a single great event but the sustained choice to follow the path of meditation and practice.

suchness: the essential nature of reality; the true mode of the being of things.

Śūnyatā: emptiness, nothingness. Metaphorically said to be "sky-like"; an all-encompassing cosmic sky.

tabula rasa: a blank sheet. The view that human beings enter the world without innate predispositions or ideas.

tariki: Other-power. Tanabe taught that salvation was possible only through the mediation of Other-power. (See *jiriki*).

Tendai **Buddhism:** a school of Buddhism originating in China teaching that Buddhahood is innate in all things.

topos: a Greek word, adopted by Nishida to mean place or locus.

transcendent: not immanent, separate from the world. A transcendent god is to be found in a separate realm apart from created things.

übermensch: Nietzsche postulated a superman who would "overcome" the values, traditions, and beliefs of his society, creating a new worldview not dependent on God.

Vedanta: a philosophy found in the ancient Vedas of India. Its basic teaching is that our real nature is divine; God or Brahman exists in every living being.

wa: harmony, especially group harmony.

zange: repentance, confession.

zangendo: metanoetics. A transcending of metaphysical philosophy usually based on reason or intellectual intuition.

Notes

Introduction

1. In the seventh century, Prince Shōtoku, Vice-Regent of the Empress Suiko, wrote the Seventeen Article Constitution in AD 604, the first political document in Japanese history. Shōtoku, who was the most responsible for the early unification of Japan, emphasized in this Constitution the importance of group harmony and consensus in settling disagreements and in reaching agreement in policy decisions. The text of Shōtoku's Constitution can be found in Wm. Theodore de Bary, ed., *Sources of Japanese Tradition,* vol. 1, comp. Tsunoda Ryusaku, Wm. Theodore de Bary, and Donald Keene (New York: Columbia University Press, 1958), 34–37.

2. "I think that we can distinguish the West to have considered being as the ground of reality, the East to have taken nothingness as its ground. I will call them reality as form and reality as the formless, respectively." Nishida Kitarō, "The Forms of Culture of the Classical Periods of East and West Seen from a Metaphysical Perspective," the final essay in his *Fundamental Problems of Philosophy: The World of Action and the Dialectical World,* trans. David A. Dilworth (Tokyo: Sophia University Press, 1970), 237.

3. James W. Heisig, *The Philosophers of Nothingness: An Essay on the Kyoto School* (Honolulu: University of Hawai'i Press, 2001), 3.

4. Ibid., 9.

5. Bret W. Davis, "Provocative Ambivalences in Japanese Philosophy of Religion," in *Japanese Philosophy Abroad,* ed. James W. Heisig (Nagoya, Japan: Nanzan Institute for Religion and Culture, 2004), 266–67.

6. Ibid., 267.

7. Heisig, *Philosophers of Nothingness,* 9. See also James W. Heisig, "The Religious Philosophy of the Kyoto School—An Overview," *Japanese Journal of Religious Studies* 17, no. 1 (1990): 57.

8. Ibid., 276.

9. Bret W. Davis, *Stanford Encyclopedia of Philosophy* (http://plato.
stanford.edu./entries/kyoto-school/) (Feb. 27, 2006, section 2.2.

10. Ibid., sec. 2.3. While it is true that most scholars either omit
Watsuji from Kyoto school membership, it is interesting that one Japa-
nese scholar of the Kyoto school, Shibayama Futoshi, not only includes
Watsuji in the membership of the school, but actually refers to him
as "a most preeminent member of the school" (in "Coping with the
Anglo-American World Order: Japanese Intellectuals and the Cultural
Crisis of 1913–1953." PhD dissertation, Yale University (Ann Arbor:
University Microfilms, 1994). Quoted in Heisig, *Philosophers of Nothing-
ness,* 276–77.

11. Heisig, *Philosophers of Nothingness,* 14.

12. Ibid.

13. Davis, *Stanford,* sec. 2.2.

Chapter 1. Nishida Kitarō

1. James W. Heisig, "The Religious Philosophy of the Kyoto
School—An Overview," *Japanese Journal of Religious Studies* 17, no. 1
(1990): 57.

2. Michiko Yusa, *Zen and Philosophy: An Intellectual Biography of
Nishida Kitar* (Honolulu: University of Hawai'i Press, 2002), xix.

3. Noda Matao, *Tetsugaku no mittsu no dentō* [*Three Philosophical
Traditions*], (Tokyo: Kinokuniya, 1984). Cited in Heisig, "The Religious
Philosophy": 57.

4. Yusa, *Zen and Philosophy,* 60.

5. Ibid., 62.

6. Ibid., 96.

7. *Sourcebook for Modern Japanese Philosophy: Selected Documents,*
trans. and ed. by David A. Dilworth, Valdo H. Viglielmo, with Augustin
Jacinto Zavela (Westport, CT: Greenwood Press, 1998), 2.

8. Yusa, *Zen and Philosophy,* 72.

9. Joel W. Krueger, "The Varieties of Pure Experience: William
James and Kitarō Nishida on Consciousness and Embodiment," in *William James Studies* 1, no. 1 (William James Society, 08/10/2011, published
online): 3.

10. William James, *Some Problems of Philosophy* (London/New York/Toronto: Longmans, Green, 1948), 50.

11. Edward C. Moore, *William James* (New York: Washington Square Press,1966), 164–65.

12. Nishida, *Inquiry,* 9.

13. Krueger, "The Varieties," 12.

14. William James, *Essays in Radical Empiricism* (Cambridge: Harvard University Press, 1976), 46.

15. Yusa, *Zen and Philosophy,* 97.

16. Nishida Kitarō, *An Inquiry into the Good,* trans. Abe Masao and Christopher Ives (New Haven and London: Yale University Press, 1990), 3.

17. Nishitani Keiji, *Nishida Kitarō,* trans. Yamamoto Seisaku and James W. Heisig (Berkeley: University of California Press, 1991), 96.

18. Ibid., 98.

19. Robert Aitken, *A Zen Wave: Bashō's Haiku and Zen* (New York and Tokyo: Weatherhill, 1978), 25. There are thirty or more English translations of this beautiful *haiku* poem, many of them with commentaries. Another of Aitken's books, *The Morning Star* (Washington, DC: Shoemaker and Hoard, 2003), 87 . . . 91. Or Takeuchi Yoshinori, "The Philosophy of Nishida," in *The Buddha Eye: An Anthology of the Kyoto School,* ed. Frederick Franck (New York: Crossroads, 1982), 185–90. Or Thomas Hoover's *Zen Culture* (New York: Vintage Books, 1978), 199–211. Hoover provides a full chapter on *haiku.*

20. Nishida, *Inquiry,* 3–4.

21. Ibid., 6.

22. Ibid., 7. In an essay, "Goethe's Metaphysical Background," in *Nishida Kitarō: Intelligibility and the Philosophy of Nothingness,* trans. Robert Schinzinger (Westport, CT: Greenwood Press, 1958), 151, Nishida writes, "It needs no saying, that poetry is originally and essentially a product of intuition, and that intuition is the essence of the poet. This is especially true of Goethe. To him, all being becomes the object of intuition."

23. Nishida, *Inquiry,* 8.

24. Ibid., 9.

25. Nishitani, *Nishida,* 98.

26. Ibid., 107. See Nishida, *Inquiry,* 56 for Abe's and Ives's translation of this passage.

27. Nishitani, *Nishida*, 107.

28. Nishida, *Inquiry*, xiv. From Abe Masao's Introduction.

29. Ibid., 19.

30. Ibid., 44.

31. Ibid.

32. Ibid., 49.

33. Ibid., 54.

34. Ibid., xvii. From Abe Masao's Introduction.

35. Ibid., 38.

36. Ibid., 43.

37. Ibid.

38. Nishitani, *Nishida*, 116.

39. Thomas P. Kasulis, *Zen Action/Zen Person* (Honolulu: University of Hawai'i Press, 1981), 71–77. Kasulis, following Zen Master Dōgen, contrasts thinking, not-thinking, and without thinking: "thinking includes most of what we typically regard as consciousness . . . the object of not-thinking's intentionality is thinking . . . itself . . . without-thinking . . . neither affirms nor denies, accepts nor rejects, believes nor disbelieves" (73–75). Like Nishida's "pure experience," without-thinking provides the "raw material" out of which thinking, reflecting, and judging develop.

40. Nishida, *Inquiry*, 158–61.

41. Ibid., 159.

42. Ibid., 161.

43. Ibid., 164, 175.

44. de Bary, Tsunoda, and Keene, *Sources of Japanese Tradition*, vol. 1, 362.

45. Ibid.

46. Nishida, *Inquiry*, 77.

47. Ibid., 175.

48. Part of a discussion Robert Carter had with Masuno Shunmyo at his Sōtō Zen temple, Kenkoh-ji, in Yokohama, Japan. The lengthy discussion took place in October 2003, when Prof. Carter was researching his book, *The Japanese Arts and Self-Cultivation* (Albany: State University of New York Press, 2008). Passages without footnotes to follow are all from this conversation.

49. Nishitani Keiji, *Contemporary Problems and Religion*, trans. Yamamoto Seisaku and Morris Augustine (in preparation), 66–67.

50. Ibid.

51. Nishitani Keiji, *Religion and Nothingness,* trans. Jan Van Bragt (Berkeley/Los Angeles/London: University of California Press, 1982), 102.

52. Ibid., 164.

53. Masuno Shunmyo, "Landscapes in the Spirit of Zen: A Collection of the Work of Masuno Shunmyo," *Process Architecture,* Special Issue 7 (1995): 10.

54. Heisig, *Philosophers of Nothingness,* 46. Heisig takes this phrase from Nishida's writings–no specific reference is given.

55. Nishida, *Inquiry,* 75–76.

56. Ibid., 82.

57. "An Interview with D. T. Suzuki," by Huston Smith (NBC 1958).

58. Nishitani, *Nishida,* 116.

59. Ibid., 110.

60. Nishida, "The Forms of Culture," 237.

61. D. T. Suzuki and Ueda Shizuteru, "The Sayings of Rinzai," *The Eastern Buddhist* 1, no. 1 (May 1973): 93.

62. Nishida Kitarō, *Last Writings: Nothingness and the Religious Worldview,* trans. David Dilworth (Honolulu: University of Hawai'i Press, 1987), 47.

63. Nishida, *Inquiry,* 81.

64. This passage is Nishitani Keiji's translation of Nishida in his study of *Nishida* previously cited, 146. In the Abe and Ives translation of the *Inquiry,* it is found on p. 81.

65. Nishitani, *Nishida,* 146.

66. "I beg of God that he make me rid of God," and "I flee from God for the sake of God," Nishitani, *Religion and Nothingness,* 64. The discussion of these ideas can be found in Meister Eckhart, *Sermon 15,* various editions.

67. Nishida, *Inquiry,* 164–65.

68. Ibid., 158.

69. From a conversation with Dr. Sen, Kyoto, Japan, at the Urasenke Foundation Headquarters, September 2003. Dr. Sen recalled that as a boy, his father used to tell him that one must continue to practice tea even after one dies. "I found this incomprehensible at the time, and thought my father a little strange. But now I understand the truth of what my father taught me [after fifty years of continual practice]. The Way of Tea is never ending."

70. James, *Essays in Radical Empiricism,* 4.

71. Nishida Kitarō, "The Intelligible World," in *Intelligibility and the Philosophy of Nothingness: Three Philosophical Essays*, trans. Robert Schinzinger. (Westport, CT: Greenwood Press, 1958), 131–32. In his "glossary," Schinzinger defines and describes "lining" as follows: "The Japanese kimono has a precious silk lining which shows at the ends. So the lining envelops, in a way, the kimono. N.[ishida] uses this word 'lining' to indicate the progress from the natural world to the psychological world and finally to the intelligible world. The higher sphere is like an enveloping lining of the lower sphere. The natural world is 'lined' with the world of psychology, and this conscious world is again lined with the intelligible world. The innermost 'lining' is the all-enveloping Nothingness" (248).

72. From a letter written by Nishida to a "colleague" and member of Nishida's "inner circle," Mutai Risaku, on Dec. 21, 1944, and translated under my direction by Tom Hino (from *Collected Works*, vol. 19 (2nd ed.), 367–68.

73. Nishida, *Inquiry*, 163.

74. Ibid., 164.

75. Ibid., 169.

76. Nishida, *Last Writings*, 76. "This is another aspect of Cusanus' infinite sphere of God in which, because there is no circumference, every point is the center. The world of the absolute present is a bottomlessly contradictory sphere that reflects itself within itself." Cusanus, or Nicholas of Kues (or Cusa) (1401–1464) was a Roman Catholic Cardinal, philosopher, jurist, mathematician, and astronomer. His spiritual or mystical writings still command respect.

77. Ibid.

78. Evil results from a partial understanding of our nature and the inability to grasp our relationship to others and to the universe at large.

79. Nishida, *Inquiry*, 104.

80. Ibid., 91.

81. Ibid., 122.

82. Ibid., 123.

83. Ibid., 124.

84. Ibid., 125.

85. Ibid., 130.

86. Ibid., 131.

87. Ibid., 132.

88. Ibid.

89. Ibid., 133.

90. Ibid., 135.
91. Ibid., 137.
92. Ibid., 138.
93. George Bosworth Burch, "Respect for Things," *Aryan Path* 31, no. 2 (Nov. 1960): 484.
94. Nishida, *Inquiry,* 141.
95. Ibid.
96. Ibid., 143.
97. Ibid., 145.
98. Ibid.
99. Nishida, *Last Writings,* 75.
100. Ibid.
101. Ibid., 74.
102. Ibid., 75.
103. Ibid., 78.
104. Ibid.
105. Nishida, *Last Writings,* 112.
106 Nishida, *Inquiry,* 81; italics mine.
107. Ibid.
108. Daisetz T. Suzuki, "An Interpretation of Zen Experience," in *The Japanese Mind: Essentials of Japanese Philosophy and Culture,* ed. Charles A. Moore (Honolulu: University of Hawai'i Press, 1967), 133.
109. Quoted in Nishitani, *Religion and Nothingness,* 64.
110. Ibid.
111. Ueda Shizuteru, "Meister Eckhart and Zen," *Journal of the Japan Society for Buddhist-Christian Studies* 4 (2005): 28.
112. Bret W. Davis, "Letting Go of God for Nothing: Ueda Shizuteru's Non-Mysticism and the Question of Ethics in Zen Buddhism," in *Frontiers of Japanese Philosophy 2,* ed. Victor Sōgen Hori and Melissa Anne-Marie Curley (Kyoto: Nanzan Institute for Religion and Culture, 2008), 223, n. 5.
113. Ibid., 223.

Chapter 2. Tanabe Hajime

1. James W. Heisig, *The Philosophers of Nothingness* (Honolulu: University of Hawai'i Press, 2001), 108.
2. Ibid., 109.

3. Ibid.

4. David A. Dilworth and Valdo H. Viglielmo, with Agustin Jacinto Zavala, trans. and eds., *Sourcebook for Modern Japanese Philosophy: Selected Documents* (Westport, CT: Greenwood Press, 1998), 98.

5. James W. Heisig and John Maraldo, eds., *Rude Awakenings: Zen, the Kyoto School, and the Question of Nationalism* (Honolulu: University of Hawai'i Press, 1995), 256.

6. Tanabe Hajime, *Philosophy as Metanoetics,* trans. Takeuchi Yoshinori, with Valdo Viglielmo and James W. Heisig (Berkeley, Los Angeles, London: University of California Press), L.

7. Ibid.

8. Ibid., LI.

9. Nishida Kitarō, *An Inquiry into the Good,* trans. Abe Masao and Christopher Ives (New Haven and London: Yale University Press, 1990), 176.

10. Ibid., 175.

11. Ibid., 176.

12. Tanabe, *Metanoetics,* LI.

13. Ibid.

14. Ibid., 221.

15. Ibid., 42.

16. Ibid., 4.

17. Ibid., 2.

18. Ibid., 3.

19. Ibid., 233.

20. Ibid., 234.

21. Ibid., 235.

22. Heisig, *Philosophers of Nothingness,* 116.

23. Ibid., 118.

24. Tanabe Hajime, in *Collected Works of Tanabe Hajime,* Vol.2 (Tokyo: Chicumo Shobō, 1964), 238. Quoted in Hase Shōtō, "The Structure of Faith: Nothingness-*qua*-Love," in *The Religious Philosophy of Tanabe Hajime,* ed. Taitetsu Unno and James W. Heisig (Berkeley: Asian Humanities Press, 1990), 98.

25. Tanabe, *Metanoetics,* 158.

26. James Fredericks, "Metanoetics: An Analysis," in *The Religious Philosophy of Tanabe Hajime,* ed. Taitetsu Unno and James W. Heisig (Berkeley: Asian Humanities Press, 1990), 57.

27. James W. Heisig, from an e-mail to Robert Carter, October 3, 2009.

28. Ibid.

29. James W. Heisig, "Tanabe's Logic of the Specific and the Critique of the Global Village," in *The Eastern Buddhist* 28, no. 2 (Autumn 1995):. 202. Available on the net at www.Nanzan-u.ac.jp/˜heisig/pdf/Tanabe-global.pdf, 4.

30. Ibid., 5: From Tanabe's "The Dialectic of the Logic of Species," in *The Collected Works of Tanabe Hajime,* Vol. 7, 261–62. Traditional two-value logic, the logic that most of us are familiar with, rests on two fundamental laws or principles. The law of identity simply states that a thing is what it is: that A = A. In an argument or discussion, nothing can be justifiably concluded if the meaning of terms is unstable and keeps shifting: "I think apples are the best fruit." "But I prefer pears." "Sure, but I mean by apples, pears."

The law of non-contradiction states that a thing either is an "X" or it is not an "X," but it cannot be both at the same time and in the same respect, for that would be a blatant contradiction. Nishida and Zen repeatedly break this law. The Zen formula, A is A, A is not-A, therefore A is A, is a famous example. However, some would argue that this formulation does not actually violate the law of non-contradiction. "First I see mountains; then I see that there are no mountains; then I see mountains again," makes perfect sense from a Buddhist perspective. We do see mountains, but at a higher level of understanding we know that they are impermanent, in flux, and are nothing. As expressions or manifestations of absolute nothingness they are really not mountains, but are empty. Given that background, then, when I look at mountains I see that they are mountains in the everyday sense, yet at another level they are not mountains at all, but are nothingness, yet because I am able to comprehend mountains in both senses, then they are now not just mountains, but are mountains! We might more precisely rewrite the formula as A = A, and A = not-A, therefore A = A! The exclamation point indicates that the final A = A is a transformed sense of "mountains." In much the same way, a physicist might say that a table is not really a (solid) object but is made of atomic particles moving at high speeds with incredibly huge spaces between them. The table is really not a table, but high-speed atoms in a spacious environment, but taking the two views together, the table is a table! for the educated mind that is aware of both senses of "table."

31. Ibid., 6.

32. James W. Heisig, *The Philosophers of Nothingness: An Essay on the Kyoto School* (Honolulu: University of Hawai'i Press, 2001), 124.

33. Nakamura Hajime, *Ways of Thinking of Eastern Peoples: India-China-Tibet-Japan,* trans. Philip P. Weiner (Honolulu: East-West Center Press [now University of Hawai'i Press], 1964), 521.

34. Ibid.

35. Heisig, "Global Village," 8. Heisig cites this as a passage from Tanabe's "A Logic of Social Existence," 6:166.

36. Ibid.

37. Ibid., 9. Heisig again cites this as a passage from Tanabe's "A Logic of Social Existence," *The Collected Works of Tanabe Hajime,* Vol. 6:155.

38. Tanabe, *Metanoetics,* 4.

39. Ibid.

40. Ibid., 5.

41. Ibid., 37.

42. Ibid., 18.

43. Ibid., 28.

44. Ibid.

45. Ibid., 30–31.

46. Ibid., 25.

47. Ibid., 120.

48. Ibid., 120–21.

49. Ibid.

50. Ibid., 152.

51. Ibid., p. 164.

52. Ibid., 158–59.

53. Ibid., 159.

54. Ibid., 171.

55. Ibid., 172.

56. Ibid.

57. Ibid., 190.

58. Ibid., 290.

59. Ibid., 291.

60. Ibid., 292.

61. Francisco J. Varela, *Ethical Know-How: Action, Wisdom, and Cognition* (Stanford: Stanford University Press, 1999), 73–75.

Chapter 3. Nishitani Keiji

1. Nietzsche "announced" the death of God in *The Gay Science* (in the fifth book, entitled "We Fearless Ones," first aphorism). It reads, "The greatest recent event—that 'God is dead,' that belief in the Christian God has become unbelievable—is already beginning to cast its first shadow over Europe."

2. James W. Heisig, *Philosophers of Nothingness: An Essay on the Kyoto School* (Honolulu: University of Hawai'i Press, 2001), 191.

3. Ibid., 183.

4. Ibid., 184.

5. Ibid., 185.

6. Ibid.

7. Ibid.

8. Nishitani Keiji, "Encounter with Emptiness: A Message from Nishitani Keiji," in *The Religious Philosophy of Nishitani Keiji*, ed. Taitetsu Unno (Nagoya, Japan: Nanzan Institute for Religion and Culture, 1989), 1.

9. Ibid., 2.

10. Heisig, *Philosophers of Nothingness*, 215. Heisig translates a recollection by Nishitani on his earlier work on nihilism: "I am convinced that the problem of nihilism lies at the root of the mutual aversion of religion and science. And it was this that gave my philosophical engagement its starting point. . . . The fundamental problem of my life . . . has always been . . . the overcoming of nihilism through nihilism."

11. Nishitani Keiji, *The Self-Overcoming of Nihilism*, trans. Graham Parkes with Setsuko Aihara (Albany: State University of New York Press, 1990).

12. Ibid. 32.

13. Ibid., 29–68.

14. Nishitani Keiji, *Religion and Nothingness*, trans. Jan Van Bragt (Berkeley/LosAngeles/London: University of California Press, 1982), 4.

15. Ibid., 3.

16. Ibid., 5.

17. Ibid., 4–5.

18. Suzuki Daisetz Teitaro, *Essays in Zen Buddhism*, First Series (London: Rider, 1949), 372.

19. Ueda Shizuteru, "Emptiness and Fullness: Śūnyatā in Mahāyāna Buddhism," *Eastern Buddhist* XV, no. 1 (Spring 1982): 19.

20. Ibid.

21. Suzuki Daisetz Teitaro, *Manual of Zen Buddhism* (London: Rider, 1956), 134.

22. Aristotle, *The Basic Works of Aristotle*, ed. with an intro. by Richard McKeon (New York: Random House, 1941), 732 ("Metaphysics," bk. 4, ch. 2 [1003]).

23. Ueda Shizuteru, "Contributions to Dialogue with the Kyoto School," in *Japanese and Continental Philosophy: Conversations with the Kyoto School*, ed. Bret W. Davis, Brian Schroeder, and Jason M. Wirth (Bloomington: Indiana University Press, 2011), 23.

24. Ibid., 24.

25. Ibid., 25.

26. Ibid., 26.

27. Ibid., 27.

28. Ibid.

29. Ibid.

30. Ibid., 28.

31. Nishitani, *Religion and Nothingness*, 17–18.

32. Ibid., 90.

33. Ibid., 5. Nishitani clarifies his use of "realize" to include both "actualize" and "understand." He continues, "I am using the word to indicate that our ability to perceive reality means that reality realizes (actualizes) itself in us; that this in turn is the only way that we can realize (appropriate through understanding) the fact that reality is also realizing itself in us; and that in so doing the self-realization of reality takes place" (5).

34. Robert E. Carter, *The Japanese Arts and Self-Cultivation* (Albany: State University of New York Press, 2008). An exploration of five of the many Japanese arts: *aikidō*, the Way of Tea, the Way of Flowers (*ikebana*), landscape gardening, and pottery. Similar expectations of the Japanese arts—that they can lead to enlightenment—can be found in Japanese calligraphy, *Noh* drama, *bunraku* puppetry, etc. Carter's book provides the philosophical background to these arts as pathways to enlightenment.

35. Taitetsu Unno, ed., *The Religious Philosophy of Nishitani Keiji* (Berkeley: Asian Humanities Press, 1989), 311.

36. Nishitani, *Religion and Nothingness*, 121.

37. Ibid., 123.

38. Ibid., 124.

39. Ibid.

40. Abe Masao, "Nishitani's Challenge to Western Philosophy and Theology," in Unno, *The Religious Philosophy of Nishitani Keiji*, 24: "As the negation of the existence of things nihility stands in opposition to existence. This means that nihility is still taken as some 'thing' called nihility . . . a *relative nothingness*."

41. Nishitani, *Religion and Nothingness*, 125.

42. Abe, "Nishitani's Challenge," 32.

43. Nishitani, *Religion and Nothingness*, 128.

44. Ibid.

45. Ibid., 148.

46. Ibid.

47. "Dependent origination," sometimes referred to as "co-dependent origination," or "interdependent origination," is a key Buddhist concept that attempts to show that causation is a complex process which describes the arising of things without recourse to permanent notions of "substance" or "selves." For anything to come into existence and to remain in existence, a "chain of causes" must continue to support it. An example often used is that of fire. Fire requires (1) fuel, (2) oxygen, (3) dryness, (4) a source of ignition, etc. If any of these antecedent conditions is absent, or if any one of them ceases to exist, then the fire will go out. The entire universe is a vast collection of "causes," with every thing, living being, or human self dependent on a specific "bundle" of causes for its continued existence.

An excellent discussion of co-dependent origination is to be found in Abe Masao, "Non-Being and *Mu*—The Metaphysical Nature of Negativity in the East and the West," in Abe Masao, *Zen and Western Thought*, ed. William LaFleur (Honolulu: University of Hawai'i Press, 1985), 125–26: "That everything is impermanent, having no eternal selfhood (self-being) and no unchangeable substance, is one of the basic principles of Buddhism. That everything is dependent on something else, that nothing is independent and self-existing, is another basic Buddhist principle. This is termed *pratitya-samutpāda*, which can be translated as dependent origination, relationality, relational origination, or dependent co-arising. The realization that everything is impermanent and dependently originating must be applied to things not only *in* the universe but also *beyond* the universe."

48. Nishitani, *Religion and Nothingness*, 150.

49. Ibid., 164. Nishitani quotes from Musō Kokushi, also known as Musō Sōseki (1275–1351), a Zen Buddhist monk and teacher, calligrapher, poet, and landscape designer.

50. Nishitani, *Religion and Nothingness,* 156.
51. Ibid., 157.
52. Ibid., 163.
53. Nisitani Keiji, "The I-Thou Relation in Zen Buddhism," in *The Buddha Eye: An Anthology of the Kyoto School,* ed. Frederick Franck (New York: Crossroad, 1982), 47–60.
54. Ibid., 48. *The Blue Cliff Records* is an "old and well-known" collection of *kōans* still used to train Zen monks.
55. Nishitani, "The I-Thou Relation," 47–60.
56. Ibid., 56.
57. Ibid.
58. Nishitani, *Religion and Nothingness,* 275.
59. Ibid., 278.
60. Ibid.
61. Ibid., 281.
62. Ibid.

Chapter 4. Watsuji Tetsurō

1. Watsuji Tetsurō's *Shamon Dōgen* (*Purifying Zen: Watsuji's Shamon Dōgen*), trans. with commentary by Steve Bein (Honolulu: University of Hawai'i Press, 2011).
2. Watsuji Tetsurō, *Climate and Culture: A Philosophical Study,* trans. Geoffrey Bownas (Japan: The Hokuseido Press, Ministry of Education, 1961), 17.
3. Ibid., 1–2.
4. Ibid., 214.
5. Ibid., 142.
6. Ibid., 136.
7. Ibid., 138.
8. Ibid., 139.
9. Ibid.
10. Ibid., 145.
11. Ibid.
12. Ibid., 150–51.
13. Ibid., 153–55.
14. Ibid., 164.
15. Ibid., 166.

16. Ibid., 206.

17. Ibid., p. 191. For an introduction to the philosophy behind Japanese landscape gardens, see Robert E. Carter, *The Japanese Arts and Self-Cultivation* (Albany: State University of New York Press, 2008), chs. 1 and 3.

18. Watsuji, *Climate*, 204.

19. Yuasa Yasuo, "The Encounter of Modern Japanese Philosophy with Heidegger," in *Heidegger and Asian Thought*, ed. Graham Parkes (Honolulu: University of Hawai'i Press, 1987), 168.

20. Watsuji Tetsurō, *Watsuji Tetsurō's Rinrigaku*, tr. Yamamoto Seisaku and Robert E. Carter (Albany: State University of New York Press, 1996), 9.

21. Yuasa Yasuo, *The Body: Toward an Eastern Mind-Body Theory*, ed. T. P. Kasulis, trans. Nagatomo Shigenori and T. P. Kasulis (Albany: State University of New York Press, 1987), 148.

22. Watsuji, *Rinrigaku*, 9.

23. Ibid.

24. Ibid., 15: "[W]e Japanese have produced a distinctive conception of human being. According to it, *ningen* is the public and, at the same time, the individual human being living within it."

25. Ibid., 124.

26. Ibid.

27. Ibid., 231.

28. Ibid., 225.

29. Ibid.

30. Confucius, *Chung-yung* (*Doctrine of the Mean*), ch. 20, 8, trans. James Legge, in *The Confucian Classics*, 2nd ed. (Oxford: Clarendon Press), Vol. 1, 406.

31. Ibid., ch. 20, 18.

32. Genpei Ninomiya, "Ethical Backgrounds in Japan and Their Bearing upon the Rise of Social Consciousness in Japan," MA Thesis, University of Chicago, 1927, 56.

33. Watsuji Tetsurō, *Climate and Culture*, 148.

34. Watsuji, *Rinrigaku*, 225.

35. Yuasa Yasuo, *The Body*, 156.

36. Sallie B. King, "Egalitarian Philosophies in Sexist Institutions," *Journal of Feminist Studies in Religion* 4 (Spring 1988): 15. King explains, "One who is *makoto* or sincere is true to her or his total life situation: one is true to oneself by knowing one's true nature which is in a condition

of absolute spiritual purity and by expressing that spiritual purity in all of one's actions. One is true to the *kami*, similarly, by living in the condition of spiritual purity which is identical to theirs. One is true to one's neighbors by doing what is right for them, again on the basis of one's spiritual purity. The concept of *makoto* thus expresses a sense of a continuum of spiritual purity which embraces both the *kami* and human being. All beings—myself, other persons, and the *kami*—are harmonized at the level of spiritual purity. Moreover, the power of *makoto* to transform the self and the world is virtually unlimited."

37. Watsuji, *Rinrigaku*, 318.

38. Quoted in "Ricoh Family Values," by Simon Partner, *Impact* 21 (June 1997), 3.

39. Hamada Hiroshi, *Achieving "CS" Number One: Oyakudachi*, trans. Simon Partner (Tokyo: Ricoh Company, Limited, 1995), p. v.

40. Ibid., 48.

41. Ibid., 49.

42. Quoted in "Ricoh Family Values," by Simon Partner, 3.

43. William R. LaFleur, "Buddhist Emptiness in the Ethics and Aesthetics of Watsuji Tetsurō," *Religious Studies* 14: 237.

44. Watsuji, *Shamon Dōgen*, 91.

45. Erin McCarthy, *Ethics Embodied: Rethinking Selfhood through Continental, Japanese, and Feminist Philosophies* (Lanham, MD: Lexington Books/Rowman and Littlefield, 2011), 39.

46. Ibid., 146.

47. Ibid.

48. The best study of the pros and cons of the members of the Kyoto School as actively encouraging Japanese involvement in World War II, as well as a strident nationalism, is a volume edited by James W. Heisig and John C. Maraldo, *Rude Awakenings: Zen, the Kyoto School, and the Question of Nationalism* (Honolulu: University of Hawai'i Press, 1994). The essays included in this excellent volume genuinely struggle with the claim that the Kyoto School philosophers were either in support of the war, or intrinsically nationalistic in their thinking. The debate is genuine, and if a conclusion is reached it is that there is nothing in the essential thrust of their writings to suggest an intrinsic militarism, although some did clearly support Japan's actions. The issue of nationalism is even more complex, given that we, too, tend to be "nationalistic" in defense of our nation and sometimes exude an air of "superiority" in praise of our way of life. *Rude Awakenings* is a volume well worth reading.

Chapter 5. Conclusion

1. Nishida Kitarō, *An Inquiry into the Good,* trans. Abe Masao and Christopher Ives (New Haven and London: Yale University Press, 1990), 61.

2. Nishitani Keiji, *Nishida Kitarō,* trans. Yamamato Seisaku and James W. Heisig (Berkeley: University of California Press, 1991), 116.

3. Discussion of the "reversed eye" appears on p. 81 of Nishida's *Inquiry;* discussion of each of us being a part of one great spirit appears on p. 166 of the *Inquiry.*

4. Tanabe Hajime, *Philosophy as Metanoetics,* trans. Takeuchi Yoshinori, with Valdo Viglielmo and James W. Heisig (Berkeley, Los Angeles, London: University of California Press), 45.

5. Nishida, *Inquiry,* 176.

6. Yuasa Yasuo, *The Body: Toward an Eastern Mind-Body Theory,* ed. Thomas P. Kasulis, trans. Nagatomo Shigenori and Thomas P. Kasulis (Albany: State University of New York Press, 1987), 66. The passage from Nishida's *Inquiry* and quoted by Yuasa is his own translation. In the Abe and Ives translation of the *Inquiry,* the passage appears on p. 32, and reads as follows: "Intellectual intuition is just that which deepens and enlarges our state of pure experience; it is the manifestation of a great unity in the systematic development of consciousness. When a scholar achieves a new idea, the moral person a new motive, the artist a new ideal, the religious person a new awakening, such a unity is manifesting itself."

7. Quoted in Yuasa, *The Body,* but no reference is supplied.

8. Tanabe, *Metanoetics,* 46.

9. Ibid.

10. Ibid., 47.

11. Nishida, *Inquiry,* 176

12. Fung yu-lan, *A Short History of Chinese Philosophy,* ed. Derk Bodde (New York: The Free Press, 1948), 1: "Sometimes when the children were just beginning to learn the characters, they were given a sort of textbook to read. This was known as the "Three Characters Classic," and was so called because each sentence in the book consisted of three characters arranged so that when recited they produces a rhythmic effect, and thus helped the children to memorize them more easily. This book was in reality a primer, and the very first statement in it is that 'the nature of man is originally good.' "

13. Nishida, *Inquiry,* 142.

14. Ibid., p. 143.
15. Ibid., 144–45.
16. Ibid., 145.
17. Ibid., 122.
18. Ibid., 125.

Selected Bibliography

Readers should be aware that James W. Heisig, Thomas P. Kasulis, and John C. Maraldo, eds., *Japanese Philosophy: A Sourcebook* (Honolulu: University of Hawai'i Press, 2011) has just been published. It is a 1,341 page volume of newly translated and never before translated writings by Japanese philosophers, including an entire section on the Kyoto School philosophers (pp. 639–798).

Nishida Kitarō

Translations of Nishida's Writings

An Inquiry Into the Good. Trans. Masao Abe and Christopher Ives. New Haven: Yale University Press, 1990.

Art and Morality. Trans. D. A. Dilworth and V. H. Viglielmo. Honolulu: University Press of Hawai'i, 1973.

"An Explanation of Beauty." Trans. Steve Odin. *Monumenta Nipponica* 42 (1987): 211–17.

"The Form of Culture of the Classical Periods of East and West Seen from a Metaphysical Perspective." Trans. D. A. Dilworth. *Japanese Religions* 5, no. 4 (1969): 26–50.

Fundamental Problems of Philosophy: The World of Action and the Dialectical World. Trans. D. A. Dilworth. Tokyo: Sophia University, 1970.

Intelligibility and the Philosophy of Nothingness. Trans. R. Schinzinger. Tokyo: Maruzen 1958. Reprint. Westport, CT: Greenwood Press, 1973.

Intuition and Reflection in Self-Consciousness. Trans. V. H. Viglielmo, with Y. Takeuchi and J. S. O'Leary. Albany: State University of New York Press, 1970.

Last Writings: Nothingness and the Religious Worldview. Trans. D. A. Dilworth. Honolulu: University Press of Hawai'i, 1987.
"On the Doubt in Our Heart." Trans. J. Shore and F. Nagasawa. *The Eastern Buddhist* 17, no. 2 (1984): 7–11.
"The Problem of Japanese Culture." Trans. M. Abe and R. DeMartino. *Sources of Japanese Tradition,* vol. 2, ed. R. Tsunoda, W. T. de Bary, and D. Keene, 350–65. New York: Columbia University Press, 1958.

Studies About Nishida

Abe, Masao, and L. Brüll. "Kitarō Nishida Bibliography." *International Philosophical Quarterly* 28, no. 4 (1988): 373–81.
Axtell, G. S. "Comparative Dialectics: Nishida Kitarō's Logic of Place and Western Dialectical Thought." *Philosophy East and West* 41, no. 2 (1991): 163–84.
Carter, Robert E. *The Nothingness Beyond God: An Introduction to the Philosophy of Nishida Kitarō,* 2nd ed. New York: Paragon House, 1997.
———. "God and Nothingness." *Philosophy East and West* 59, no. 1 (January 2009): 1–21.
Knauth, L. "Life is Tragic—The Diary of Nishida Kitarō." *Monumenta Nipponica* 20, no. 3–4 (1967): 335–38.
Nishitani Keiji. *Nishida Kitarō.* Trans. Yamamoto Seisaku and James W. Heisig. Berkeley: (Nanzan Studies in Religion and Culture), University of California Press, 1991.
Takeuchi Yoshinori. "The Philosophy of Nishida." In *The Buddha Eye: An Anthology of the Kyoto School,* 179–202. New York: Crossroad, 1982.
Ueda Shizuteru. "The Difficulty of Understanding Nishida's Philosophy." *Eastern Buddhist* 28, no. 2 (Autumn 1995): 175–82.
Wargo, Robert J. J. *The Logic of Nothingness: A Study of Nishida Kitarō.* Honolulu: University of Hawai'i Press, 2005.
Yusa, Michiko. *Zen and Philosophy: An Intellectual Biography of Nishida Kitarō.* Honolulu: University of Hawai'i Press, 2002.
See the "Memorial Issue" for Nishida Kitarō, in *Eastern Buddhist* XXVIII, no. 2 (Autumn 1995).
See *Sourcebook for Modern Japanese Philosophy* (see main entry in "General Background" section) which contains five translated essays by Nishida.

Tanabe Hajime

Translations of Tanabe's Writings

"The Logic of the Species as Dialectics." Trans. D. A. Dilworth, Taira Sata. *Monumenta Nipponica* 24, no. 3 (1969): 273–88.

Philosophy as Metanoetics. Trans. Yoshinori Takeuchi, Valdo Viglielmo, and James W. Heisig. Berkeley: (Nanzan Studies in Religion and Culture), University of California Press, 1986.

See *Sourcebook for Modern Japanese Philosophy* (see main entry in "General Background" section), which contains three translated essays by Tanabe.

Studies About Tanabe

Heisig, James W. "Tanabe's Logic of the Specific and the Critique of the Global Village," *Eastern Buddhist* 28, no. 2 (Autumn 1995), 198–224.

Kiyozawa Manshi. "The Great Path of Absolute Other-Power." In *The Buddha Eye: An Anthology of the Kyoto School,* ed. Frederick Frank, 232–35. New York: Crossroad, 1982.

Ozaki, Makoto. *Individuum, Society, Humankind: The Triadic Logic of Species According to Hajime Tanabe.* Leiden: (Japanese Studies Library), Brill, 2001.

Suzuki Teitaro Daisetz. "Ápropos of Shin." In *The Buddha Eye: An Anthology of the Kyoto School,* ed. Frederick Frank, 211–20. New York: Crossroad, 1982.

Unno, Taitetsu, and James W. Heisig, eds. *The Religious Philosophy of Tanabe Hajime: The Metanoetic Imperative.* Freemont, CA: (Nanzan Studies in Religion and Culture), Asian Humanities Press, 1990.

Nishitani Keiji

Translations of Nishitani's Writings

On Buddhism. Trans. Yamamoto Seisaku and Robert E. Carter. Albany: State University of New York Press, 2006.

"The Personal and the Impersonal in Religion," Part 1, in *Eastern Buddhist* 3, no. 1 (1970): 1–18; Part 2, in vol. 3, no. 2 (1970): 71–88.

"Reflections on Two Addresses by Martin Heidegger." In *Heidegger and Asian Thought,* ed. Graham Parkes. Honolulu: University of Hawai'i Press, 1987.

Religion and Nothingness. Trans. Jan Van Bragt. Berkeley and Los Angeles: University of California Press, 1982.

"Science and Zen." In *The Buddha Eye: An Anthology of the Kyoto School,* ed. Frederick Franck, 111–37. New York: Crossroad, 1982.

The Self-Overcoming of Nihilism. Trans. Graham Parkes with Setsuko Aihara. Albany: State University of New York Press, 1990.

"The I-Thou Relation in Zen Buddhism." In *The Buddha Eye: An Anthology of the Kyoto School,* ed. Frederick Franck, 47–60. New York: Crossroad, 1982.

Studies About Nishitani

Dallmayr, Fred. "Nothingness and 'Sunyata': A Comparison of Heidegger and Nishitani." *Philosophy East and West* 42, no. 1: 37–48.

Horio Tsutomu. "Nishitani's Philosophy: The Later Period." *Zen Buddhism Today* 14: 19–32.

Maraldo, John C. "Emptiness, History, Accountability: A Critical Examination of Nishitani Keiji's Standpoint." *Zen Buddhism Today* 15: 97–118.

Marra, Michael. *Modern Japanese Aesthetics: A Reader* (chapter 8 deals with "The Kyoto School and Nishitani Keiji"). Honolulu: University of Hawaii Press, 1999.

Parkes, Graham. "Nietzsche and Nishitani on the Self-Overcoming of Nihilism." *International Studies in Philosophy* 25, no. 2: 51–60.

Unno, Taitetsu, ed. *The Religious Philosophy of Nishitani Keiji: Encounter With Emptiness.* Berkeley: Asian Humanities Press, 1989.

See the "In Memoriam" volume for Nishitani Keiji, *Eastern Buddhist* XXV. no. 1 (Spring 1992).

See *Sourcebook for Modern Japanese Philosophy* (see main entry in "General Background" section), which contains three translated essays by Nishitani.

Watsuji Tetsurō

Translations of Watsuji's Writings

Climate and Culture: A Philosophical Study. Trans. Geoffrey Bownas. Tokyo: Hokuseido Press, 1961. Reprinted by Greenwood Press, Westport, CT, 1988.

"Japanese Ethical Thought in the Noh Plays of the Muromachi Period." Trans. David A. Dilworth and Umeyo Hirano. *Monumenta Nipponica* 24 (December 1969): 457–98.

Purifying Zen: Watsuji Tetsurō's Shamon Dōgen. Trans. Steve Bein. Honolulu: University of Hawai'i Press, 2011.

Rinrigaku: Ethics in Japan. Trans. Yamamoto Seisaku and Robert E. Carter. Albany: State University of New York Press, 1996.

Studies About Watsuji

Bellah, Robert N. "Japan's Cultural Identity: Some Reflections on the Work of Watsuji Tetsurō." *The Journal of Asian Studies* 24, no. 4 (1965): 573–94.

Bernier, Bernard. "1942—National Communion: Watsuji Tetsurō's Conception of Ethics, Power, and the Japanese Imperial State." *Philosophy East and West* 56. No. 1 (January 2006): 84–105.

Couteau, Pauline. "Watsuji Tetsurō's Ethics of Milieu." In *Frontiers of Japanese Philosophy,* ed. James W. Heisig, 269–90. Nagoya, Japan: Nanzan Institute for Religion and Culture, 2006.

LaFleur, William R. "An Ethic of As-Is: State and Society in the *Rinrigaku* of Watsuji Tetsurō." In *La société civile face à l'État dans les traditions chinoise, japonaise, coréenne et vietnamienne,* ed. Léon Vandermeersch, 453–64. Paris: Études thématiques, 3 École française d'Extrême-Orient, 1994.

———. "Buddhist Emptiness in the Ethics and Aesthetics of Watsuji Tetsurō." *Religious Studies* 14 (1978): 237–50.

Mayeda, Graham. *Time, Space and Ethics in the Philosophy of Watsuji Tetsurō, Kuki Shōzō, and Martin Heidegger.* New York: Routledge, 2006.

McCarthy, Erin. *Ethics Embodied: Rethinking Selfhood through Continental, Japanese and Feminist Philosophies*. Lanham, MD: Rowman and Littlefield, 2010.

———. "Towards a Transitional Ethics of Care." In *Neglected Themes and Hidden Variations*, ed. Victor Sōgen Hori and Melissa Anne-Marie Curley, 113–28. Nagoya, Japan: Nanzan Institute for Religion and Culture, 2008.

Nagami Isamu. "The Ontological Foundations in Tetsurō Watsuji's Philosophy: *Kō* and Human Existence." *Philosophy East and West* 31, no. 3 (July 1981).

Odin, Steve. "The Social Self in Japanese Philosophy and American Pragmatism: A Comparative Study of Watsuji Tetsurō and George Herbert Mead." *Philosophy East and West* 42, no. 3 (July 1992): 475–501.

General Background

Abe Masao. *Zen and Western Thought*. Ed. William R. LaFleur. Honolulu: University of Hawai'i Press, 1985.

Carter, Robert E. *Encounter With Enlightenment: A Study of Japanese Ethics*. Albany: State University of New York Press, 2001.

———. *The Japanese Arts and Self-Cultivation*. Albany: State University of New York Press, 2008.

de Bary, Wm. Theodore, ed. Compiled by Tsunoda Tyusaku, Wm. Theodore de Bary, and Donald Keene. *Sources of Japanese Tradition*, vols. 1–2. New York: Columbia University Press, 1958.

Dilworth, David A., and Valdo H. Viglielmo, with Agustin Jacinto Zavala. *Sourcebook for Modern Japanese Philosophy: Selected Documents*. Westport, CT: Greenwood Press, 1998.

Frederick Franck, ed. *The Buddha Eye: An Anthology of the Kyoto School*. New York: Crossroad, 1982.

Hamada Hiroshi. *Achieving CS Number One: "Oyakudachi."* Trans. Simon Partner. Tokyo: Ricoh Company, 1995.

Heisig, James W. *Philosophers of Nothingness: An Essay on the Kyoto School*. Honolulu: University of Hawai'i Press, 2001.

———, and John Maraldo, eds. *Rude Awakenings: Zen, the Kyoto School, and the Question of Nationalism*. Honolulu: University of Hawai'i Press, 1995.

Herbert, Jean. *Shintō: At the Fountain-head of Japan*. London: George Allen and Unwin, 1967.

Ives, Christopher. *Zen Awakening and Society.* Honolulu: University of Hawai'i Press, 1992.

Kasulis, Thomas P. *Intimacy or Integrity: Philosophy and Cultural Difference.* Honolulu: University of Hawai'i Press, 2002.

———. *Zen Action/Zen Person.* Honolulu: The University of Hawai'i Press, 1981.

———. "The Kyoto School and the West: Review and Evaluation." *Eastern Buddhist* 15, no. 2 (1982): 125–44.

Loy, David. *Nonduality: A Study in Comparative Philosophy.* New Haven: Yale University Press, 1988.

Moore, Charles A., ed. *The Japanese Mind.* Honolulu: An East-West Center Book, The University Press of Hawai'i, 1967.

Odin, Steve. *The Social Self in Zen and American Pragmatism.* Albany: State University of New York Press, 1996.

Parkes, Graham, ed. *Heidegger and Asian Thought.* Honolulu: University of Hawai'i Press, 1987.

———, ed. *Nietzsche and Asian Thought.* Chicago: University of Chicago Press, 1991.

Picken, Stuart D. B. *Shintō: Japan's Spiritual Roots.* Tokyo and New York: Kodansha International, 1980.

Piovesana, Gino. *Recent Japanese Philosophical Thought: 1862–1962: A Survey.* Tokyo: Sophia University Press, 1968.

Suzuki Daisetz T. *The Awakening of Zen.* Ed. Christmas Humphreys. Boulder: Prajna Press, 1980.

———. *Zen and Japanese Culture.* Princeton: Princeton University Press, Bollingen Series LXIV, 1973.

Varela, Francisco J. *Ethical Know-How: Action, Wisdom, and Cognition.* Stanford: Stanford University Press, 1992.

Yuasa Yasuo. *The Body, Self-Cultivation, and Ki-Energy.* Trans. Shigenori Nagatomo and Monte S. Hull. Albany: State University of New York Press, 1993.

———. *The Body: Toward an Eastern Mind-Body Theory.* Ed. T. P. Kasulis. Trans. Nagatomo Shigenori and T. P. Kasulis. Albany: State University of New York Press, 1987.

The seven recent volumes from the Nanzan Institute for Religion and Culture dealing with the Kyoto School in particular, but also covering much of modern Japanese philosophy are as follows:

Japanese Philosophy Abroad. Ed. James W. Heisig. Nagoya: Nanzan Institute for Religion and Culture, 2004.

Frontiers of Japanese Philosophy. Ed. James W. Heisig. Nagoya: Nanzan Institute for Religion and Culture, 2006.

Neglected Themes and Hidden Variations: Frontiers of Japanese Philosophy 2. Ed. Victor Sōgen Hori and Melissa Anne-Marie Curley. Nagoya: Nanzan Institute for Religion and Culture, 2008.

Origins and Possibilities: Frontiers of Japanese Philosophy 3. Ed. James W. Heisig and Uehara Mayuko. Nagoya: Nanzan Institute for Religion and Culture, 2008.

Facing the 21ˢᵗ Century: Frontiers of Japanese Philosophy 4. Ed. Lam Wing-keung and Cheung Ching-yuen. Nagoya: Nanzan Institute for Religion and Culture, 2009.

Confluences and Cross-Currents: Frontiers of Japanese Philosophy 6. Ed. Raquel Bouso and James W. Heisig. Nagoya: Nanzan Institute for Religion and Culture, 2009.

Classical Japanese Philosophy: Frontiers of Japanese Philosophy 7. Ed. James W. Heisig and Rein Raud. Nagoya: Nanzan Institute for Religion and Culture, 2010.

Index

Abe Masao (1915–2006), 12, 91, 116, 195n40, 195n47, 199n6
absolute, the, 82, 86–87, 98. *See also* One, the; relative
  as absolute nothingness, 70–71
  divine manifestations of, 41
  and mediation, 74
  and negation, 55
  as self-contradictory, 45, 48–49
  union with, 54 (*see also* mysticism)
absolute affirmation. *See* affirmation
absolute emptiness. *See under* emptiness
absolute mediation. *See under* mediation
absolute nothingness. *See under* nothingness
action-faith, 61, 81–82
action-faith-witness, 81, 85, 175
action intuition, 28–29, 61, 158–60, 173
action of no-action, 82
Adam and Eve, 43, 46–47
adversarial, 141–42. *See also* consensus
affirmation, 115, 74
aidagara (betweenness), xxi, 125, 141–43, 173. *See also* betweenness

aikidō (way of harmony), 113, 131, 147, 173, 194n34. *See also* Japanese arts
aikidōka (student of *aikidō*), 147, 173
Allah, 39
Amida Buddha. *See under* Buddha
an sich (Ger, in-itself), 85, 173. See also *en-soi*; in-itself
analogies (fire, sword, eye, water). *See under* in-itself
Ancient Japanese Culture (Watsuji), 127
anicca (Pali: impermanence), 167. *See also* impermanence; *mujō*
Anselm of Canterbury (1033–1109), 7
antithesis, 56
Aquinas, Thomas (1225–1274), 7
artist vs scholar, 27
Aristotelian, 67
Aristotle (384–322 BCE), 49, 109, 127, 175
arrogance, 62–64, 68, 71–72, 80–83, 154, 162, 163. See also *hubris*
attachment, 123
attitudes, 132, 134, 138, 141, 144, 148, 152, 168. *See also* values

Augustine (354–430), 7
authentic existence, xiii

background, 59, 106, 114, 144,
    169. *See also* foreground
basho (place or field), 14, 25,
    58–59, 109, 173. *See also*
    Logic of *Basho*; *topos*
and betweenness, 140, 146
as deep self, 42
and kimono, 33
logic of, 45, 76
and Tanabe, 65, 81
three types, 38
Bashō (1644–1694), 23, 33, 116
be-ification, 114, 165
being, is emptiness, 114 (*see also*
    emptiness, is being)
and Western culture, 5 (*see also*
    nothingness, and Eastern
    cultures)
beings, 115, 122, 174, 179,
    198n36. *See also* things
and Being, xiii
being[s]-in-nothingness, 85–86
interconnection of, 88
and nothingness, 155, 161
original mode of, 165
relative, 74, 81–83
are Śūnyatā, 115
Being and Time (Heidegger), 13,
    132
Bein, Steve, 127
Bergson, Henri (1859–1941), xiii,
    20–21, 77, 93, 127, 174, 175
and duration, 20–21
and immediate experience, 20
and intuition, 20–21
Berkeley, George (1685–1753),
    25, 105

betweenness, xxi, 125, 135–38,
    140–47, 150, 152, 168–69,
    173, 178. *See also aidagara*;
    gen; *under* nothingness
Beyond Good and Evil (Nietzsche),
    131
Bhattacharya, K. C. (1875–1949),
    10
Bible, the, 92
Blue Cliff Records, The (ancient
    teachings), 121, 196n54
Bodhisattva (Buddhist saint),
    74–75, 174
body-mind, 150–51, 158–60,
    173. *See also under* oneness,
    of mind and body
Boehme, Jakob (1575–1624), 56
both/and logic, 45, 84, 136–37.
    See also either/or logic; nei-
    ther/nor logic; two-value logic
Bownes, Geoffrey, 129
Brahman, 181. *See also* God
Brentano, Franz, (1838–1917),
    127
Buber, Martin (1878–1965), 32
Buddha, 21, 39, 41, 49, 52, 61,
    70, 76, 85, 107, 135, 152,
    170
Amida, xv–xvi, 69, 72–73, 152,
    173, 177
becoming a, 85
-hood, 174, 180, 181
-nature, 41, 71, 84, 86, 88, 174
-self, 88, 164
*Buddha Eye: An Anthology of the
    Kyoto School, The* (Takeuchi),
    13
Buddhism, x, xi, xvii, 1, 5, 6, 10,
    97, 181. *See also* Kegon Bud-
    dhism; Shin

Buddhism; Shingon Buddhism;
   Tendai Buddhism; Zen
   Buddhism
   and attitudes, 168
   Chinese, 139
   and dependent origination, 74,
      87, 117, 195n47
   and emptiness, 112
   emptiness and Watsuji, 151,
      170
   and evil, 49
   and impermanence, 76, 135, 167
   influence on Japanese culture,
      127
   Japanese, and ethics, 121–24
   and the Kyoto philosophers, 9,
      11
   and Nishida, 13, 21
   and suffering, 104
bunraku (puppetry), 194n34
Burch, George B., 51, 54
Busse, Ludwig (1862–1907), 13
busshō (Buddha-nature), 41, 174.
   See also Buddha, nature
Byron (1788–1824), 126

calligraphy. See Japanese arts
Camus, Albert (1913–1960), 92
Carter, Robert E., ix–xi, xvi–xvii,
      186n48, 191n27, 194n34,
      197n17
carving out, 43
causation, 15, 195n47
centrifugal. See under evil
centripetal. See under good
Cézanne, Paul (1839–1906), 46
chadō (way of tea), 113, 174,
      187n69
ch'eng (Chinese: sincerity), 139.
   See also makoto; sincerity

Christianity, 38–39, 69, 96–97,
      126, 157
   collapse of, 96–97
circuminsessional interpenetration,
      117, 122, 166, 174. See also
      interpenetration
climate, 128–30, 132, 135, 141,
      143, 148, 167–68, 174, 175.
      See also fūdo
Climate and Culture: A Philosophi-
      cal Study (Watsuji), 128–29,
      132
co-dependent origination. See
      dependent origination
compassion, xv, 85, 120–24, 147.
      See also Great Compassion;
      love
   as concern, 88
   as expected, 142
   and the good, 170
   hindrances to, 89
   in the household, 167–68
   a model of, 174
   as natural, 162
   and the no-self, 145
   and Other-power, 151
   as selfless, 137, 150, 164
   as spontaneous, 144
   true meaning of, 166
   as a virtue, 139
confession, 67, 71–72, 80, 86–87
Confucianism, xvii, 1, 6, 138–41,
      151, 162, 174
Confucius (551–479 BCE), 139,
      174
Confucius (Watsuji), 128, 174
consciousness, xiii, 28, 35–36, 55,
      73, 159, 164–65
   apart from, 108
   background of, 103

consciousness *(continued)*
  cause of, 49
  contents of, 155
  cosmic, 38
  division of, 25
  everyday/ordinary, 46, 98,
    102–103, 112, 115, 118–19,
    164–65
  and experience, 22–23, 31, 49,
    105
  field of, 108, 111–12, 115
  God's, 30
  individualistic, 133
  internal demands of, 162
  nondual, 104
  object of, 156, 173
  objects in, 111
  organization of, 50
  phenomena of, 27, 29
  and phenomenology, 63
  as pure experience, 19
  reality as activity of, 34
  as removed from content, 42
  and self-consciousness, 47
  structure of, 179
  systematic development of, 199
  as thinking, 186
  transformation of, 6
  true, 74
  unity of, 39
consensus, 141–42, 146, 149,
    183n1. *See also* adversarial
"Coping with the Anglo-American
    World Order: Japanese Intel-
    lectuals and the Cultural Cri-
    sis of 1913–1953" (Futoshi),
    184n10
cosmic consciousness, 38, 156
creativity, 44, 53

Cusana. *See* Nicholas of Cusa
Cusanus. *See* Nicholas of Cusa

damnation, 96
dance. *See* Japanese arts
Daoism, xi, 5, 6, 139, 174
Darwin, Charles (1809–1882), 13
Dasein (being-in-the-world), 133,
    174
Davis, Bret W., on de-mysticism,
    10, 57, 166–67
de Bary, Wm. Theodore, 183n1
deep nature, 49, 53. *See also* deep
    self
deep personality, 51
deep self, the, 34, 103–105 (*see
    also* deep nature)
  as deep reality, 58
  identical with God, 37
  listening to, 52
  as pure experience, 38
  an undifferentiated place, 42
deeper self, 8, 49, 58, 98,
    102–103, 112
Dejima, (artificial island port) 1
delusion, xv–xvi, 49. *See also*
    self-deception
de-mysticism, 55, 57, 174. *See
    also* non-mysticism
dependent co-arising. *See* depen-
    dent origination
dependent origination, 74–75,
    117, 174, 176, 195n47.
    See also circuminsessional
    interpenetration
Descartes, René (1596–1650), 7,
    25, 29, 127
despair, 67–68, 84, 91, 95–96,
    98, 102, 110, 113, 164. *See*

also hopelessness; meaninglessness; nihilism
Dharma, the (law, teaching),
151–52
dialectic, xiv, 14, 45, 65, 73,
75–76, 136–37, 174,
191n30. *See also* Hegel; *soku
hi*; thesis-antithesis-synthesis
differentiation, 47
Dilthey, Emile, 127
direct experience, 34, 177, 180.
See also immediate experience;
intuition; pure experience
beyond words, 39
and internal necessity, 50
and intuition, 37
as pure, 27
as a standard of good conduct, 49
and unity, 35
distinctions, 29–30, 35–37, 47,
173, 178
conceptual, 7
foundational, 144
prior to all, 19–20, 169
of self and other things, 26–27
dō (way, path), 40–41, 113, 158,
174
Dōgen (1200–1253), xiv, xvii,
165, 186n39
on forgetting the self, 137
and Nishida, xii
and Watsuji, 127, 151–52
and without thinking, 30, 156
Dostoevsky, Fyodor (1821–1881),
92
double aperture, 44. *See also*
double vision
double negation. *See under*
negation

double vision, 107, 118. *See also*
double aperture
dualism/duality, 20, 27, 35, 59,
106, 135, 175, 178. *See also*
nondualism/nonduality; subject and object
of Creator and created, 38–39
and mysticism, 54–55
and non-duality, 137
of self and world, 108, 144–45
dual-nature, 135–37, 152. See
also dual structure
dual structure, 136, 143. See also
dual nature
duration, 20–21, 174
Durkheim, Émile (1858–1817), 127

Eckhart, Meister (1260–1328),
xiv, 47, 55–57, 93, 155, 175,
187n66
and the Godhead, 52, 56
and mysticism, 175
and nothingness, 109
prayed to be rid of God, 39
"Education Times," 16
"Egalitarian Philosophies in Sexist
Institutions" (King), 197n36
ego, xv–xvi, 7, 26, 34, 51, 57,
87–88, 158
as centrifugal motion, 49
-consciousness, 102
isolated, 48, 119, 134
-less, xv
-self, 50, 74, 88, 98, 112, 117,
120, 165, 169, 178
egoism, 51. *See also* individualism
either/or logic, 45, 76, 84, 136. *See
also* both/and logic; neither/
nor logic; two-value logic

élan vital (French: vital force or impulse), 21, 175
Embodied Ethics (McCarthy), 150
emotion, 42, 111, 132, 168
empiricism, 63
  radical, 18, 179
emptiness, 17, 169, 175, 176, 178, 181. See also *mu*; nothingness; Śūnyatā
  absolute, 114–15
  is being, 114. See also being, is emptiness
  and betweenness, 137, 144
  is form, 57, 107, 115. See also form, is emptiness
  and the ordinary world, 95
  and relationships, 146
  and relative and absolute nothingness, 114–16, 155
  and self, 120
  and self-realization, 112–14
  and Śūnyatā, 110, 165
  and the Ten Ox-herding Pictures, 104–106
  is things, 91, 115 (*see also* things, as empty)
  and Watsuji, 151, 170
en-soi (French: in-itself), 85, 175. See also *an sich*; in-itself
energetism, 49, 175
enlightened, awareness, 33, 59, 102, 106–107, 180
  becoming, 40–43, 165
  experience, 145
  person, 39, 45, 102, 106–107, 118, 120, 124, 173
  intuition, 158
  state, 160

enlightenment, 123, 174, 175, 176, 180, 194n34. See also *kenshō*; oneness; *satori*; Zen Buddhism
  attaining, 40–43
  and Dōgen, 151–52
  and empiricism, 18
  on the field of Śūnyatā, 113–14
  and History, 73
  in-itself, 85–86
  and intellectual intuition, 158
  and the Japanese arts, 31–32, 113, 132, 174, 176
  as oneness, 54, 56, 103
  and the oneness of all things, 39
  path to, 98–108, 120 (*see also* Ten Ox-herding Pictures)
  and personal transformation, 11, 53
  and pure experience, 19
  and Shinran, xv–xvi
  and stereoscopic vision, 45, 106
  sudden, 180
  and the Ten Ox-herding Pictures, 98, 102–105, 107, 120
  as transformative, 20 (*see also* self-cultivation; transformation)
entity, fixed, 42
  as a nonentity, 118
epistemology, 64–65, 125
estrangement, 49. See also separation
ethical action, 82, 88
ethics, 179. See also morality; *rinri*
  and absolute nothingness, 87–88

of becoming the other, 84, 121, 166
and body-mind, 150–51
as the central focus of philosophy, 78
and Confucianism, 139, 138–39
as effortless and spontaneous, 51
environmental, 166
and ethical action, 80
and evil, 46–53
and forgetting the self, 50
and interconnectedness (see under interconnectedness)
and metanoetics, 83, 86 (see also under metanoetics)
of naturalness, 83
and Nishida, 165–66
only route to true, 87
ordinary, 123–24
rational, 82
and religious transformation, 85
and relationships, 138, 144
selfless, 120–21, 123–25
social, 87
as the study of man, 134–35
the state as the culmination of, 152
and Watsuji, 127–28, 132–33, 151–52, 166–69
Ethics (Watsuji), 128, 133, See also *Rinrigaku*
Ethics as the Study of Man (Watsuji), 133
eudaimonia (Greek: goal of life as happiness), 49, 175
European nihilism. *See under* nihilism

everyday self. *See under* self
evil, xv, 47, 52, 82, 85, 97, 144, 154, 162, 178, 188n78. *See also* immorality
and arrogance, 83
as centrifugal motion, 48, 53
Christian perspective of, 96
as contrary to the demands of personality, 50
ethics and, 46
and the Garden of Eden, 43, 46
and human freedom (see freedom)
human nature as innately, 71–72, 83, 163 (see also under human nature)
origin of, 48
potential for, 161, 163, 169
as present in the good, 52
evolution, 42, 48, 53, 175
existentialism, xiii, 83, 94, 164
and being, 64
and existential choice, 108
and existential nihilism, 118
and in-itself, 85
existential predicament, 91–92, 102
experience, xiii
nondual, 40, 54
pure (*see* pure experience)
three types, 54

faith, 69, 85, 95, 151–52, 157
and the death of subjectivity, 61
and Nishida, 154
in Other-power, 62

faith *(continued)*
  power of, 160
  as release, 62
  and religion, 156
  resurrection of the self through, 69–70
family, Japanese, 131–32, 136, 139–41, 150, 152, 169. *See also* home
Fichte, Johann Gotlieb (1762– 1814), 65
filial piety, 131, 139–40. *See also* loyalty
finger, pointing at the moon, 36, 157
five obligations, the, 139. *See also* Confucianism; virtues, the
flow, 19–21, 27, 42, 76, 104, 107, 136
flower, becoming the, 25, 31, 33–34, 39, 59, 123, 165, 173
flower arranging. *See ikebana*; Japanese arts
for-itself, 87. See also *für sich*; *pour-soi*
foreground, 59, 106, 144, 169. *See also* background
form, is emptiness, 57, 107, 115 (*see also* emptiness, is form)
  is formless, 107, 118
  as reality, 36, 183n2
formless, the, xi, 36, 45, 47, 57–58, 107, 118, 124, 155, 157, 161, 183n2
  as form (*see under* form)
  as reality, 36, 183n2
  self, 58, 169

formlessness, 36, 45. *See also* nothingness
forms, and de-mysticism, 59
  differentiation of, 47
  of existence, 53
  and formless awareness, 42
  formlessness of, 58
  and personality, 50
  as self-expressions of the form- less, 45
"Forms of Culture of the Classi- cal Periods of East and West Seen from a Metaphysical Perspective, The" (Nishida), 183n2
Francis of Assisi, Saint (1182?– 1226), 92, 123
Fredericks, James, 61
freedom, 15, 74, 80, 85, 110, 175, 179
  and evil, 80
  and mediation, 83
  and Other-power, 80
Fundamental Problems of Philoso- phy: The World of Action and the Dialectical World (Nishida), 183n2
fūdo (climate), 129, 174, 175. *See also* climate
Fujita Masakatsu, 12
Fung yu-lan (1895–1990), 162, 175, 199n12
für sich (German: for-itself), 85, 175. See also *pour-soi*

garden, Japanese, 32–34, 40–41, 130, 132. *See also* Japanese arts

Garden of Eden, 43–44, 46–48.
See also Paradise
Gay Science, The (Nietzsche),
193n1
gen (the space between), 135,
175. See also betweenness
gensō-ekō (returning to this
world), 71, 175. See also
ōsō-ekō
God, 58, 64, 70, 97–98, 123,
163–64, 181, 188n76
belief in, 108
city of, 87
is dead, 91, 95–96, 110, 164,
193n1
and Eckhart, 56, 175, 187n66
found within, 37
and the Garden of Eden,
43–44, 46
and the Godhead, 39, 175
as hypothetical, 37
as immanent, 38
as immanent-transcendence/
transcendent-immanence,
38–39
infantile notion of, 30, 35
as kami, 131, 176
knowing versus loving, 157
and mediation, 81
movement away and toward,
48, 55
and mysticism, 57
the nation as a manifestation
of, 65–66
Nishida on, 37
and nothingness, 36, 41
as oneness, nothingness, 44, 89
and panentheism, 179

and pantheism, 179
as penultimate, 36
relative vs absolute, 53
as self-contradictory identity,
52–53
self-expressions of, 25, 40
as transcendent, 38, 80
as the true self, 38
undermined, 108
union with, 54 (see also
mysticism)
as unity, 30–31, 35
as unity within, 156
will of, 52, 162
as the world, 47–48
God And Absolute Nothingness
(Nishitani), 94
Godhead (Gottheit), 39, 52, 56,
175. See also Gottheit
Goethe, Johann Wolfgang von
(1749–1832), 24, 185n22
"Goethe's Metaphysical Background" (Nishida), 185n22
good, 52, 163
as centripetal motion, 48, 49,
53
conduct, 51
greatest, 50
human nature as innately, 71,
163 (see also under human
nature)
potential for, 161, 163, 169–70
Gottheit (Godhead), 52, 175. See
also Godhead
grace, 70, 75, 173
Great Compassion, 84, 87. See
also compassion; love
Great Death, 80–81, 175

Great Doubt, 111, 114, 164
ground, of reality, 19, 36–37, 52,
    56, 61, 111, 144, 175, 183.
    See also *grund*; home-ground
group harmony. *See under*
    harmony
grund (German: ground), 56, 175.
    See also ground; home-ground

haiku, 23, 31, 46, 113, 176,
    185n19
hakarai (figure things out), xv
Hamada Hiroshi (CEO, Ricoh
    Company, Ltd.), 149
harmony (*wa*), 50, 122, 147–49,
    152, 169, 181. See also
    oyakudachi; *wa*
    and Confucius, 139
    family model of, 141
    group, 147, 183n1
    of herder and ox, 104
    and mediation, 71
Hartmann, Nicolai (1882–1950),
    14
Hatano Seiichi (1877–1950), 127
Heart Sutra, 57
Heaven, 96
Hegel, G. W. F. (1770–1831),
    xiv, 14, 65, 75–76, 127, 174.
    See also dialectic; *soku hi*;
    thesis-antithesis-synthesis
Heidegger, Martin (1889–1976),
    7, 13, 127, 174
    and Nishitani, xiii–xiv, 93, 164
    and Tanabe, 64, 66
    and Watsuji, 132–33, 150
Heisig, James W., x, 5–6, 8, 12,
    187n54, 193n10, 198n48,
    201
    on absolute mediation, 75

on interrelatedness, 73
Kyoto School as world philoso-
    phy, 8, 153
on Nishida, 14, 65
on Nishitani, 91–94
on Tanabe, 64–65
on Tanabe and morality, 78
on thinking as transformation,
    11
Heraclitus (535?–475? BCE), 46
Herder, Johann Gottfried (1744–
    1803), 128
herd morality, 79
heresy, 58
Hino, Tom, 188n72
Hinduism, 5
Hisamatsu Shin'ich (1889–1980),
    11, 58
*History of Japanese Ethical Thought,
    The* (Watsuji), 133
Hobbes, Thomas (1588–1679),
    148
home, Japanese, 131–32. *See also*
    family
home-ground, 104–106, 115,
    165, 174, 175, 176. *See also*
    ground; *grund*
    as authenticity, 144
    as circuminsessional interpen-
    etration, 122, 166
    and deep connection, 33
    and ethics, 124
    and fire, 116
    as a giant web, 117
    and nothingness, 118–19
    as suchness, 114
Honen (1133–1212), 69
hopelessness, 84, 92, 96, 162,
    166. *See also* despair; mean-
    inglessness; nihilism

Huayan Buddhism. See *Kegon* Buddhism
hubris (arrogance), 72. *See also* arrogance
human beings, 32, 75, 83, 89, 96–97, 143, 151–52, 166, 172, 177, 181
  as actualized, 170
  and compassion, 149
  and dual-nature, 133–37
  and evil, 53
  the greatest, 51
  as good and evil, 161, 163
  and original sin, 43, 154
  as self-expressions of the Buddha, 41
  as transformed, 70–71, 87
  and value, 95
humanism, 151, 170
human nature, 71, 161–63
  as essentially good/evil, 71 (*see also* evil; good)
Hume, David (1711–1776), 15, 105
Husserl, Edmund (1859–1938), xiii–xiv, 63–64, 127, 179
Huxley, Thomas Henry (1825–1895), 13

idealism, 27, 64
identity of self-contradiction, 25, 44–46, 48, 49, 52–53, 59, 107, 135, 143, 180, 188n76
ikebana (art of Japanese flower arranging), 176, 194n34
immanent, 35, 38, 81, 176, 181. *See also* transcendent
immanent-transcendence. *See under* God

immediate experience, 20, 28, 70, 81, 108, 114. *See also* direct experience; intuition; pure experience
immorality. *See* evil
impermanence, 164. See also *anicca*; *mujō*
  and emptiness, 104, 111, 114, 191n30
  and the identity of self-contradiction, 53
  and reality, 21, 76, 135, 167
  and the self, 195n47
Indian philosophy, 10
individuality, xiv, 48, 51, 75, 118, 122, 126, 136–37
individualism, 51, 127, 134. *See also* ego
Indra's Net. *See* Jewel Net of Indra
ineffable, the, 36, 56. *See also* God; nothingness; One, the in-itself, 25, 85–86, 108, 113, 116–17, 118–19, 173, 175. See also *an sich*; *en-soi*; selfness; suchness; thusness
analogies (fire, sword, eye, water), 116, 119, 124
Inquiry into the Good, An, (Nishida), xiii, xix, 4, 20–21, 23, 30, 35, 49, 68, 155, 157, 160, 199n3
intellectual intuition. *See under* intuition
interconnectedness, 8, 164, 174, 176. *See also* circuminsessional interpenetration; interrelatedness; oneness; unity
  and the absolute, 41
  and ethics, 88, 123, 132, 134

interconnectedness *(continued)*
    in the home, 168
    and interdependence, 117–18
    and the self, 144, 166
    social, 148
interdependence, 117, 174, 176
interdependent origination. *See*
    dependent origination
interpenetration, 33, 117,
    119, 122, 166, 179. *See*
    also circuminsessional
    interpenetration
interrelatedness, 73–75. *See also*
    interconnectedness; oneness;
    unity
intuition, 20–21, 24, 36, 61, 157,
    159, 176–77, 178, 185n22.
    See also direct experience;
    immediate experience; pure
    experience
    action-. *See* action intuition
    as deepest knowledge, 37
    enlightened, 158
    of facts, 24
    of faith, 157
    of God, 37, 56
    intellectual-, 17, 28–30, 69,
        155, 158–60, 176, 181,
        199n6
    knowledge through, 30
    multiple meanings of, 28, 30,
        160
    and non-philosophy, 67
    of the unseen, 33
Islam, 39
I-thou, 32–34, 121
"I Thou Relation in Zen Bud-
    dhism, The," 121

James, William (1842–1910), xiii,
    18–20, 42–43, 179
    on pure experience, 42–43
Japanese arts, 7, 31–32, 40–41,
    103, 113, 147, 150–51, 174,
    194n34, 197n17
*Japanese Arts and Self-Cultivation,
    The* (Carter), 186n48,
    194n34, 197n17
Japanese militarism, xv
Japanese slogans/sayings, 2, 3, 49,
    139
Japaneseness, 77
Jewel Net of Indra, 75, 87, 176.
    See also net metaphor; web
    metaphor
jinen (spontaneous, natural), xvi
jiriki (self-power), xv, 67, 176. *See
    also* Other-power; self-power;
    tariki
jissen (praxis), 109
Jōdo Shinshō (the Pure Land
    School), 69, 180. *See also*
    Pure Land Buddhism; Shin
    Buddhism
Jordan, Michael, 159
Judaism, 39
Judgment Day, 96

Kaku-an Shi-en, 98
kami (god, divine), 131, 139,
    149, 176, 198n36
Kant, Emanuel (1724–1804),
    xiv, 14, 28, 63–64, 72, 122,
    127–28, 158, 176. *See also*
    Neo-Kantianism
Kasulis, Thomas P., ix, xvii, xxi, 156,
    171, 186n39, 199n6, 201

Kegon Buddhism, 157, 176
Keisei (voice of the valley stream),
   93
kendō (way of swordsmanship),
   113, 176
kenshō (seeing into one's true
   nature), 17, 162, 175. See
   also enlightenment; satori
Kierkegaard, Søren. (1813–1855),
   xvii, 69, 127, 179
kimono, 33, 39, 176, 188n71
kimono metaphor. See under
   lining
King, Sallie B., 148, 197n36
kinship, 19, 30, 33 39, 148
knower and known, 38, 43, 164,
   112
kōan (a Zen puzzle), 17, 39, 41,
   86, 121, 165, 176–77, 179,
   196n54
Koeber, Raphael von (1848–
   1923), 13
Kōkai (774–835), 180
kokoro (mind/heart), 32, 41, 142,
   158, 168, 177
Kōsak Masaaki (1900–1969), 11
Koyama Iwao (1905–1993), 12
Krueger, Joel W., 19
Kuki Shōzō (1888–1941), 10
"Kyoto School" (Davis), 167
Kyōzan Ejaku, 121–23, 165–66

LaFleur, William R. 125, 151,
   195n47
landscape gardening. See garden,
   Japanese. See also Japanese
   arts
Lao Tse (604–531 BCE), 174

Last Writings: Nothingness and the
   Religious Worldview (Nishida),
   xiii, 52
law of identity, 191n30
law of non-contradiction, 191n30
laws of Heaven, 139
lining, of the kimono, metaphor,
   33, 39, 155, 188n71
   and nothingness (see under
   nothingness)
Linji (?–866), xii
Locke, John (1632–1704), 105
logic of basho, 45
"Logic of Basho" (Nishida), 65,
   76
"Logic of Social Existence, The"
   (Tanabe), 65
"Logic of Species" (Tanabe),
   65–66
Logic of Species (or the Specific),
   Tanabe's, 65–66, 75, 82, 191.
   See also Logic of the Specific
Logic of the Specific, Tanabe's,
   75, 78. See also Logic of
   Species
logos (Greek: word), 32–33, 177.
   See also morotomo
love, 31, 32, 47, 68, 82, 97, 109,
   130–31, 173. See also compassion; Great Compassion
   and faith, 62
   as other-centered, 122–23, 166
   of self, 97
   selfless, 123, 130–31
   transforming, 71
   as union, 31, 51–52
loyalty, 1, 62, 77, 130–31, 139–
   40, 152. See also filial piety

Mahāyāna (a sect of Buddhism), 110, 176
makoto (sincerity), 145–47, 177, 197–198n36. See also ch'eng; sincerity
Malkani, J. R., 10
many, the, 14, 43–45, 47, 52, 54, 76, 107. See also One, the; things
Maraldo, John C., 198n48, 201
martial arts. See Japanese arts. See also aikidō
Masao Abe. See Abe Masao
Masuno Shunmyo, 32–34, 40–41, 186n48
materialism, 27
McCarthy, Erin, 150
meaninglessness, 110–11, 171, 178. See also despair; hopelessness; nihilism
  abyss of, 92, 164
  and Dōgen, 152
  and Nietzsche, 96–98
  as nihilism, 102, 107
mediated knowledge, 108
mediation, 70–75, 80–82, 84–85, 161, 173, 176, 177, 181. See also Other-power; repentance
  absolute, 72, 74–76, 86
  and ethics, 83, 87
  and freedom (see under freedom)
  rational reflection as, 79
  reciprocal, 87
meditation, 13, 21, 130
  and the deeper self, 7–8
  and the Japanese garden, 132
  the practice of, 40–41
  and the samurai, 167

and the Ten Ox-herding Pictures, 102–103
  and unity, 156
  Zen, 35, 40, 179–80
  meditative disciplines, 20, 113, . See also Japanese arts
Meiji era (1868–1912), 1–4, 177
Meiji Restoration. See Meiji era
Mencius (372–289 BCE), 162, 177
Meno, The (Plato), 163
meta (Greek: beyond, after), 67, 177
metanoia (Greek: repentance, change of heart), xv–xvi, 86
metanoesis, 67, 81, 86, 177
metanoetic awareness, 61
metanoetic society, 87
metanoetics (Greek: beyond reasoning), 66–67, 69, 71–72, 80–81, 85–86, 160
  ethics of, 83–86
metaphysics, 24–25, 30, 125, 177
Mill, J. S. (1806–1873), 13
mind/heart. See kokoro
mindfulness, 41, 176–77, 180
monism, 20
Moore, Edward, 18–19
morality, 53, 78. See also ethics; rinri
  God-given, 96
  selfless, 137, 144
  true, 137
morotomo (to gather), 32–33, 177. See also logos
mu (emptiness), 17. See also emptiness; nothingness; Śūnyatā
muchness, 18, 42, 45
mujō (impermanence), 167

mushin (no-mindedness). *See* no-mindedness

Musō Kokushi (1275–1351), 33, 195n49

Musō Soseki. *See* Musō Kokushi

Mutai Risaku, 188n72

mysticism, 37, 54–59, 84–86, 93, 155–57, 174, 177, 178. *See also* oneness

myth of eternal recurrence, the, 97

Nāgārjuna (c. 150–250), 10

nakama (a system of relations guiding human associations), 134, 177. *See also* rin

Nakamura Hajime (1912–1999), 77

Namu Amida Butsu ("I Take Refuge in Amida Buddha"), 61

Nanzan Institute for the Study of Japanese Religion and Culture, xx–xxi, 12, 171, 207

nation, 51–52. *See also* Logic of Species
  as a manifestation of God, 65–66
  as the locus of the specific, 78–79

Natsume Sōseki. *See* Sōseki Natsume

negation, 36, 55, 57, 104, 109, 144, 195n40
  absolute, 68
  double, 115, 136–37, 143
  negation of, 137
  of the self (*see under* self)
  neither/nor logic, 84. *See also* both/and logic; either/or logic; two-value logic

Nembutsu (practice of repeating the name of Amida Buddha), 69, 86, 177

Nembutsu Buddhism. *See* Shin Buddhism

Neo-Buddhism, 9

Neo-Confucianism, 162

Neo-Kantianism, xiii, 63–64

Neo-Platonism, 157, 177

net metaphor, 73–75, 87, 157, 165, 174. *See also* Jewel Net of Indra; web metaphor

Nicholas of Cusa, (1401–1464), 48, 188n76

Nicholas of Kues. *See* Nicholas of Cusa

Nietzsche, Friedrich (1844–1900), xvii, 14, 93, 126, 131, 179
  announcing God is dead, 95–96, 193n1
  and existentialism, 83, 92, 164
  and nothingness, 109
  overcoming nihilism through nihilism, 96–97
  and overman (*übermensch*), 97, 181
  and traditional values, 108
  and values, 95–97

Nietzschean Studies (Watsuji), 126

nihilism, 91–92, 102, 107–108, 110, 115, 178, 193n10. *See also* despair; hopelessness; meaninglessness
  path out of, 96–97, 111–12, 118, 164, 193n10
  European, 95–97

Nihilism (Nishitani), 94

nihility, 91, 95, 97, 108, 110–11, 114–15, 178, 195n40

nin (human being, person), 135,
178
ningen (human being), 135–38,
143, 149–50, 168–69, 178,
197n24. *See also* betweenness
as both the individual and the
social, 152
nirvana (Sanskrit: state of perfect
peace), 44, 57, 174, 178
is samsara, 44, 57, 107, 115,
180. *See also* samsara, is
nirvana
Nishida Kitarō (1870–1945), ix–
xiv, xix, 5–6, 8–10, 13–59
and action-intuition, 61
career of, 4, 11
dialectical logic. See *soku hi*
and enlightenment, 113
and intellectual intuition,
199n6
and law of non-contradiction,
191n30
and lining, 188n71
and Nishitani, 92–94, 98, 118,
125
as philosophical genius, 13, 59
and Tanabe, 63–65, 67–71, 73,
76–77, 81, 84, 88–89, 125,
153–67, 169–71
and the Ten Ox-herding Pictures, 107
translations of, ix
and Watsuji, xvi–xvii, 127–28,
143–44, 146, 151, 169–71
Nishida Kitarō Zenshu (Nishida's
Complete Works) (Nishida), 35
Nishitani Keiji (1900–1990), 11,
12, 68, 91–124, 128, 144–
45, 153, 167, 175, 187n64

and circuminsessional interpenetration, 165–66, 174
and Dōgen, 30, 156
and Eckhart, 55
and existentialism, 164
and formless self, 169–70
on god, 38
influenced by, xii–xiv
and I-thou, 32–33
and nihilism, 193n10
and Nishida, 22
and reality, 194n33
and Zen practice, 9
"Nishitani's Challenge to Philosophy and Theology," (Abe),
91, 195n40
no-mindedness (*mushin*), 31, 178
Noda Mateo, 14
Noh drama, xvii, 194n34
noesis (Greek: thinking, reasoning), 67, 178
"Non-Being and *Mu*—The Metaphysical Nature of Negativity
in the East and the West"
(Abe), 195n47
nondual, awareness, 54, 112–14,
150, 164. *See also* nondual-
ism/nonduality; oneness
connection, 144
consciousness (*see under*
consciousness)
experience (*see under*
experience)
merging, 137
oneness (*see under* oneness)
perspective, 144, 175
unity, 38
no-self, 165–66. *See also* true
self

non-mysticism, 55, 57–59, 107,
178. *See also* de-mysticism
non-self. *See under* self
nondualism/nonduality, 88, 112,
137, 144, 151, 175, 178. *See
also* dualism/duality; subject
and object
nothingness, 41, 56, 94–95, 104,
151–52, 157, 167, 175, 176,
181. *See also* betweenness;
emptiness; formlessness; *mu*;
Śūnyatā)
absolute, 10, 19, 35–40, 43,
49, 53, 57–59, 70–76,
79–87, 105, 109–15,
155–56, 159, 161, 165–66,
173, 177, 178, 191n30
acting in the world, 166
as background, 45, 59, 103,
106, 114, 144, 169
and being, 120
as betweenness, 137, 144, 146,
169 (*see also* betweenness)
beyond God, 37, 39
beyond nihility, 115
critique of, 82, 84–85, 110
definition of, 109–10, 144
and Eastern cultures, 5, 183n2
as essential defining quality,
11
the eyes of, 46
as formless, 45
and God, 36–37, 39
in history, 109
idea of, xvi, 10
as lining, 106, 118, 155,
188n71
logic of, 191n30
manifest as creation, 98

and mediation, 70, 72, 80–81,
161
negation of, 57
Nishida and Tanabe on, 68,
160–61
and the non-self self, 122–23
as not a thing, 165
nothingness-qua-love, 68
as one with being, 114
as Oneness, 43
and Other-power, 159
the problem of, 94–95
qua-relative, 86
realization of, 112
relative, 38, 91–92, 115–18,
155, 161, 173, 178, 195n40
(*see also* nihilism; nihility)
as the self, 120, 122
self-manifestations of, 58
things as, 107
as transformative, 70, 72–74
as the ultimate ground, 19
as the unity within, 156
Watsuji and, 143–45, 169–70
*Nothingness Beyond God: An Intro-
duction to the Philosophy of
Nishida Kitarō, The* (Carter),
x, xxi
not-thinking, 186n39. *See also*
without-thinking
nullification, 114
nyūmon (entry gate; introduction), x
functions of, xi

object logic, 55–56
objectivity vs subjectivity. *See*
subjectivity vs objectivity
Ōhashi Ryōsuke, 11–12

on (obligation), 138, 178
One, the, 14, 43–45, 47, 57, 76, 107, 146
becomes the many, 118
oneness, of all things, 31–32, 39, 43–44, 119, 175 (*see also* enlightenment; interconnectedness; unity; Zen Buddhism)
becoming, 59
breaking, 44, 47
and de-mysticism, 54–57
and the everyday self, 111–12
experience of, 34, 103–104, 151
and ineffability, 19
as interconnection, 168
intimacy of, 137
of body and mind, 8, 40, 131–33, 142, 159–60, 168 (*see also* body-mind)
and mysticism, 177
nondual, 137
original, 46–48
and no-mindedness, 178
as unity of all things, 30
original sin. *See under* sin
ōsō-ekō (going to), 71, 178. See also *gensō-ekō*
Other-power, 153, 164, 173, 175, 177, 181. See also *jiriki*; Other-power; self-power; *tariki*
and absolute nothingness, 161
compassion of, 151
and the critique of Nishida, 159–60
the dictates of, 88
and ethics, 83, 85
faith and, 62

and freedom (*see under* freedom)
and grace, 80
guidance of, 81–82
and mediation, 82
as new direction, 67–68
not a thing, 74
and the power of nothingness, 70–71
and reason, 154
and rebirth, 72
and resurrection, 87
and salvation, 71, 82
and Shin Buddhism, 84
as the solution, 163
submission to, 84
and transformation, 75
Outline of Science (Tanabe), 63
overman (*übermensch*), 97, 179. *See also* superman; *übermensch*
Ox-herding Pictures, the. *See* Ten Ox-herding Pictures
oyakudachi (helping others), 149–50, 179. *See also* harmony; *wa*

painting. *See* Japanese arts
panentheism (God is in everything), 38–39, 179
pantheism (all is God), 38–39, 179
papermaking. *See* Japanese arts
Paradise, 43–44, 46–47, 69. *See also* Garden of Eden
Buddha's, 69
paradox, 37, 68–69, 114, 116, 176
Pascal, Blaise (1623–1662), 69
permanency. *See* impermanence

Perry, Commander Matthew
   (1794–1858), 2
phenomenology, xiii, 63–64, 179
*Philosophers of Nothingness: An
   Essay on the Kyoto School*
   (Heisig), x, 5, 153
philosophy, German romantic, 13
   and religion (*see under* religion)
Philosophy as Metanoetics (Tanabe),
   xv, xix, 66, 82, 155
"Philosophy as Metanoetics: An
   Analysis" (Fredericks), 61
"Philosophy of Nishida, The"
   (Takeuchi), 13
"Philosophy of the Kyoto School,
   The" (Tosaka), 5
Philosophy of Science (Tanabe), 63
Pilgrimage to Ancient Temples
   (Watsuji), 127
Plotinus, 177
Plato (427?–347? BCE), 14,
   49–50, 98, 127, 163, 171,
   177. *See also* Neo-Platonism
Platonist, 67. *See also*
   Neo-Platonism
poetry. *See* haiku; Japanese arts
pottery making. *See* Japanese arts
Pound, Roscoe (1870–1964), 154
pour-soi (French: for-itself), 85,
   179. See also *für sich*
practice, 7–8, 40. See also *dō*;
   Japanese arts; self-cultivation
pragmatism, 179
pratātya-samutpāda (Sanskrit:
   dependent origination),
   195n47. *See also* dependent
   origination
praxis (*jissen*), 109
Primitive Christianity (Watsuji), 128

"Prolegomenon to a Philosophy
   of Religion" (Nishitani), 94
puppetry. *See* Japanese arts
pure experience, 14, 18–29,
   36–38, 155, 178. *See also*
   direct experience; immediate
   experience; intuition
   and abstractions, 42–43
   deepening of, 158
   and de-mysticism, 58
   and enlightenment experiences,
      113
   and intellectual intuition,
      199n6
   as letting go of the subjective, 31
   and Nishitani, 165
   as a pathway to reality, 35
   prior to judgment, 113
   reason vs empiricism vs experi-
      ence, 30
   and Tanabe, 76
   and the Ten Ox-herding Pic-
      tures, 103–104
   as unifying activity, 25, 29–30,
      35
   as unifying power, 24–30, 37,
      50
   as unifying principle, 29–30, 34
   and Watsuji, 144
   and without thinking, 186n39
"Pure experience, cognition, will,
   and intellectual intuition"
   (Nishida), 17
Pure Land, xvi, 71, 87, 173, 178.
   See also Shin Buddhism
Pure Land Buddhism, xii, xv,
   9, 61–62, 69, 84, 154,
   157, 160, 1. *See also* Shin
   Buddhism

Purifying Zen: Watsuji Tetsurō's Shamon Dōgen (Watsuji), 127
radical empiricism. *See under* empiricism
rationalism, 63
realization. *See* enlightenment
real nature, 88, 163, 181. *See also* true nature
reason, and ethical transformation, 82
reason vs empiricism vs experience. *See under* pure experience
reason vs experience, 7
rebirth, xvi, 68, 70, 72, 80–81. *See also* resurrection
Record of Linji (Linji), xii
reine Wissenschaft (German: pure science), xiii
relationality. *See* dependent origination
relational origination. *See* dependent origination
relative, the (beings), 68, 71, 74, 81, 83, 86. *See also* absolute, the
relative beings, 74
relative nothingness. *See under* nothingness
religion, 22, 61, 69, 92, 108
as culmination of knowledge and love, 68
and doubt, 97
and ethics, 86
as faith, 7, 156 (*see also* faith)
as focus, 125
as human network, 151, 170
of India, 56

and morality united, 52
and nihilism, 193n10
Nishitani's definition, 97–98, 112
as panentheism, 37–39
and philosophy, 6–8, 10–11, 18, 89, 95, 171
as a reaction to meaninglessness, 97
Watsuji and, 128, 167
Religion and Nothingness (Nishida), x, xiv, xix, 94, 120–21, 187n66
Religious Philosophy of Nishitani Keiji, The (Taitetsu), 91
Religious Philosophy of Tanabe Hajime, The (Taitetsu and Heisig), 61
repentance, xv, 62, 64, 67, 69–70, 72, 80, 83–88, 161, 173, 181. *See also zange*
repetition, 179
resurrection, 61, 68–69, 80–85, 87. *See also* rebirth
"Revering the Teaching of Master Nishida." 65
reversed eye, 37, 56, 156, 199n3
ri (principle), 134, 179
Rickert, Heinrich (1863–1936), 63
Riehl, Alois (1844–1924), 63
rin (fellows, company), 134, 179. *See also nakama*
rinri (ethics), 134–35, 138, 168, 179. *See also* ethics; morality
rinrigaku (ethics, moral philosophy), 179
Rinrigaku: Ethics in Japan (Watsuji), xix, 125, 128. *See also Ethics*

Rinzai. *See under* Zen
Rude Awakenings: Zen, the Kyoto School, and the Question of Nationalism (Heisig and Maraldo), 198n48
Russo-Japanese war, 17

sakoku, (locked or chained country), 1, 180
salvation, 62, 69–71, 74–75, 82–83, 126, 152, 176, 181
samsara (Sanskrit: this ordinary world), 44, 57, 180
   is nirvana, 44, 57, 107, 115, 180 (*see also* nirvana, is samsara)
samurai, 3, 130–31, 140, 160, 167
Sanshō Enen, 121–23, 165–66
Satan, 48–49, 52–53
satori (illumnination), 41, 84, 180. *See also* enlightenment; *kenshō; satori*
Scheler, Max (1874–1928), 127
Schelling, Friedrich Wilhelm Joseph (1775–1854), 65, 92
Schiller, Friedrich (1759–1805), 127
Schinzinger, Robert, 185n22, 188n71
scholar vs artist. *See* artist vs scholar
Schopenhauer, Arthur (1788–1860), xvii, 14, 126–27
"Schopenhauer's Pessimism and Theory of Salvation" (Watsuji), 126
seer and seen, 27, 106
Sein (German: being), xiii

Seindes (German: thicket of beings), xiii
self, the, 35, 115–16. *See also under* ego; true self
   and activity, 42
   annihilation of, 55, 144
   attachment to, 123
   and the body, 150
   -centeredness, 119–20, 165
   deep (*see* deep self)
   deeper, 8, 17, 26, 49, 58, 88, 98, 102–103, 112, 120
   dissolving of, xvi
   and Dōgen, 165
   dying to, 82
   as emptied/empty, 31, 91, 122, 166
   as end in itself, 122
   and ethics, 49–53
   everyday, 57–58, 102, 104, 111–12, 122
   extending, 160
   forgetting, 137, 165
   formless (*see under* formless)
   as formless, 58
   as God, 55–56 (*see also* true self)
   improvement of, 50
   -in-itself, 108
   letting-go of, 69
   making the self a Buddha, 152
   negation of, 31–33, 83–84, 108, 144
   and nihility, 111–12
   no consciousness of, 47
   non-self, 119, 122–24, 169–70
   not-a-self, 58, 88, 119, 124
   as nothingness (*see under* nothingness)

self, the *(continued)*
  and nothingness, 73–74, 120
  one with emptiness, 120
  as original, 118–20
  and other, 38, 164, 173
  as realized, 85
  as represented, 108
  resists all explanation, 120
  resurrection of *(see* resurrection)
  selfish, 51, 122, 165 *(see also* selfishness)
  selfless, 42, 88, 145, 164–66, 170 *(see also* selflessness)
  shift to, 95
  transformed, 70–71, 198 *(see also* transformation)
  true- *(see* true self)
  and the universe, 162
  without a self, 158–59
self-abandonment, and philosophy, 81
self and other, 38. *See also* subject and object
self-consciousness, 14, 25, 47, 61
self-contradictory, 8, 44, 46–49, 52, 135, 143, 152, 180, 188n76
self-contradictory identity. *See* identity of self-contradiction
self-cultivation, 7, 37. *See also* transformation
self-deception, xv. *See also* delusion
self-empowerment, 162–63. *See also* self-power
self-identity of contradiction. *See* identity of self-contradiction
selfishness, 51, 83, 122, 127, 142, 163, 165. *See also under* self

selflessness, 150, 170
  and betweenness, 137
  and ethics, 120–24
  as fellow-feeling, 168
  as formless awareness, 42, 144–45
  and nothingness, 164–66
  and resignation, 130
  as selfless power, 160
  as selfless self, 88
selfness, 116–17. *See also* in-itself; suchness; thusness
Self Overcoming of Nihilism, The, 96
self-power, 67–68, 72, 82–84, 153–54, 157, 159–62, 166, 176. See also *jiriki*; Other-power; self-empowerment; *tariki*
self-realization, 52
self-transformation. *See* transformation
Sen, Dr., 187n69
separation, 48. *See also* estrangement
Sermon 15 (Eckhart), 187n66
sesshin (a gathering of the mind, intensive Zen workshop), 9, 180
Seventeen Article Constitution, The, 183n1
Shamon Dōgen (Dōgen, the Monk) (Watsuji), xvii, 127
Shibayama Futoshi, 184n10
Shimomura Torataro (1900–1995), 11
Shin Buddhism (Pure Land Buddhism), xii, xv, 9, 69, 84–87, 161, 177, 179, 180. *See also* Pure Land Buddhism

and Other-power (*see under* Other-power)

Shingon Buddhism, 157, 180

and enlightenment, 180

shinjin (faith, true entrusting), xv

Shinran (1173–1262), xii, xiv–xvi, 62, 69, 81, 151–52, 180

Shintō, xi, 1, 6, 10, 126, 139, 148–49

Shintōism, 5, 139, 151, 168, 180

Shōgun (military commander), 2–3, 177

Shokoku-ji temple, 93

Short history of Chinese Philosophy, A (Fung), 199n12

Shōtoku, Prince (574–622), 3, 183n1

Shūkyō to wa nanika (*What is Religion?*) (Nishitani), xiv

sin, 64, 71–72, 82–83, 163

original, 43, 71, 80, 154

sinful nature, 82–83, 88

sincerity, 50, 139, 141, 145, 147–48, 168, 177. See also *ch'eng; makoto*

slogans. *See* Japanese slogans

social ethics. *See under* ethics

Socrates (469–399), 52, 127, 171

soku hi (and yet; is and is not), 44–45, 51, 56, 59. *See also* dialectic; Hegel; identity of self-contradiction; *soku hi*; thesis-antithesis-synthesis

Sōseki Natsume (1867–1916), 92, 127, 138

Sōtō. See under Zen

Sourcebook for Modern Japanese Philosophy: Selected Documents

(Dilworth, Viglielmo and Zavela), xx, 12, 171, 201

Sources of Japanese Tradition (de Bary), 183n1

Spencer, Herbert (1820–1903), 13

species, xiv, 76, 81, 83, 87. *See also* Logic of Species; Logic of the Specific; specific

specific, (vs universal), xiv, 75, 78–79, 83, 87. *See also* Logic of species; Logic of Species; species

Spiritual Development of the Japanese People, The (Watsuji), 128

stereoscopic vision. *See under* enlightenment

Study of Aristotle, A (Nishitani), 94

subject and object, distinction, 23, 25, 27, 28, 35, 38, 113, 173 (*see also* dualism; nondualism/nonduality; subject and object)

union of/become one/merging, 31, 51, 56, 162, 164, 176

subjectivism, 108

subjectivity vs objectivity, 27

suchness, xvi, 105–106, 112–16, 118, 164–65, 180. *See also* in-itself; selfness; thusness

Śūnyatā (Sanskrit: emptiness), 91, 95, 164, 175, 181. *See also* emptiness; *mu*; nothingness

as absolute emptiness, 114–15

as absolute nothingness, 115, 165

and becoming the other, 121–22, 166

Śūnyatā *(continued)*
is beings, 115
and ethics, 121, 123–24
and the Great Doubt, 114
and home-ground, 106, 114,
117–19, 165
and intimate encounters, 33
and nihilism, 110–15
and suchness, 105–106, 113,
165
and the Ten Ox-herding Pictures, 118
superman, 179, 181. *See also*
overman; *übermensch*
Suzuki, D. T. (1870–1966), x, xii,
35, 36, 55–56, 92, 103
Suzuki Shigetaka (1907–1988), 12
sword making. *See* Japanese arts
swordsman, 28, 130, 160, 173.
See also samurai
swordsmanship. See *kendō*
synthesis, 56

tabula rasa (Latin: blank sheet),
143, 181
Takeuchi Yoshinori (1913–2003),
xv, 9, 13
Tanabe Hajime (1885–1962), xi,
xiv–xvi, 6, 61–89, 93–94,
173, 177, 181
and absolute nothingness, 109
critique of Nishida, 155–61
emphasis on faith, 151, 154
first generation of the Kyoto
School, 11–12
a follower of Shinran, 151
and human intrinsic evil,
161–64
inspired by Shin Buddhism, 9

and Nishitani, 164, 166
pro-war activities, 65–66
similarities to Nishida, 153–55
took religion as a focus, 125,
128
and Watsuji, 166–67, 169–70
Tannishō (a collection of Shinran's
sayings), xii
tariki (Other-power), 67, 80.
See also *jiriki*; Other-power;
self-power
tea ceremony. See *chadō*; Japanese
arts
Ten Commandments, the, 163
Tendai Buddhism, 157, 181
Ten Ox-herding Pictures, the,
58–59, 98–108, 111–12,
118, 120, 145
tetsugaku nyūmon (an introduction
to philosophy), xi
theory of recollection, Plato's, 163
thesis-antithesis-synthesis, 65, 76,
174. *See also* dialectic; Hegel;
soku hi
things, 11, 107, 113, 116, 135,
156, 164, 166, 168–69. *See*
also forms; many, the
and *basho*, 42
connectedness of, 8, 75, 132,
174
and consciousness, 29
as constitutive element, 117
created, 57
deeper richnes of, 20
and dependent origination,
195n47
empirical form of, 44
as empty, 91, 114–15, 118,
122

and the eye, 42
flow of, 104–105
and formlessness, 45
God inherent in, 38
and home-ground, 117–19,
    122
interconnectedness of, 144,
    146, 164
and interrelatedness, 74
light of, 120
lining of, 155
and Masuno, 34
as nothing, 118
oneness of, 19, 32, 29, 43, 45,
    54, 59, 118, 175
origin of, 103
and place of arising, 58
as present, 111
as represented, 108, 112
as self-expression of the Bud-
    dha, 41
self in, 123
self not a, 74
source of, 48
suchness of, 14, 114, 118
are Śūnyatā, 115
and the Ten Ox-herding Pic-
    tures, 106
as unique, 117–18, 165
unity in, 25–26, 29–31
things-in-themselves, 108
Thou. See I-thou
Thought and Experience (Nishida),
    92
thusness, 106. See also in-itself;
    selfness; suchness
Thus Spoke Zarathustra
    (Nietzsche), 93, 96
Tokugawa Shōgunate. See Shōgun

topos (Greek: field), 14, 25, 58,
    81, 146, 181. See also basho
torii (gateway), x–xi
Tosaka Jun (1900–1945), 5
transcendent, 35, 38–39, 81, 159,
    179, 181. See also immanent
transcendent-immanence. See
    under God
transformation, 80–89, 159, 175.
    See also self-cultivation
    absolute, 73, 87
    from a closed to an open soci-
        ety, 79
    by confession and repentance,
        80–89
    as endless potential, 49
    and enlightenment, 11, 20, 40,
        53
    ethical, 122
    existential, 61–62
    and faith, 62
    and freedom, 85
    on the inside, 122
    of the intellect, 40
    and mediation, 70–71, 83–84,
        177
    and loving actions, 82
    of nothingness, 72–75
    and Other-power, 87, 161
    personal, 53, 171
    and philosophy, 6–7
    pragmatics of, 89
    and reason (see under reason)
    and reason, 81
    reciprocal, 137
    self-negating, 86
    of society, 87–89
    of the student, 39
    and Śūnyatā, 124

transformation *(continued)*
and the Ten Ox-herding Pictures,
107
and thinking, 11
transformative power, 70, 73–74
transformed self. *See under* self
Treaty of Peace and Amity, the, 2
true consciousness. *See under*
consciousness
true nature, 17–18, 41, 175, 181,
197n36
of reality, 27
true self, 170, 174. *See also* deep
self; no-self
as absolute nothingness, 53, 82
and becoming other things, 119
and circuminsessional interpenetration, 166
and God, 38
as inherently good, 154, 162
and pure experience, 26, 50
as reality, 52
and the Ten Ox-herding Pictures, 59, 103
and transformation, 70, 74, 80,
82, 88, 164
Tsujimura Kōichi, 12
two-value logic, traditional,
191n30. *See also* both/and
logic; either/or logic; neither/
nor logic
*Two Sources of Morality and Reli-
gion* (Bergson), 77

übermensch (German: overman),
97, 179, 181. *See also* overman; superman
Ueda Shizuteru (1926–), xix,
12, 55–58, 93, 106–107,
109–10, 118, 178

Ueshiba Morihei (1883–1969),
173
unification, 56
unified awareness, 24, 28
unifying activity. *See under* pure
experience
unifying factor, 39
unifying power. *See under* pure
experience
unifying principle. *See under* pure
experience
union, mystical, 55, 56
unity. *See also* interconnectedness;
oneness
of all things, 19, 30–31, 40,
103, 156–57, 176
of body and mind, 8, 142, 168
of consciousness, 30–31, 39
divine, 51
God as, 31, 35, 38, 47–48
in home and family, 131
and intellectual intuition, 28,
199n6
principle of, 25, 156
and pure experience, 24–26, 158
of religion and morality, 52
of the self, 50, 111
as self-contradiction, 44–46, 143
and the Ten Ox-herding Pictures, 103, 111
and true ethics, 144
underlying all awareness, 28
universal, the (vs the specific), 83
universalism, 51–52
Unno Taitetsu, 114

values, 78, 179, 180. *See also*
attitudes
cluster of, 148
cultural, 4, 134

eclectic mix of, 1
and the family, 141
in the home, 131–32
and Japanese gardens, 132
and Nietzsche, 95–97, 181
and nihilism, 95–97
and personality, 50
traditional, xi, xvii, 108, 164
Varela, Francisco J., 88–89
Varieties of Religious Experience
(James), 18
Vedanta, 157, 181
virtues, the, 139. *See also* Confucianism; five obligations, the
vital force or impulse. See *élan vital*

wa (harmony), 141, 147–48, 181.
See also harmony, *oyakudachi*
Watsuji Tetsurō (1889–1960),
xvi–xvii, xix, 9–10, 11–12,
125–153, 166–70, 174,
184n10
*Watsuji Tetsurō's Rinrigaku: Ethics
in Japan* (LaFleur), 125
Watts, Alan (1915–1973), x
way of flowers. *See* Japanese arts
way of tea. See *chadō*; Japanese arts
ways (*dō*). See *dō*
Ways of Thinking of Eastern Peoples
(Nakamura), 77
weaving. *See* Japanese arts
web metaphor, 74–75, 117, 157.
See also Jewel Net of Indra;
net metaphor
whole, the, 40, 46–48, 98, 118,
156–57, 171, 176
of experience, 20–24, 42
expressions of, 53

as formless, 45
and its individual parts, 76
an integral part of, 34
manifestations of, 146
and the one and many, 136
wholeness, 22
without-thinking, 30, 103–104,
139, 156, 173, 139, 186n39.
See also pure experience;
not-thinking
will to power, 95, 97
witnessing, 82
woodcarving. *See* Japanese arts
World War II, ix, 3, 62, 64, 66,
77, 94, 152, 198n48

Yamazaki, master, 93
YHWH, 39
Yuasa Yasuo, 132–33, 140, 149,
199n6
Yusa Michiko, 16
Yüeh-shan Wei-yen (745–828),
156

zange (confession and repentance), xv–xvi, 67–72, 80,
83, 87–88, 181. *See also*
repentance
zangedo (metanoetics), 69, 177,
181. *See also* metanoetics
zazen (seated Zen meditation),
180
Zein und Zeit (Being and Time)
(Heidegger), 13, 150
Zen, Buddhism, xv, xxii, 16–17,
20–21, 31, 98, 157, 173,
174, 176, 178
and Dōgen, 30
and enlightenment, 18–19, 40,
56, 85, 86, 179–80

Zen, Buddhism *(continued)*
and Great Death *(see* Great
Death)
and Great Doubt *(see* Great
Doubt)
and the *kōan*, 39
and logic, 191n30
meditation, 40, 180
and mysticism, 56–57, 155,
161
and natural ethics, 84
and Nishida, 5, 9, 14–20, 22, 33
and Nishitani, 92–94
and oneness, 19
and Pure Land Buddhism, 61,
154, 160
Rinzai, xii, 41, 179–80

and self-power, 68–69
Sōtō, 32, 41, 127, 180, 186n48
and Tanabe, 84–86
and teaching, 21
temples, x
and the Ten Ox-herding Pictures, 58
training, 18–19, 22, 35, 40–41,
68, 105 *(see also* meditation)
and without thinking, 186n39
Zen and Western Thought (Abe),
195n47
*Zen no Kenkyō (Inquiry Into the
Good)* (Nishida), 20
zettai-mu (absolute nothingness),
109. *See also* nothingness,
absolute

2959986R00129

Printed in Great Britain
by Amazon.co.uk, Ltd.,
Marston Gate.